CHOICES

The Handbook to Core Values Consciousness

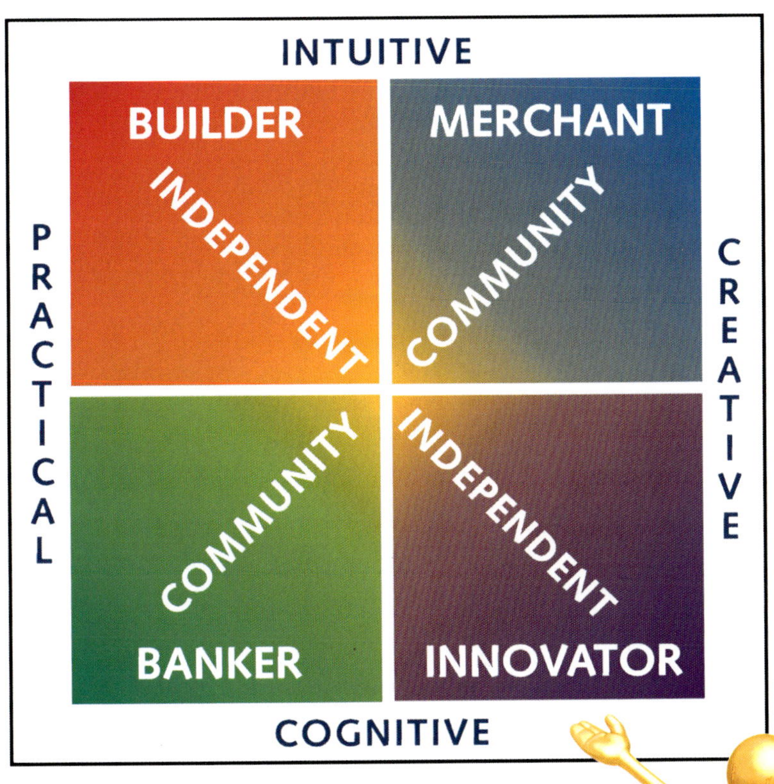

Lynn Ellsworth Taylor

Dedicated to my sons Greg and Doug
whose lives are a joy to me.

CHOICES
The Handbook to Core Consciousness

Copyright 2010 Lynn Ellsworth Taylor.
All rights reserved.

This book or any part thereof may not be reproduced by any means, written or mechanical, or be programmed into any electronic retrieval or information storage system without permission in writing from the author except in cases where short passages are used solely for the purpose of review in periodicals, television, and radio. This book is intended for personal use only. Any repetitive use of the *CVI*™ assessment and training information by companies and individuals requires a license from the author and Elliott Bay Publishing, Inc.

First Printing October 2010
Library of Congress Publication Data
Taylor, Lynn Ellsworth, 1949–

1. Choices
The Core Values Consciousness Handbook

ISBN-0- 978-0-9822647-0-6 (Paper)

ISBN-0-978-0-9822647-1-3 (Download version)

Manufactured in the USA by Elliott Bay Publishing, Inc.
October 2010

ACKNOWLEDGEMENTS

Sue Daniels has served as content editor, project manager, and creative assistant for Choices. Sue found the Gold Guys and helped with all of the selections and production issues. Sue has been a master at helping me put my intuitive writing into a form that is more understandable to the readers of Choices. Without her work Choices would likely remain unpublished.

My sincere appreciation and thanks also go to Sandy Kolberg, Ph.D. for her Introduction and to Chip Conley, author of Peak for his foreword to this book.

Thanks also to Max Scott for his illustrations, and to Glenn Jansen for the design, layout and perfection of form for Choices.

FOREWORD
by Chip Conley, author of
Peak: How Great Companies Get Their Mojo from Maslow

CHOICES

Finding Your Place of Highest and Best Contribution

I've spent the past quarter-century building a hotel company based upon helping my 3,500 employees live up to their calling. Psychologist Abraham Maslow spent thirty years of his life studying human potential. He did this in order to identify the common drivers that cause (or allow) people to be peak performers in their business careers.

In my book, PEAK, I attempted to bring Maslow's conclusions and prescriptions for implementation into business organizations in the twenty-first century. It is my profound belief that by paying attention to man's search for meaning and the impact of that personal pursuit of success, a great deal of momentum is added to businesses and individual lives.

Taylor's work has focused on developing a methodology for characterizing and quantifying what Maslow called the innate unchanging nature of each person. The goal for Taylor has been to learn how to consistently put people into a work role in which the work, the tasks of the job, are a natural expression of this innate nature. It has been Taylor's premise that if this were consistently accomplished, the human productivity bell curve (20% of the people create 80% of the value) could be turned upside down.

In this book, he has provided a new level of understanding of the human psyche and how it operates, a new pathway to higher consciousness—all in the context of helping people find the right job that will lead to fulfillment. The end result of this job-matching process is an organization that more naturally rises toward being a more actualized company. Interestingly, six of the top eight of the "world's most admired companies" (as defined by Fortune magazine's annual poll) are companies I profiled in PEAK.

In ***Choices***, Taylor has given us a personal road map for developing a life that is centered in conscious development of what he calls our *Real Core Values Self.* By striving to put ourselves into the right roles at work and in our personal lives, he is showing us more concretely what the peak of Maslow's "Hierarchy of Needs" pyramid is all about.

He has colorized this highest point of individual development. He has given us a new framework within which to understand and master our individual pursuits. He has shown us an effective and affecting means to find fulfillment and purpose during our brief time on earth.

Taylor's *Core Values Index*™ comes to life in ***Choices***. This assessment (the *CVI*™) provides the first clear picture of each person's innate unchanging *Core Values Nature*™. This makes it possible for the first time to consistently match the right person with the right job. The methodology for this important business optimization methodology is presented in his first book, *The Core Values Handbook*. His successful work with more than 200 turn-around business projects over the course of twenty years has provided a strong validation of his *CVI* and his *Taylor Protocols*™.

Now in ***Choices*** we understand how these important personal and business successes actually happen, inside the individual. New definitions of the human ego and our adapted personalities provide a lynchpin for new knowledge about our inner nature. Taylor effectively illuminates the deepest fears in people, the negative emotions that cause internal shifting between *Core Value Energies*™ and the destructive shift into ego-based conflict.

His book, ***Choices***, leads us to understand that these troublesome elements in our human nature are, in fact, the keys to our adult consciousness. Fears excite personality and self-protection, but they also provide a wake-up call to our *Real Core Values Self*. By showing us how to listen to these wake-up calls, and how to use *Core Values Consciousness*™ to decide *who* we want to *be* any moment, Taylor presents a new pathway to adult consciousness and meaningful living.

Taylor unfolds a tried and proven means for self-discovery and self-mastery. This is practical guidance about how we can each become the person we are meant to become; how to allow our adapted personalities to fall away; giving all of our attention to the work at hand through a commitment to being *who we are*.

In many ways this new approach to enlightenment is a fulfillment of Maslow's work and a new significant contribution to the development of a modern positive psychology. Dr. David Mashburn's evaluation of the *CVI* and the *Taylor Protocols* provides a good frame within which to enter this book.

"The Core Values Index has done an excellent job at capturing some of the innate core traits of the person's unchanging nature. Several experts in optimal human functioning such as Abraham Maslow, Peter Drucker, and Marcus Buckingham have described these core traits as an "inner bent," "propensity," or "core wiring." Because of this, Taylor Protocols is able to make a compelling and convincing connection between the essential nature of each person and the tasks and contributions that are inherent in his/her work."

As an individual seeking to make a profound difference in my society, I am committed to making thoughtful application of Maslow's valuable psychological and human development premises. I find ***Choices*** to be a significant and highly beneficial new work. In many concrete ways, Taylor is launching and adding fuel to the fires of what he calls the *Better Work-Life Revolution.* He is turning the business world inside out and upside down.

If ***Choices*** and its author are given a little room to breathe, they will breathe new life into the way people relate to their jobs. They will also breathe new understanding about the way businesses can most beneficially relate to their people.

Taylor has brought into a single united effort the pursuit of sustainable profits for a company and the search for meaning for an individual. He shows that these goals are not mutually exclusive. I am excited to see how this all unfolds in the next few years. Thank you, Lynn, for the new breath of life you have brought to me through your books and your dedicated work.

INTRODUCTION by Sandy Kolberg, Ph.D.

CHOICES

Occasionally a book comes along that marries theory with practice, a book that connects with how life works and how we human beings are able to function successfully in a world that seems unpredictable and chaotic.

Choices is such a book. Lynn Taylor presents a practical way to look at how the human organizing system works; how we can each *be who we really are* and live in conscious awareness and choice. How we can live in the state of contribution instead of getting and taking through personality conflicts.

It is interesting to follow the theories of some of the great thinkers of our time to trace the evolution of the human organizing system to its culmination in Taylor's book, ***Choices.*** In following these thinkers, one finds the basis for discovery of the four *core values* and the six secondary traits that make up the *Core Values Index*™, the basis of the book and Taylor's work.

In his stages of life, Carl Jung talked about "knowing" as the way a child develops his first acknowledgment of someone or something. In that moment of knowing, the child begins the process of consciousness. As the child continues to make connections between his perceptions of things and the context in which they exist, he creates his reality. That reality exists through the teachings, training, and practice he receives, ultimately culminating in his consciousness of self.

As the child develops, he creates the self that interplays between his inner self and the outer world of values and culture. This interplay becomes his authentic self or persona. Perhaps Jung best describes this as personal unconsciousness and collective unconsciousness. The whole operating structure, what Taylor calls the *Human Operating System*™, is universal in nature and function, yet individually differentiated by each individual's attitudes and by the way they are predisposed to see the world outside of themselves, and then by which aspect of their inner nature they choose for effective functioning at any moment.

The progression of thinking continued through Maslow's *Toward a Psychology of Being.* Maslow, through Humanist Psychology theory saw human potential as both being and becoming, culminating in actualized humans. In order to realize the self-actualized state, man had to meet basic inner needs and evolve through a series of warping experiences to become self-actualized in a manner that allowed him to express himself freely in his culture.

Maslow saw these needs as life, safety and security, belongingness, affection, respect, self-respect, and self-actualization. He felt that man had an intrinsic inner nature that was in some ways fixed and unchangeable and could be studied quantitatively and structured. It is in Maslow's work on personality and motivation that one finds the idea of the healthy individual. Maslow's work not only defined our idea of human needs but also of the potential for high-performing teams and productivity in organizations, if people were allowed to develop to their self-actualized potential.

Carl Rogers, the founder of the Human Potential Movement, added to the phenomenological, existential, person-centered body of knowledge of the time through his works, *On Becoming a Person* and *A Way of Being.* Notably what Rogers added to the body of literature was the notion of "the good life" as a process and not as a state of being. As a process, specific choices are made through openness to experiences and the desire to live in the moment.

A distinction here for Carl Rogers was the desire for man to trust himself in the evolution of his experiences, to manage conflicting views, perceptions, and his consciousness, and then to set a course of action ultimately becoming fully functioning human beings. The shift from looking at man from the scientific psychologist's theoretical perspective to the general acceptance of self-awareness of the emotional self by the layperson brought the literature to the public in the 1960s and 70s.

Following the "good life" theories and the shift out of the focus on mental illness, the natural progression was to positivist psychology and mental wellness. The work in the discovery of innate knowledge has prompted current empirical psychologists like Martin Seligman, who coined *learned helplessness*, Ed Diener, who is known for studying human well-being and happiness, and Mihaly Csikszentmihalyi, who is known for his studies in human happiness, creativity, and most importantly, *flow* to define modern psychology.

Seligman is often noted as the father of Positivist Psychology and its focus on human nature, and the possibility that man can be happier, more satisfied, and more engaged in life choices. Implicit in this emerging area are the potential for man to be authentic and his desire for a good life.

What becomes interesting is that the new theorists are also writing popular works and speaking to wide academic and public audiences. The integration of theory into popular literature allows deeper integration of these principles into society as a whole. Authors like Peter Senge, who founded the concept of the learning organization and systems thinking and who purported the *Ladder of Inference*, and Chris Argyris, who developed single, double, triple loop learning, are bringing focus for lay people to study and understand these thinking processes rather than focusing on fixing behaviors. This shift brings a new understanding of conscious and unconscious behaviors to the forefront of contemporary conversation.

Other authors like Marilee Adams, *Change Your Questions: Change Your Life*, help people understand the innate unchanging nature of people and help them make appropriate choices, away from judger behaviors to learner behaviors. The ultimate goal is to help people understand how to be who they really are from values-based thinking. Ken Wilber, in his book, *The Simple Feeling of Being: Embracing Your True Nature*, explores our innate awareness into our very being. Wilber is a master at bringing Eastern and Western philosophy together with modern psychology leading our thinking to our spiritual connections and higher levels of consciousness.

Where values-based thinking and self-awareness leads is to the fulfillment of a psychology of being through *Core Values Consciousness*. Lynn Taylor's work with the *Core Values Index* survey and now the book, ***Choices***, is a shift away from reaction to contribution. It is a natural extension from the psychological thinking and theory to the practice of *being*.

It is choosing to be a specific energy ". . . in the room" by living consciously in our *core values*. It is the ability to use our self-awareness to let go of negative belief structures and fear. It is negotiating conflict with strategies that honor our deepest *core values*.

Taylor's focus becomes one of intentionality. It is the fulfillment of becoming a person by shedding personality behaviors and making a higher contribution to our society through reaching our highest level of consciousness. This works to lift each person into a role that allows each of us to make our highest and best contribution—our spiritual calling.

Choices is the natural progression from theory to practice. Taylor has provided a new characterization and quantification of the innate nature in people. He has found an effective way to make this innate nature accessible as a recipe of *core values* capacities—the capacity to *be* different kinds of energy, to make different kinds of contributions. He presents this as a universal journey toward self-knowledge, self-actualization, and ultimately, loss of self-consciousness in meaningful work. You are invited to take this journey in learning about our conscious and unconscious self and about the innate *core values* that comprise the *real self* in each of us.

The Core Values Pathway to Higher Consciousness

In this book, ***Choices***, the handbook to *Core Values Consciousness*™, we are going to present a carefully designed map of this pathway.

The first portion of the book is a description of the *Core Values Index*™, and the four *core values*, the six *types of contribution*, and the way the *Core Values Nature*™ of people operates at the conscious and unconscious level. Part of this new knowledge will be a clear picture of your own innate unchanging nature and the built-in capacities you have. You will also learn about the life challenges that are *wired* into your *innate nature.*

In order for you to participate fully in this book and get the most out of it, you will need to take the *Core Values Index*, available at www.taylorprotocols.com.

You will want to learn not only your own *core values* but also the *core values* of others and how all types of people operate and interact. With this knowledge you can become more conscious of your own choices and more aware of the choices that others are wired to make.

In addition to the four *core values*, you will also be introduced to the six *types of contribution*. Three of these *contributions* you will be more strongly geared to use as your strategies for success. But you will want to learn as much as you can about all six of the *contribution types*. With this knowledge you will be able to make a more conscious choice to draw upon the different contribution strategies when needed. You will also be able to more easily identify the different contribution strategies when they are being used by those around you.

It is important for you to know and understand your dominant and secondary *core values*. It is just as important for you to understand the *core values* that are not your dominant nature, because these *core values* are the dominant way of being for other people in your life. They are also a good explanation of why you have challenges in certain kinds of situations and certain kinds of work or life activities. By learning and understanding all four of the *core values*, you will be able to more easily choose to shift into any of the *core values* when you want to.

In this book, ***Choices***, you will have the opportunity to learn how your emotional patterns affect and interact with your *Core Values Nature*, and what you can do about this. ***Choices*** will help you easily identify what your deepest anxieties and fears are, and how these fears and anxieties can cause you to shift into a negative conflict mode.

You will learn to recognize your fears and anxieties, that what triggers you to shift into your negative conflict mode is also the secret to becoming more conscious in your life. This is the key to making conscious choices that are more effective and that keep you operating in alignment with your deepest *core values*.

You can learn how to easily shift from *being* one of your more dominant *Core Value Energies*™ into *being* a very different kind of energy in the room—all by simply being conscious of the different *core values* that comprise your unique *Core Values Nature*.

Core Values Consciousness is designed to show you how to lift yourself to your highest and best contribution.

We will do this by helping you see the incredible human creature that you are and how you are wired to operate as an adult Homo sapiens *being*.

The second half of the book is designed to help you see how to take *this new consciousness you have learned* into your own life and begin making more conscious and more highly accountable choices. The major choices we will explore with you are:

What *core value* you choose to be at the present moment.

What and how you choose to learn.

Who you choose as your life partner.

How you choose to operate as a parent.

What is your primary calling?

What in this world gives you a sense of meaning and purpose?

What are your deepest passions?

What are your highest skills?

What job is right for you?

What are your deepest fears?

This book is designed to be a life-long guide, a new, more workable and understandable description of how human life is meant to operate. It is meant to help you get a clearer picture of yourself, how you are currently making choices, and how you can intentionally and consciously make more-effective choices beginning today.

Finally, this book is designed to teach you the most adult lesson of all: *who* to consciously choose to *be* at each important moment of life—giving you a straightforward pathway to higher consciousness and greater success in living.

I want you to know *who you are*, how to operate more consciously and therefore more effectively. I want you to be the incredible presence in the room that you are meant to *be*, creating the life that you are here to create for yourself and for others.

This leads naturally to knowing and doing your *Real Work*™. It leads to higher success by society's standards. It leads to greater success by spiritual standards. You will be better prepared to make conscious decisions that lead to better outcomes. You will be more skilled at identifying ineffective behavior sooner. You will learn how to make better choices about yourself in real time. You will learn to employ all of your innate *Core Values Nature* for greater success and in service of your highest callings and your passions.

You will learn how to improve *what you are*—your skills and talents—for better delivery of *who you are* to society.

The end result for you will be a life lived more consciously and effectively with a deeper sense of meaning and purpose in everything you do. In the end, you will have lived a life that you will judge to be fulfilled. You will have learned to claim and live your own unique life and you will be happier and more beneficial to others in the process.

Welcome to Choices, your pathway to *Core Values Consciousness.*

Enjoy.

Lynn E. Taylor
President
Taylor Protocols
www.taylorprotocols.com

TABLE OF CONTENTS

1

Life Is Simple

We come into this world with just three things:

1. **What we are:** Our talented physical presence, which includes mental, psychological, and emotional attributes, including our adapted personality.
2. **Who we are:** Our innate unchanging nature, a unique recipe of *core values energies*, and…
3. **Time:** The time we are given to be *who we are*, and to make our *highest and best contribution.*

Throughout our lives there is one thing we do over and over again; we make *choices.* We observe the circumstances in our surroundings, and we choose what action to take or we choose not to take action. Acting or not acting are both choices we make.

We observe or choose not to observe the results of our chosen actions and our new circumstances. Then we choose again what action to take. We all do some of this consciously. But most of us do most of this reactively, without conscious acknowledgment or thought.

Acceptance of the simplicity of life as described above greatly increases the difficulty of life. Why?

If I accept that I only do one thing, and that one thing is to make choices, then I must also accept that the current circumstances of my life are the result of the choices I have made. Being accountable for my own life is irritating and difficult.

It is apparent when looking at my life that I have made many less-than-effective choices. Accepting this also is difficult. Learning how to make choices today in a different way than I made choices yesterday is difficult. Learning how to observe life, people, and circumstances from a different perspective, so that I can make different choices today, is frustratingly difficult.

Learning to accept responsibility for the state of my life tomorrow is frightening and difficult.

Maybe this is why M. Scott Peck in his first major work, *The Road Less Traveled*, began that book with the words, "Life is difficult."

I don't know about you, but I have not found life to be easy or fair.

We humans are not equally endowed physically, mentally, emotionally, or even psychologically, nor are we given an equal beginning. We are born into a variety of cultures, economic situations, and family circumstances. Some of these environmental situations are friendly and nurturing. Some are hazardous to health and happiness.

However, there is one level of fairness that does exist: we are all given the power to *choose* how to respond to life's circumstances.

We long for fairness in the life situations described above. We struggle against the fact that our lives are what they are as a result of choices we have made and that we have the power to change our lives by simply making different choices.

Do you want total responsibility for the level of happiness in your life?

I know that a part of me still does not want this ultimate responsibility. I would like to blame my disappointments and frustrations on other people, or on God.

This is not a workable or useful belief. It makes all of the unsatisfactory situations in life God's problem or a problem created by God or fate. If I *choose* to believe this, I excuse myself from any accountability for the presence of any particular challenge in my life.

I excuse myself from future consequences created by the way I handle this situation, since it's God's fault. If I *choose* to hold onto this belief, I also excuse myself from taking responsibility for each current and future trial/test/situation/result.

I have to choose to give up the ineffective belief that my life's difficulties were set up by God, or by chance, and that I, therefore, give up the right to complain that this life is unfair. Otherwise I am committing that age-old commitment to perfect insanity: trying to do the same things today that I did yesterday, with the expectation that I will get a better result tomorrow.

I don't enjoy having full responsibility for my own life.

It is easier to hope for fairness, point to difficult situations, and excuse myself for being less than happy and less successful with my life than I would like to be. It is easier to hope that at any moment my luck will change, or that God will reach down and just make things better for me at this time in my life, when I am feeling a little discouraged and feeling too sorry for myself to decide to make a different choice and start down a different path.

That's the bad news. The good news is that we are offering in this book a new way to make these difficult things much easier. The revolutionary *Core Values Index*™ and the other tools in this book provide a new understanding of the way choices are made and how the increase in *Core Values Consciousness*™ can lead to full self-actualization and personal fulfillment.

Almost forty years ago, after serving as a substitute teacher for one year with high expectations of obtaining a permanent teaching position,

I found myself without a teaching job in the greater Seattle area. The Boeing Company had suffered a significant downturn and had laid off 37% of its workforce, causing a huge downturn in the Seattle economy seemingly overnight.

I, like so many others, found myself leaving town, reading the billboard beside the freeway that said, "Will the last one to leave Seattle, please turn out the lights?"

This was not an auspicious beginning for a young man who had a college degree and teacher certification, and nowhere to go. I had worked my way through college as a journeyman window cleaner; so hard work was not strange to me.

I chose to leave Washington State in search of opportunities. Boise, Idaho, was my first stop along my open road to the future. After working for two years in various positions, I once again found myself without a professional job, so I talked the general manager of the Roadway Inn in Boise into giving me the job as bellman and limo driver. I began making $1.10 per hour, along with tips that netted me enough to live on.

One night I picked up the president of H. K. Ferguson and brought him back to his room at the Roadway Inn. We started talking. He learned that I was a poet with one book published, a photographer, and a college graduate with no place to use my best talents. Two days later he hired me as a new Project Reporter, and I started the long exodus to Cleveland, Ohio.

When I arrived in Cleveland, I had five dollars in my pocket. It was late Friday afternoon, after 5:30, when I finally got to the downtown offices of H. K. Ferguson. I had been forced to spend my last $800 dollars on rebuilding the clutch and transmission of my 1964½ Ford Mustang, because it didn't like pulling a U-Haul trailer 3,000 miles across this great country.

I finally got someone to open the Ferguson Company doors for me, and the last HR person in the office offered to let me sleep on his couch until I could start work on Monday.

The reception on Monday morning was cool at best. No one could find any instructions regarding my employment. When they finally did find my file, the long-time HR manager signed me up as a new Project Recorder. He showed me to my seat at a workbench in a huge engineering bullpen. My assignment was to transfer by hand the hours on each engineer's time sheet onto the ledger for each client project—right name, right hours, right job number.

This brings us to the beginning of my life-long journey to a position that would allow me to make my highest and best contribution. It was the inkling edge of my path to *Core Values Consciousness.*

At noon, I walked into the HR office and asked to see the manager. He was kind enough to sit down with me. I told him there was a mistake—that I had been hired as a Project Reporter, not a Project Recorder. I was there to take photographs, and to write articles and publish their newsletter.

He insisted that there was no mistake and that I should go back to my seat. When the president returned the next week, we would all straighten things out.

I stood my ground and told him that I was certain of my position and that I was not willing to return to that three-legged stool in the bullpen. Not even for the rest of the day. I had not traveled across this country to transfer numbers from one piece of paper to another. We compromised. He gave me an advance of $100 and told me to check in each morning, while he tried to contact the CEO.

Two years later I had produced a huge new project proposal, written numerous monthly newsletters, visited dozens of construction sites, and taken thousands of pictures. In addition to my basic job, I had assumed the responsibilities of three other people as they resigned. I had received three promotions and four pay raises along the way.

If I had accepted the wrong seat on the three-legged stool in the engineering bullpen, I would have been saying no to my own life. I would have been denying my own value. I would have been delaying my development, and

I would have set myself up for a much longer and more uncertain pathway to my place of highest and best use.

Before I leave this personal story, it is important to note that there was absolutely nothing wrong with the Project Recorder job—for someone else. But it was just not even close to a fit with my innate *Core Values Nature*. For someone else that position would have been a perfect fit—his or her *Real Work*™—but not for me.

Many years later I created the *Core Values Index* and its inherent revelation of the *Human Operating System*™ that exists in all of us. I found myself helping one of my clients through one of his critical life path choices . . .

I was standing outside Charlie's company with him one sunny Seattle afternoon. I had suggested we take a walk in an attempt to get him to talk a little more openly with me.

I wanted to connect Charlie with the earth around us, trying to distract him from his nearly total focus on his business that was currently in a critical, near-death condition. We walked and talked for nearly an hour, during which I heard his litany of situations, people problems, money worries, and personal failures. He was feeling trapped without any reasonable strategy to change his situation. He was tired, deeply, emotionally, and spiritually tired.

"I'm in so deep now," he began. "The IRS is putting a lien on my home. My wife is upset. I've already gone into bankruptcy once. Now, here I go again. My bookkeeper thinks she can run the company better than I can. My foreman is threatening to work for another company that has taken half my customers from me already. There's nothing I can do."

"This world is a big and open place to live," I said to him. "If you wanted to, you could easily just put your life aside, take a little cash, get on a bus or hitchhike, and leave everything that is making you unhappy.

You are talented enough. You could land in Southern California, take a new name, find a simple job, go back to school, take an art course. You could take a job on a fishing boat that docks in South America, land in Rio, and just disappear. You would then rebuild your life and set things up so you are happy—for a while."

"I know I could."

"Then why don't you?"

The silence was long and deep.

"Maybe you won't do that because you like a lot of your present life. Maybe you also know instinctively that you could rebuild a life anywhere, but after a while you are likely to remake your current circumstance. You have created a wonderfully complex, difficult, interesting, mind-bending, challenging situation here, one that really tests your mettle as a man."

"You're right," he asserted. "I don't want to leave. I want to keep everything I have. But I'm going to lose everything."

"Since you are choosing to stay in your present life, why don't you choose to make the best of it? Once you have chosen to stay where you are, with all of the frustrations, unfairness, and imperfect people around you, you can't claim to be unfairly at the mercy of all of the bad things around you.

"You have chosen to stay in the current situation."

"Put your heart and mind back into it and work on the things that you can change. You will feel a lot less fearful if you get really busy making things different. Get to work creating something instead of working to defend and protect what you already have."

"Sure," Charlie said, "but I am spending my days fighting with creditors, arguing with the bookkeeper, and threatening employees for mistakes they have already made and for their future likely mistakes."

"You are a *creative*, *intuitive*, *independent* person with the capability of starting and losing one company, only to start another, which you also grew into a multi-million-dollar business. Look at all of the things you had to do well in order to get back into this situation where failure is even possible.

Most people never put themselves at risk in business, and most that do never grow their company to this level. "

"You are *creatively* talented. People come to you again and again because they like the work you do. You are an intelligent, *creative*, gregarious presence on this earth, with a company that you created. You have a contribution to make. Make it."

His response was to shake my hand, thank me for the walk, and, while looking me in the eye, a spark flickered in his. He said, "Well, I have some important things to do. I'd better get to it."

Calling after him, I said, "Do things differently today than you did yesterday." He grinned and waved. "And," I added, "remember that every decision based upon fear is a wrong decision."

When we find ourselves critically appraising our current circumstance; finding the unfairness in it all; when we are feeling unloved, ignored, or unable to make things different—it is helpful to ask ourselves whether we are going to remain where we are.

Am I going to complete the drama I have been creating? Or, am I going to choose to leave, drop all of the current nonsense, desert the current situation, and start again somewhere else?

Once this question is asked and answered, there is no rational way to deny complete accountability for the life we have chosen. There is only one thing for us to do: look around, see what needs to be done, what positive effect might be gained through choosing a different action, and then choose to act.

My client in the story above did not succeed in saving his company, even with our help. He did manage to merge his customer base with another business owner who was much better at the operations side of business. He now owns 30% of a growing, successful business. He stuck things out and continued to make a *creative* and energetic contribution, to the best of his ability. He chose a different action and began to make many choices differently, and that opened up his new partnership opportunity.

Now, let's look at the choices we all are required to make that have the greatest impact on the circumstances of our lives. Let's learn where we can improve our decision-making process and how we can change the results of our lives.

We have discovered new information about how every one of us operates at the deepest levels of human existence. We have discovered some real secrets about how we can make *choosing* an easier and more effective activity. We have developed some tools that will help you quickly gain greater mastery of this essential life process. We are going to make your life of choices much easier than it now is.

2

How We Got to Be the Way We Are

Each of us is born with a different emotional, psychological, physical, spiritual, and mental dispensation, also known as our nature or our character. This innate design of each person may be rooted in our DNA, our genetic makeup, or it may be that our inner person is some yet misunderstood spiritual presence with these unique features, or possibly some mixture of the two.

Regardless, we are at once a unique person, and also a Homo sapiens creature with characteristics similar to other Homo sapiens creatures.

Part of our creature package is an instinct for survival. We instinctively know that being cold is uncomfortable and dangerous, that falling into a crevasse is life threatening, that survival without food, air, and water is not possible.

As children, we cry when we are cold and wet. We cry when we are hungry and when we feel in danger of falling, but as adults in this contemporary world, we no longer live in dark caves surrounded by dangerous creatures. We no longer have the sense of imminent danger every day and all night long. In fact, by the time we are five or six years old, we seldom need our quick survival response to the most basic life threats.

We are born with a conscious and unconscious mechanism that enables us to shift from one part of our *Core Values Nature* into another. This is how we survived and modified ourselves into our personality (the way we have chosen to show up). By the age of eight or nine, this personality is well formed. This adapted mode of behavior is a warped version of our *Real Core Values Self*™. It is the result of our need to protect ourselves and to set each of us up for some level of social success.

As adults, we become tuned in to our society, we have survived as a creature. Our innate fears have served us well, but they don't simply go away because there are no physical survival threats to excite these fears. Our survival instinct continues to monitor everything around us. We, as instinctual creatures, look out into the world with fearful eyes. The same protective fear that kept us from stepping into a crevasse now actively surveys the social world we are entering, and we begin constructing our social survival and approval strategies.

This self-generated, slightly warped version of our *real* innate *Core Values Nature* is our best answer to early challenges from our environment and from our family/community unit. It is the mission of our survival instinct to protect us, to provide instant responses when under duress and to keep us from harm and want.

The human creature spends more time in infancy and complete dependency than any other creature on earth. The relative size of a toddler compared with an adult could be compared to an adult who is facing an 18-foot giant. If this giant entered a room in which you and I were sitting, neither of us would resist doing anything the giant seemed to want us to do. We would focus a great deal of our attention on reading every movement, every expression, every action, and response of this giant.

The total dependency of a child and the unpredictable nature of people, as well as the size difference, all serve to make adaptation to the needs, preferences, and wants of the adults in our child world an absolute necessity.

Dependency also contributes to the fact that our adaptation into an acceptable personality is a fear-based process. The result of the fear-based development of our behavioral pattern is what we commonly call our personality, or the behaviors that we have selected as the least likely to result in death or abandonment.

Each of us is born with a unique *Core Values Nature*—a special mixture of *power*, *love*, *wisdom*, and *knowledge* energies. We each develop different social strategies, different personal characteristics, different sets of social mores and ethics that tend to harmonize with our *Core Values Nature*.

As dependent children with our unique *core value*–based view of the world, we attempt various responses to life circumstances, mostly relying on our predominant values. Some of these responses bring good results that are effective or acceptable, and some create a completely new set of problems.

Some of our responses are not found acceptable by our parents, grandparents, teachers, or older siblings, so we adjust our behavioral self to meet the unique life circumstances into which we are born. We adjust by unconsciously shifting from one *Core Value Energy*™ to another.

Over time these instinctual, fear-driven survival strategies become a well-formed personality, one based in fear and in stimulus-response dramas. Our self-made personality is a warped version of our *Real Core Values Self.*

The personality we exhibit and rely upon for continued guidance as adults is a set of beliefs, attitudes, and ideas about the relative effectiveness of our innately directed *Core Values Strategies*™. These beliefs justify our decision to act in certain ways based upon certain circumstances. We now have a fixed set of beliefs about ourselves. This is a set of beliefs about why it is better to act in ways that I would not naturally choose, a set of beliefs that cause me to be a person different from my most innate *Core Values Nature*.

To learn *who we are* at the deepest level, we must observe our adult world through adult eyes and make conscious decisions about the most effective responses—those responses that are most likely to yield the most desirable outcomes. Our mission is to learn how to make conscious choices in our daily activities, so our lives become intentional and optimized for maximum contribution with the least amount of wasted emotional and social energy.

When we begin to make these conscious choices in our daily lives, we can then begin to consciously deny our fear-based beliefs and recapture and learn to effectively express our most innate natural energies. This is the requirement for anyone who wants to live a life that is rewarding, fulfilled, and personally satisfying.

3

What Kind of Chooser Are You?

We are each a unique blend of spiritual *core value* preferences and strategies. This innate nature born out of basic genetic and psychological dispensations can be understood as innate *Core Values Nature—power, love, wisdom,* and *knowledge*—each *core value* having a different strategy for making choices and taking action.

I call this innate unchanging nature, the *Real Core Values Self* (or *Core Values Nature*). To help us differentiate this self from our adapted personality. It is composed of the four *Core Value Energies*™ that make up our basic human nature.

Each *core value* has a different primary contribution to make. These *core values* are all found in each of us at different levels of preference or intensity of energy. Another way to think of this is that we each have different levels of capacity to *be* the presence of each of the *core values.*

Based on our *Core Values Index* assessment, our *Core Values Nature* is represented as 72 value (character) points. For instance, one person might be characterized as having 25 value points centered on *power,* 20 on *love,* 15 on *wisdom,* and 12 on *knowledge.* The larger the number of value points in each quadrant the greater the person's reliance upon the beliefs, strategies, and social contributions that arise from and are built upon that *value.*

The practical way of saying this is that the higher scores show our greater capacity to *be* that *Core Value Energy* at any given moment

The person illustrated above, with a high score centered on *power*, will most often respond to circumstances from a *power* strategy. This person will go after what he wants mostly from a *power*-based position with *love* being his second most likely response or strategy. This same prioritization exists in our sense of mission and purpose, the primary contribution of each *core value* being the value itself, *love* or *knowledge*, *wisdom* or *power*.

Our unique recipe of *core values* is the essential makeup of *who we are*. Our unique blend of *Core Value Energy* makes us a unique and specific kind of presence in the room. This is what I believe Abraham Maslow was pointing toward in his book, *Toward a Psychology of Being*. We each have a unique *Core Values Nature* that is our *being*. Our *being* is the only thing that truly matters in our adult Homo sapiens lives.

In simplest form, we are born to learn *who we are* (to know our being) and to express *who we are* through the capabilities and talents that compose *what we are*, contributing *who we are* to our society. In other words, we are each born to contribute some unique mixture of *power*, *love*, *wisdom*, and *knowledge* into our world, according to our innate blend of these *core values*.

We know that we are all raised by parents or guardians who have spiritual and, therefore, social values that are different from ours and from each other. Parts of our selves were highly valued by our parents, and parts of ourselves were not valued very highly. In some cases, our *core values* selves as well as other value-based character traits were seen and reacted to as disturbing, undesirable, and sometimes unacceptable. The greater the disparity between those traits that are highly praised and acknowledged and those traits that are ridiculed and punished, the greater the adaptive demand for the child.

The end result of this adaptation is the development of behavior and thought patterns that are governed not by the innate values, but rather by the stimulus-response mechanisms that the child adopts. We also adopt those behaviors that are effective in obtaining *desired* results within our child's small society.

In this process of adapting to our environment we become *warped* into our personalities. We are *warped* out of our real value structures and into adaptive, ego-based personality belief/response systems. This is the personality we carry with us into the adult world. Our survival instinct has worked overtime, developing this *warped* personality, encroaching into our sociological, psychological, and spiritual domains as if our lives depended upon it.

As we progress into adulthood, we each find that our fear-based personality may cope quite well in society much of the time; we have, after all, survived until now. But we also find that most of our responses to current adult circumstances and situations are driven, not by conscious choices, but by our emotionally adopted survival strategies.

These personality-driven actions and reactions often do not align well with our *core values* makeup. This leaves us with more problems to fix tomorrow, and with more reactive decisions for our survival instinct to make. We also struggle with reduced self-respect and a reduced sense of personal effectiveness in our choice-constructed world. We have a developed personality that is far less valuable and far less able to make a contribution in an adult world than our innate *Real Core Values Self.*

When someone in authority raises an eyebrow in a specific way, and we interpret that unconscious gesture the same way we used to interpret our mother's raised eyebrow—this is disapproval, anger, a forewarning of harsh words, embarrassment, or shame our response to this present reminder of an authority figure comes without thought and causes a reaction similar to the one we utilized to deflect the *power* of mother. Sometimes this reaction may be so strong we appear to others to be reacting totally out of relative balance with the current situation.

This kind of defensive response is not particularly effective in our current adult relationships and sets up an amazing sequence of new challenges. All of these challenges are uncomfortable, fearful, and equally open to misinterpretation by those with whom we are interacting, because we feel at risk.

Our survival instinct flares into full force, and we find ourselves meeting a socially innocuous situation with inappropriate gestures, thoughts, words, and actions.

The survival instinct that served us so well in the past and helped us construct a personal strategy for survival (that is, a personality) becomes our dictator ego, to the degree we choose to allow this warped personality strategy to remain in control of our lives.

Years ago I was one of the product managers in a medical equipment company. Each week we would sit with the senior executives of the company and present our latest sales, product development, research results, and other progress updates. I was the youngest on the team and this was my first product management position.

My boss was very good about pushing each of the product managers forward and allowing us to make our own presentations. He was also good, I found out quickly, about keeping out of the line of fire when stern, threatening challenges came from the executives, especially from the CEO.

In one particular meeting, the CEO came down hard on one of my conclusions—that the product he had designed was unreliable, was too costly to build, and that we were losing money on every unit sold. My recommendation was that it should be dropped as a product and replaced with a better product from a competitor.

The CEO, without raising his head from playing with a small windup toy that he was releasing onto the conference table, said, "Get him out of my sight. I never want to see this guy again." He then turned to my boss and shouted, "Remind me now why you insisted we rehire this guy." You see, I had already been fired and rehired twice. This was my third strike. I was rehired the next day.

The really interesting part of this story was the extremely different reactions that I and my boss each had to this in-your-face conflict. By this time I was used to being the scapegoat and used to facing the "firing squad." My boss, however, was now in the line of fire.

His ears flushed bright red. He started gripping his meeting papers into a wrinkled mess. His cheeks started to blotch. We could practically hear his heart pounding.

As a fellow product manager told me later—I had been fired and summarily dismissed from the meeting and was out packing my personal items when my boss came unglued—"He was almost wheezing when he started talking. He tried to defend you for the first second, and then he just caved and said he would have you clean your desk. Then he started coughing and excused himself from the meeting."

What some people say when they have had an experience like this is, "I was just beside myself."

An interesting expression, don't you think? Because this is exactly what is happening. This is the survival instinct at work. It is sending out a survival warning. Our bodies and personalities respond instantly as we are completely disconnected from our *Real Core Values Self*—and we are now acting from creature survival instinct in a situation that is not life-threatening. We are literally *being* beside our *real* selves.

Our universal challenge is to discover the nature of our *Real Core Values Self* (our unique mixture of *core values*) and to live a life that honors the unique person we are, nurturing our own spiritual growth and building a life that leads to fulfillment and happiness. We are designed to be able to know *who we are* and to constantly learn, honing our talents and skills, so we can contribute our unique energy through work and social participation, making our highest and best contribution.

It is not possible to be happy when we are acting in a manner that is not a true reflection of our basic person, even when those actions receive praise, adulation, or high material compensation. Happiness and fulfillment are only derived from actions that are harmonious with our inner makeup.

We only achieve peace and joy when we are doing our *Real Work*, or when we are playing or participating with others without fear and without any help from our adapted personality behaviors.

This is what positive psychology calls congruity. I am being *who I am* designed to *be*, expressing myself freely without concern, without fear.

4

Your Innate Unchanging Nature

The reactive and proactive strategies set off by each *Core Value Energy* are completely different from each of the other strategies related to *Core Values Energies*. Here is the essential nature of the four *core values* in brief.

Builder: Core Value is Power

The application of personal energy to create a positive (desired) result.

People with dominant *builder* values most often choose to react to situations from a position of *power*. The innate strategy is to *intuitively* see what is happening, take immediate *intuitively* chosen actions, cause a measurable effect, and then take another *intuitive* action based upon the results.

When *power*-based individuals sense a strong threat and become anxious and fearful, their ego-driven response is to overpower, to *intimidate*, make the danger go away, or to destroy whatever appears dangerous. When *builders* feel good about themselves, when they are experiencing high self-respect (the results of their actions are positive and worthy of their effort), they are experienced by others as pure positive energy that is directed at a task: innocent, motivating, and effective.

Power's Catalytic Value™ is *Faith*

The belief that I know what to do now; I will cause the desired effect, and I will know what to do after causing these results.

Builders have a primary *Catalytic Value* that directly corresponds with their *power* value. This *faith*, as defined above, is required. It allows *builders* to take the *intuitive* action they are compelled by their *power*-based nature to take. When the *faith* value is in full force, *builders* feel free to continue acting. They are confident that they are making the contribution to this world they are here to make. This condition of *being* creates high self-respect and generally does not create fear in others.

When a *builder* loses *faith* in her *power*, or if she loses *faith* in her *intuitive* urges to invest personal energy and take *intuitively* driven actions, she begins to feel *powerless* (impotent). The *builder* becomes afraid to take action, afraid to invest her considerable energy into her work. Her personal respect suffers, contributing further to her sense of frustration and impotence, deepening her loss of *faith*.

Merchant: Core Value is Love

The nurturing of the *core values* in one's self and in others. This *love* includes all people, things, aesthetics, art, music, and all aspects of human interaction with others and with the universe at large.

Love is not a weak, caretaking drive. *Love* is not a doormat. *Love* is not romantic passion. It is not polite words or actions. *Love* is not hugs and kisses, although these actions can be natural expressions of *love*.

People with dominant *merchant* values typically choose to react to situations from a position of *love*. The tactic is to build alliances and relationships that strengthen available resources and open a greater range of response options. They build relationships that strengthen positional advantage and focus others on long-term opportunities. They shift energy away from momentary conflicts and threats. *Merchants* measure all considered actions by their likely contribution to, or detraction from, *love* between all parties and within one's self.

When *merchants* perceive themselves to be threatened, or if they perceive themselves or others to be unloved and disregarded, they become anxious. Their response to their fear is to manipulate relationships to maintain or to secure approval, to make the enemy evil and worthy of disregard, to cut off unsupportive people and recruit supportive people, thereby diffusing or overwhelming the energy of threatening forces.

Merchants gather the troops around themselves, surviving through the creation of social and influential forces rather than through personal power and conflict. When *merchants* are experiencing high self-respect, they are recognized as skillful communicators, *loving* supporters, and inspired visionary leaders.

In order for *love* to be experienced, a *merchant* must be able to discern the *truth* about current situations. Am I presenting a *true* picture of myself to others? Are they really the persons they are presenting themselves to be? Do I know what I want, what motivates me? Can I trust what is motivating the people around me? If a *merchant* senses a lack of *truth* in relationships and situations, all *love* that might otherwise be experienced is doubted or dismissed entirely.

Love's Catalytic Value is *Truth*

The conviction that my perception of the way things are is accurate and real. I can trust what I see. I can believe what I am experiencing. I can see and understand the way things are.

If they really knew *who I am*, they would not *love* me.

When a *merchant* has worked very hard to gain acceptance and approval, the *merchant* discounts all *love* received from others. Even real *love* from others is discounted because acceptance and approval was earned by the personality, earned by specific performance that was designed to gain attention and acceptance through *manipulation*.

When a *merchant* begins to doubt his or her perception of *truth*, there can be no acceptance and recognition of *love*. Self-respect is diminished.

Innovator: Core Value is Wisdom

The ability to *see* with the five senses, to observe all aspects of a situation, to understand and to conceive, reason out, and contribute the best strategic response or solution.

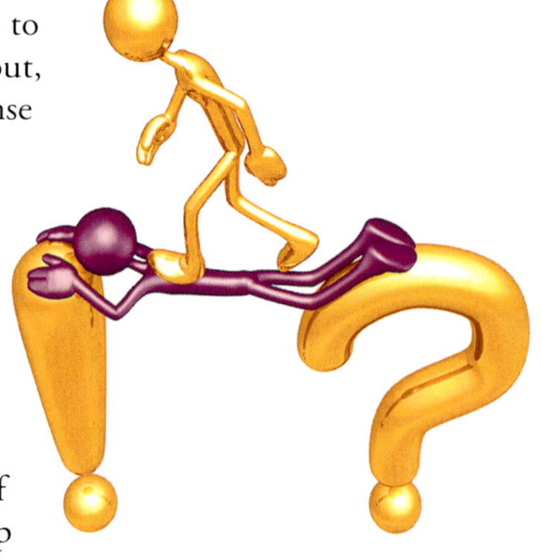

Wisdom sees the way things are and knows what to do about it.

People with dominant *innovator* values tend to react to all situations from the posture of *wisdom*. The tactic is to make a thorough assessment of all related issues and elements, develop an effective plan, and refuse to decide or participate in taking action until an effective response can be designed. *Wisdom* observes the way things are, asks questions and leads brainstorming sessions, and experiments, in order to understand what the problems are and how best to address them.

When a threat is perceived, *innovators* work to undermine the social and emotional *power*, *knowledge*, and *love* (relationships) of others through *interrogation*. They stubbornly ask questions until others are made to look unwise, unworthy of support, and are frozen in indecision.

Interrogation tends to create confusion in others, forestalling decisions and thereby slowing the rate of actions in others. This approach deflects direct *power* through confusion, breaks up relationship structures, and humiliates those who have carefully structured a *knowledge* base or who are defending a preferred strategy.

When *innovators* are feeling solid self-worth, their *wisdom* attracts other people. *Innovators* make their careful assessments, design systems, and derive solutions, causing forces to line up on the side of the "best idea."

Wisdom's Catalytic Value is *Compassion*

The ability to remain true to one's self in relationships and in situations regardless of the passions and reactions of others. The ability to understand, empathize, and accept the behavior of others and of one's self.

Because *innovators* are able to understand why another person is behaving in a certain manner, it is easier for them to remain calm and observant, even when others are acting negatively. It is easier for them to detach from the other person's actions. They can see that the conflict is not about him against me, it is about which *core value* perspective is most needed, which *Core Values Strategy* is most appropriate for the situation.

In order for an *innovator* to honor the *wisdom core value*, he or she has to remain inquisitive and curious. The first requirement is to see and understand the way things are. To do this, all information and evidence has to be observed, accepted, and put into the possible response mix. An *innovator* is therefore compelled to remain observant and dispassionate even when the negative passion of another is directed toward the *innovator*.

When an *innovator* loses *compassion* for others, the *innovator* is cut off from any chance to be the *wisdom* in that circumstance, and his personal respect is diminished. At this point the *innovator* does not feel *compassionate* and interprets the actions of others as a threat and reacts in fear, exciting the *interrogation* strategy.

Banker: Core Value is Knowledge

The what, how, and why of things. The collection of organized provable facts concerning any subject, process, or thing.

The first *bankers* may have been the individuals in each primitive group who learned to cover the embers of a fire with ashes, pressing the coals against a large log, preserving the sourcc of fire and fuel, banking the fire until morning.

Persons with dominant *banker* values rely on fundamental and accumulated *knowledge*. The tactic is to carefully record and analyze past and current facts, conserve energy and resources, and constantly build material and intellectual value. This is the strategy of *bankers* who are experiencing high self-respect.

When *bankers* feel threatened, they become *aloof* and *judge* others to be unworthy of *knowledge*. They back away from open conflict, say yes when they mean no. They buy time and build back-room political alliances around their treasure of information and preserved resources. They are passively aggressive and undermine the authority and leadership of others who are judged to be unjust or too ignorant to support.

They create fear in others through the disclosure of historic evidence that causes others to delay action. They prove to others that the person who is now perceived by the *banker* as a threat is unjust and therefore must be resisted, all influence destroyed. From a position of proof and fear, *knowledge*-based people change the choices that others would normally make and thereby focus resistance and destructive energy against perceived threats to *justice*.

Knowledge's Catalytic Value is *Justice*

The judgment that appropriate and fair actions are being taken, and that there is equal access to vital knowledge and resources.

Since the *banker* requirement is to acquire and provide *knowledge*, these people become the repository for garnered facts and information. They use this *knowledge* to make certain vital resources are not wasted, that everyone has appropriate access to resources, and that the society around them applies the garnered *knowledge* appropriately.

There is no sense of fulfillment in the *knowledge*-based person until the *knowledge* is needed and appropriately applied to current situations. True fulfillment comes only when the *banker's knowledge* has made a measurable difference in results.

Knowledge-based people feel honored when they are asked for the knowledge they have, when it is needed most. But the person in charge has to also actually read the information, change his decisions based upon the knowledge offered, and the outcome of this better choice-making must be deemed positive and just—then and only then are *knowledge* people fulfilled in their mission.

Bankers are therefore in a position to develop facts about given situations and prove the presence of or lack of *justice*. This contribution of *knowledge* and *justice* to their world is the source of self-respect for *bankers*.

When *bankers* feel they are not treated appropriately and can prove it with facts—when they have evidence that their *knowledge* is not being put to good use or being used to harm—they move from a sense of *justice* to *injustice*, which allows them to *judge* others and withdraw or become *aloof* from the situation by withholding their *knowledge* and their participation.

Using their information from this negative position, a *banker* is able to lay the blame and shame on others. *Bankers* will undermine the confidence of people who are unjust leaders of people.

This tactic requires little effort on the part of *bankers* since they remain emotionally *aloof* in this process. Others are intimidated by this tactic, and social power returns to the one with *knowledge*. When *bankers* lose the sense of *justice* for themselves or others, they lose their commitment to gain and disseminate *knowledge*, and their personal respect is diminished.

5

We Warp into a Personality

We come into this world as predominantly *merchant love, builder power, innovator wisdom*, or *banker knowledge* with an inscribed recipe of the other *core values*—a unique recipe of *love* and *power, wisdom* and *knowledge*. We have a uniquely weighted preference for reliance upon each of the *Core Values Strategies* and tactics. This gives us a unique perspective and a unique set of inter-related strategies and tactics to use.

A complete personal picture of the innate unchanging person is only accessible through the *Core Values Index*, which deduces each individual's relative motivation to make certain kinds of contributions: *intuitive* or *cognitive, creative* or *practical*, and *independent* or *community*. All together this *Core Values Nature* is a unique *Real Core Values Self*.

Those who parent us are either very similar to us or very dissimilar, sometimes even very opposite. Our *Real Core Values Self* is inscribed in us at birth and contains our deepest motivational drivers. The challenge of life is that we find ourselves with a certain *Core Values Nature*, planted on this earth into a culture and family setting in which other members have different unique *Core Values Natures*.

There is always the added ingredient that our parents (and other dominant influencers) have their own childhood warping to contend with, and often pass along their dysfunctional warping to us. We all come into a unique environment. This adds texture and richness to the life-long puzzle that is ours to solve.

As children we are subject to the dominance, protection, and nurturing of those around us. We have no choice but to adapt. We are required by innate survival instincts to adapt to them.

Through the interplay of our *Core Values Nature* in relationship with the personalities and behaviors and the *Core Values Nature* of those around us, we are influenced by the socio-economic conditions in our lives. We evolve into our ego-based personalities through a highly refined process of adaptation—a fear-based choice process that is driven by our survival instincts.

We attempt to meet the challenges of life and try to obtain the necessities of life through our instinctive strategies that derive directly from our inner nature. Sometimes this natural strategy is effective. If so, we continue to use that strategy when similar circumstances arise. When our primary *Core Values Strategies* are not effective in getting us the things we want, and when they attract neglect or abuse, we shift instinctively to a secondary value strategy, or to lesser preferred value strategies. In this way we manage to secure safety and comfort, acceptance, approval—survival.

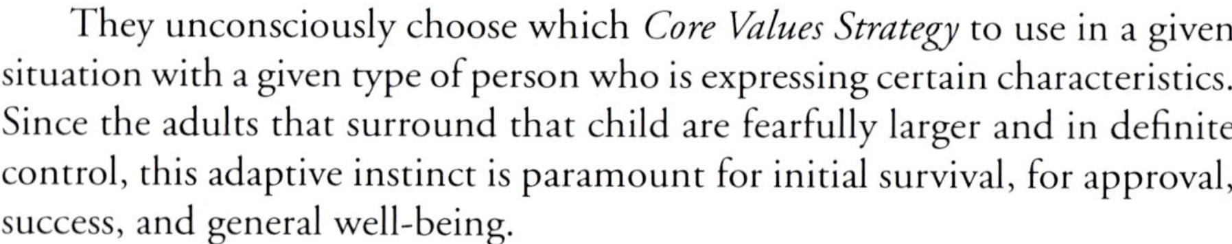

This native adaptability demonstrates the reality that human children make unconscious choices.

They unconsciously choose which *Core Values Strategy* to use in a given situation with a given type of person who is expressing certain characteristics. Since the adults that surround that child are fearfully larger and in definite control, this adaptive instinct is paramount for initial survival, for approval, success, and general well-being.

We each build from this personal experience of action, reaction, interaction, a set of beliefs, attitudes, and ideas—our personal truth, regarding the relative success and reliability of our innate self, our *Real Core Values Self*—when faced with life's challenges.

This set of beliefs and attitudes becomes an ego-driven, fear-based screen through which we view life.

We judge the people and environment around us, make decisions that derive directly from our personal set of beliefs, and take actions—shifting out of primary *Core Values Strategies* into alternate strategies based upon our ego-driven fears and judgments.

The end result is a set of stimulus-response behaviors that we consistently exhibit and rely upon for safety and comfort. This set of unconscious behaviors creates a personality—the way we as individuals are choosing to show up in life. People around us will say, "That's just the way she is. That's her personality."

Every time we unconsciously choose to follow this adapted behavior pattern, we reinforce our reliance upon it and become more and more emotionally attached to that behavior. We eventually come to rely on these patterns so absolutely that we identify with the behavior—we see it as a true expression of self. Our unconsciously designed personality becomes our conscious identity.

Positive Warping

If the value structures of mom and dad, sister and brother are the same as our own, our behavioral choices are constantly affirmed even in situations where the strategies inherent in a different value set would produce better, more effective results. To the degree that this occurs, we become overly affirmed in our dominant values and our lesser values may be almost completely ignored.

Like the negative warping, this positive warping also causes us to make inappropriate judgments and to take ineffective action out of stimulus-response patterning, yielding results that are ineffective, dissatisfying, and unfulfilling.

Since we tend to hold one or more *Core Value Energies* in greater quantity than the others, we naturally choose to start most actions and reactions from the strategies that are driven by these values. We become better at living in alignment with these preferred values, so we become still more comfortable—to the final point, that we tend to continue operating in alignment with our dominant *core values*, even when those strategies are not the best or the most effective in a given situation.

We continue to do these things unconsciously until we start feeling anxiety about our effectiveness or safety. If we do not wake up into consciousness at these decision points, we tend to hold to our first chosen course until we push ourselves over the edge of anxiety and into fear. This causes us to unconsciously shift into a *Negative Conflict Strategy*™; the one that is aligned with and is a pretense of the dominant *core value* that we have been warped into relying upon too much.

Negative Warping

Since the value structures of mom and dad are different from our own, much of who we are, many of our values and the resulting choices, are to some degree diminished, not affirmed, or even ridiculed. We learn to hide those unappreciated parts of ourselves and adjust our behavior to present more acceptable parts of ourselves and our behaviors. We are required to deal with our parents whether they are being a clean version of their innate *Core Values Nature*, or acting out some personality pattern.

Whether we are overly affirmed in our dominant values or restricted in expression of our dominant values, we all end up a little *warped*. We are either pressed to rely more heavily on values that mirror a dominant parent or we are encouraged to diminish those parts of ourselves that are not valued, or may be ridiculed or stamped out by a dominant parent.

Note: All adults and older siblings are dominant in the child's universe.

Situations arise that make us feel fearful and threatened. We construct our own unique personality based upon our instinct to survive, to obtain sustenance, and to maintain social acceptability. We construct our ego-based personalities on a foundation of fear and protective strategies. This process serves us very well as long as we reside within the constructs of our family of origin and our original small community.

?????????????????????????

Our natural survival instinct (ego) is forced to choose an instant response that is either effective or ineffective. The ego (survival instinct) constantly expands its range of influence to include all social, political, emotional, and psychological issues. Our egos choose from our *Core Values Nature*—first from the dominant, then the secondary, and finally third- and fourth-level *Core Value Energies.*

We adapt, choose reactions and responses which are deemed most effective at the time, and begin building a new personality (stimulus-and-response behavior set), one that is intended to help us survive in this world without too much harm, possibly structured for future success. This structuring of the personality is directed by the ego whose mission is to assure our survival, our safety, and our comfort.

My mother, for instance, was a strong *builder/innovator*, highly *independent*, directive, decisive, and *powerful*. My father is a *merchant/innovator/banker*, soft spoken, connecting, prudent, and careful, slow to decide and careful in the choice of actions. I, as a *merchant/innovator/builder*, had no hope in competing with the *power*-based Goddess/Mother in my life who towered over me and was fully in charge of my survival.

Although I have some strong *builder* drivers in me, I learned that these traits were not desirable, not allowed by my mother, and not respected or loved by my father. My father's clear message was that only *love* is important and that constant self-sacrifice was essential under the edicts of his definition of *love*. This made my *power* urges unacceptable to both parents upon whom I depended.

After all, to be a *builder* energy was to be like my mother, and she was too overwhelming to compete with or to tolerate (within a *merchant/love* value structure) much of the time. She did not have a great respect for the *love*-based *merchant* in me since her life strategies were mostly driven by *power*. But she liked my nonresistant, affectionate *merchant* characteristics and enjoyed the presence of me as a *loving*, responsive, and *creative* child. I acquiesced to her power and won favor. My brothers took her on, confronted her power and were often defeated and won very little favor from her.

These *merchant* characteristics, driven by *love*-based values were far more tolerable to her than any *power*-based strategies that might have challenged her *power* position. So I warped myself into an extreme *merchant*, diminishing the likelihood that I would face conflict with my *power*-based mother and assuring the *love* and approval of my *merchant* father.

This was an effective strategy for me as a child, so effective that I outperformed my brothers in obtaining parent approval. This competitive success caused them to dislike or hate me as a child, a restriction of relationship with my brothers that continues to plague me, even today.

As an adult, living in the adult world where effectiveness in business dictates freedom of choice in other areas of one's life, my *warped* personality was not always helpful in obtaining success and was sometimes downright embarrassing. I found over time that to be successful in business I would need to allow more of the *builder-power* energy to come through and diminish the extreme portions of my carefully constructed *merchant* behaviors.

I had to become more decisive, less fearful of conflict, and more willing to accept another person's anger. I had to learn to exert myself and take control when appropriate and to take decisive action, cause an effect, and deal with the consequences.

I had to learn that it was tolerable, often effective, and sometimes necessary to act in a manner that others might dislike—when those actions were honorable (in my judgment) and effective in creating the desired results. These new choices were not comfortable for my ego-based, *merchant* strategies–preferred personality.

As I learned to bring forward my natural *power* energies, I also learned to love these energies in others. *Powerful* women have become a welcome and respected presence in my life, and *power*-based men are revered for their amazingly simple and *powerful* approach to living. All of this opening to *power* has enhanced the effectiveness of my life.

By learning to un-warp my negative attitudes toward *power*, I have made my *wise love* strategies more effective. I have deepened my relationships with others dramatically. My business success has re-doubled several times.

We are each given this kind of life problem to work out. It is one of the primary questions of our life on earth: Who am I really? What is my meaning and purpose here? How can I be more effective in getting the things I want, in achieving the fulfilling successes I desire? How much have I warped away from my deepest, most innate *core values* in response to the dynamics of my childhood? Which parts of me are the natural parts and which are the results of the warping?

Note: Even if we have perfect parents, totally free from personal agenda, the fact that children have a *Core Values Nature* that is different from their parents would still cause the warping process due to the deep dependency the human creature has on its original family.

The Universal Life Process

The simple course of life is a building up of the personality self, directed by the survival instinct (ego) in response to fear. In the first stage of adulthood most of us validate this essential warping by continuing to practice the strategies and tactics that are driven by our ego-based personality.

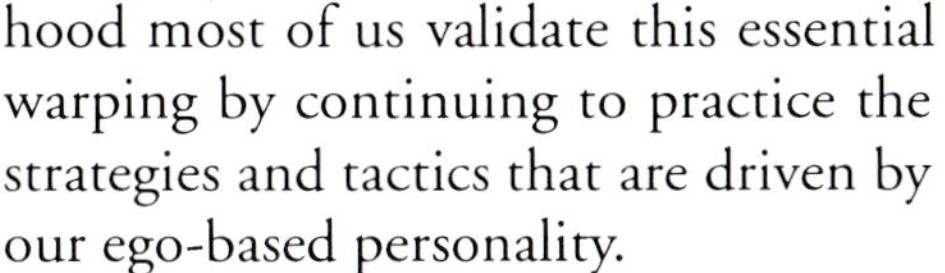

We make constant unconscious choices to remain true to our adapted beliefs, attitudes, and ideas that rationalize our personality. We become ever more emotionally committed to and psychologically attached to our ego-based personality.

This stage is followed by the slow uncovering and discovery of the true self, the *Real Core Values Self*, and the slow death of the ego-constructed personality. As we become more rationally conscious, and choose to return consciously to full expression of our *Real Core Values Self*, we allow our true person, our unique recipe of *love*, *power*, *knowledge*, and *wisdom* to emerge and be fully actualized.

This leads us into a role in life in which we can make our highest and best contribution. Fulfillment and meaning and a sense of purpose are all dependent upon our success in achieving this death of personality and full expression of our innate *Real Core Values Self*.

The single most critical skill to learn while
mastering this life process, is to . . .

MAKE EFFECTIVE CONSCIOUS CHOICES CONSTANTLY

6

Choosing to Become More Concious and Intentional

As a general rule we continue to choose our mostly unconscious manner of living until the pain of continuing is greater than our fear of seeing the truth about ourselves and making different choices. We are terrified of acknowledging accountability for our lives. We do not want the blame for those aspects of our life we deem to be unsuccessful or embarrassing.

When we allow our warped personality strategies to remain in control of our lives, as adults we find ourselves unable to make different choices on the fly. We find it hard to consciously observe our own actions, to note our ineffectiveness as it happens, or to choose to take control of our lives, one moment and one choice at a time. Instead we remain trapped in patterns of behavior that are not effective in getting us what we now want as adults.

In our *Taylor Protocols*™ training and development classes I often refer to the story attributed to the founder of Alcoholics Anonymous.

One night a man awakened from deep sleep and could not get back to sleep. So even though it was 2:00 in the morning, he got up, got dressed, and went out his front door. At the first street corner, he turned right and continued along the sidewalk, then turned right again at the next street corner.

As he walked he found himself turning left at the next street, right at the next, left again, right again, until he had zigzagged his way to a particularly dark street in a strange part of town. Turning right into that dark street, he walked quickly toward the lighted street corner ahead, but suddenly found himself falling into a deep hole.

Bruised and shaken, he climbed up out of the hole, returned home, and fell back to sleep.

The next night he once again awakened after midnight, restlessly got up and dressed, left his home, turning right at the first street corner, and zigzagged himself once again into the particularly dark street. He walked quickly until he came to the dark hole in the street and fell in.

The next night was the same.

The question to ask is . . .
"How long would ***you*** continue to do this?"

Yet, isn't this the very pattern of behavior we find ourselves in with certain individuals in certain situations in our lives? Don't we all fall into step with old patterns of behavior—stimulus and response with a given person or situation—until we find ourselves falling into a dark hole of negative reactions and attack strategies, acting as if our lives depended upon the outcome of an innocuous situation or social skirmish? Don't we feel negative feelings and say silently to ourselves some set of beliefs and rationalizations that make this kind of circumstance the other person's fault?

Some of us consider ourselves to be more mature than this. This may be true for some. But this side of perfection—the side I constantly find myself on—this tendency to hold our own behavior in the best possible light, while visualizing shadows in the other person's personality, remains a challenging aspect of our adult world.

Be careful not to dismiss too quickly the reality of the hold your personality (ego) has on you.

Remember our discussion about our emotional commitment to the beliefs, attitudes, and ideas that justify our personalities? These beliefs and attitudes are the ones that cause a CEO in a given company to keep people employed for him who are not effective in their work. Another CEO may find herself intolerant of anyone who does not meet her emotionally charged rigid standards of organization or punctuality, sending incredibly talented, hard-to-replace individuals to the competition.

Even these recognized leaders find themselves under the spell of their own carefully constructed ego-driven personalities. The next question to ask ourselves: "Is it possible to make conscious choices that would extract us from such repeated episodes?" If yes, then why do we continue in these hurtful, ineffective behaviors?

Ego: A New Definition

The human ego is our innate creature survival instinct automatically responding to nonsurvival, social situations. Our egos operate at the subconscious level, governing our personality's choice of reactions to specific situations from a position of fear.

The innate survival mechanism that exists in each of us, as it does in all of earth's creatures, performs its work effectively at the physical level. We stop and listen if we feel ourselves being followed at night on a dark street. We clench our fists and our adrenal glands begin pumping, actually increasing the strength of our muscles when we feel threatened. We are able to run faster, jump higher, and fight harder when our instinctual survival mechanism is activated. But most of the time in our modern world we do not find ourselves in *physical* jeopardy.

The fact is that most people do not learn to live significantly beyond this instinctual stimulus-response level of existence. We venture from our cloistered family settings into the larger society and find ourselves in competition for attention, approval, acknowledgment, learning, skills, jobs, comforts, and life mates. When these important, but not survival-critical elements, appear to be threatened by others, we respond from an instinctual survival fear.

Our survival instinct begins to construct safe responses aligned with the warped personalities we have developed throughout our childhood—building life strategies around these circumstance and emotional dramas. We become a well-designed, ego-driven personality that is a little warped and uncomfortable.

Personality: A New Definition

Personality is the adapted version of a person's *Real Core Values Self*, warped for safety reasons by the survival instinct (ego) to protect us from harm in our physical and social environment. The personality is an emotionally charged set of behaviors that are rationalized by attitudes, beliefs, and ideas about why it is better to be *who I am not*, rather than to be *who I really am.*

As we move from total dependence to a self-sufficient socialized person, our survival instinct continues to do its work. The ego that was born out of the survival instinct now has dominion over our personality, the way we are choosing to show up. Our personality is the result of unconscious choices made in response to the fears encountered in childhood reaffirmed by the ego and transferred by the ego into social situations in adulthood.

This happens in alignment with our survival mechanisms. The emotionally loaded behavior patterns and the events that call them up are stored in our brain stem, so that the incoming signals from our ears, eyes, skin, and nose can be monitored. When something that the ego deems to be threatening gets into this screen, there is only one thought allowed, only one action or response suggested, and it is suggested with the same weight that our autonomic nervous system commands our heart to beat its next beat.

All of our actions and behaviors are rationalized by the beliefs, attitudes, and ideas we hold to be true about our experiences. We are emotionally committed to believe our unique view of reality. This justifies our personality reactions.

Our personality is governed from the subconscious level by our ego and not by our innate *Real Core Values Nature*. It keeps us doing the same thing we did yesterday, today.

As children we chose from our innate *core values* which value strategy was most likely to be effective in a given circumstance. This happens in a perfectly designed manner, the same way within each of us. We have a built-in wiring that prefers one *Core Value Energy* over the others. The most dominant *Core Value Energy* is usually the first energy we employ in each situation. If this doesn't succeed, then we shift unconsciously to the second-level *core value*, etc.

We can only operate in alignment with one of our innate *core values* at any given moment. We tend to rely upon and continue to operate in alignment with our most dominantly held *core values*, until we experience anxiety that we are not getting the results we want. We are wired to shift from one *Core Value Energy* to another whenever this anxiety occurs. This assures maximum effectiveness as an adult.

The anxieties come to our conscious attention by showing up in our physical body as a tight shoulder, a clinched jaw, red ears, flushed cheeks, pounding heart, shortness of breath. The anxiety and its physical messages is designed to cause us to become conscious of the need to stop being our most comfortable dominant *Core Value Energy* and shift to a more effective *Core Value Energy*.

If we shift from our dominant *Core Value Energy* to our secondary *Core Value Energy* when we are experiencing anxiety, we are able to continue operating effectively in alignment with this innate way of being. We can continue to be and act in alignment with our *Real Core Values Nature.*

When we stick with our dominant *Core Value Energy* (keep trying to be *power, love, wisdom,* or *knowledge)* even when we are being ineffective—when we continue this beyond anxiety into the belief that we are not adequate in our most important *core value*—this anxiety turns to fear. We then shift into our *Negative Conflict Strategy.* The *Negative Conflict Strategy* for each *core value* is a defensive pretense of that *core value.* The *power* energy turns into *intimidation. Knowledge* becomes *aloof judgment. Wisdom* becomes *interrogation,* and *love* turns into *manipulation.*

The excitation of the *Negative Conflict Strategy* is designed to serve the needs of our personality, to protect us, and to help us get what we want.

Our personality is a mixture of these personally chosen modifications to our *core values* self. We each have a unique puzzle to work on—how to un-warp ourselves, how to live our lives consistent with our *Real Core Values Self* rather than our fear-based, ego-driven personality.

Many of us get stuck in the process of trying to solve this puzzle, forgetting that the puzzle doesn't matter, only the desired result—to *be* the person we were created to *be,* and to make our highest and best contribution to our world.

This is the primary center of modern positive psychology, to shift our focus from trying to overcome old traumatic experiences and emotional problems, toward an understanding of our innate unchanging nature. Instead of working to change our bad behaviors and fix our wounded spirits, the first emphasis of the positive psychology approach is to encourage discovery of one's *real self*, and to seek to bring this unique nature into full fruition and positive contribution.

It was Abraham Maslow with his seminal book, *Toward a Psychology of Being*, who now takes the center ground as the founding father of positive psychology. He spent thirty years working to understand why some people are engaged in the work that they do, and why others are not. In this effort he uncovered an important revelation of how people tend to operate—relative to their wired in needs.

He disclosed this new thinking as a pyramid of prioritized needs that most of us with college education learned about in Psych 101.

Redefining Peak Experience

It is important that we understand this critical internal structure of human needs and desires. This has been accepted by most as a very reasonable description of human experience. The *Core Values Index* and the *Human Operating System* it reveals, provides a new understanding of the very top of this pyramid, and also illustrates how our innate unchanging nature leads us into and through the various levels of human development, toward full actualization of *who we are* and *why we are here*.

The Peak Experience that Maslow talked about is related to a person achieving full self-actualization. This means that a person comes to know himself and is in the process of perfecting himself, and mostly, of being himself. Then the work that he does, the contribution he makes, requires his highest skills, his best self, and his most focused attention. This causes the fully actualized person to make his highest and best contribution. It is the experience of making this purpose-filled contribution that we believe best describes what Maslow called Peak Experiences.

In *Toward a Psychology of Being*, Maslow points toward this apex of human experience and says that only a few achieve it and then only occasionally, and seemingly almost accidentally.

We now have strong evidence regarding the elements of human life that comprise this peak experience phenomenon. We assert that it need not be merely occasional and certainly need not rely upon chance. We propose a new definition.

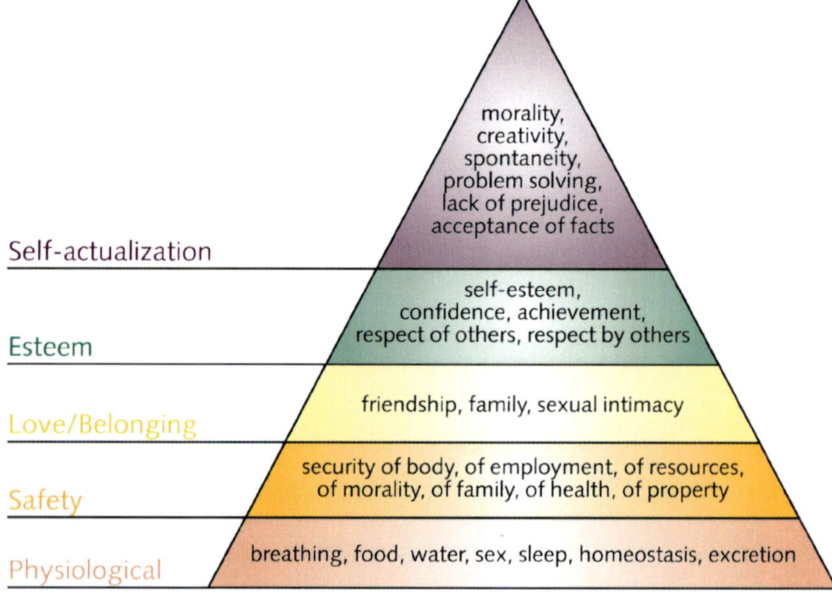

A New Definition of Peak Experience

When an individual . . .
contributes the pure energy of his innate unchanging
***Real Core Values Self* to his society, delivered through**
his strongest well-honed skills and talents,
in the role to which he is called by his innate nature,
in which his highest wired-in passions are enlivened
by work that captures his focused interests,
. . . this person has peak experience.
He is making the highest contribution he is able
to make at this point in his life.
For some this experience is a regular and almost
constant state of life.

Peak Experiences are the natural result of a life committed to *Core Values Consciousness*. The graphic that follows illustrates the top segment of Maslow's Hierarchy of Needs triangle, that shows a person moving through a series of steps that begins with physiological survival needs and culminates in a need for meaningful existence, through which one becomes fully actualized as an individual.

In other words, as each person advances in life through each phase of needs awareness and satisfaction, he constantly approaches the ultimate purposeful life—a fully actualized life (I became what I was *meant to become*, and did what I was *meant to do*. I *am being who I really am*, doing the *Real Work* I am *called to do*.) This is not a linear progression in which a person graduates forever into the higher level of being. We shift in and out of these levels of need based not only upon our own maturation, but also based upon the surprises that life holds for us in circumstances; those that are difficult and those that are filled with grace and high rewards.

Our Self-Actualization graphic is the breakout of Maslow's top triangle (his peak). The *Core Values Index* and our work with more than 200,000 people over the course of twenty years has led us to a new understanding of Peak Experience. This is built upon a new understanding and explication of what a fully actualized human life is. We call this top of the human needs pyramid the activation of self-actualization. We have learned which human nature elements must be engaged in order for self-actualization to be achieved.

The *Core Values Index* provides the first clear picture of the nature of the innate self and an easy way to measure the relative *Core Value Energies* in each person's unique *Real Core Values Self.* The power of this is to provide a simple and fast way to uncover the *real self* quickly and to understand it. This new and refreshing understanding then provides a clear way to begin leading a more conscious existence. Dr. David Mashburn has studied more than 2,300 different assessments and makes this statement regarding our *Core Values Index*:

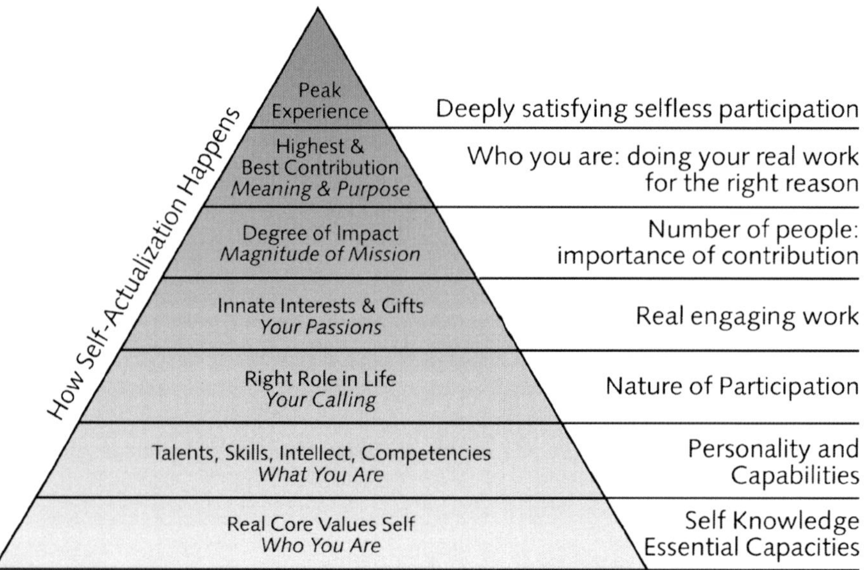

The Core Values Index has done an excellent job at capturing some of the innate core traits of the person's unchanging nature. Several experts in optimal human functioning such as Abraham Maslow, Peter Drucker, and Marcus Buckingham have described these core traits as an "inner bent," "propensity," or "core wiring." Because of this, Taylor Protocols is able to make a compelling and convincing connection between the essential nature of each person and the tasks and contributions that are inherent in his/her work.
Dr. David Mashburn

David Mashburn, Ph.D., has over twenty years' experience as a clinical psychologist, teaching assessments at the graduate level, and is an Organizational Consultant who is also Adjunct Professor of Business at Seattle Pacific University, in Seattle, Washington.

We are wired in our *Core Values Nature* to be made aware of dysfunctional or ineffective behavior through anxiety. We are designed to be made aware of the need to shift from being our current chosen *core value* into being one of our other *Core Values Strategies.* We will usually choose between our dominant and secondary *core value* and occasionally from our third- and fourth-level *core values.*

This is how we as children adopted our personality tactics and strategies unconsciously. The anxiety/fear cycle is the key to optimizing our effectiveness as an adult. It provides us the switch that turns on our conscious awareness and allows us to always choose consciously which *Core Value Energy* to be at this next moment.

So instead of working so hard to try to discipline ourselves to behave better, we are now able to become consciously aware of the motivating *core value* we are being at this moment. We can be significantly assisted through the *Core Values Index's* clear characterization of this innate nature, to understand what it feels like to operate in each of our most preferred *Core Values Strategies.*

This automatically causes a person to see himself in a positive light, even when he is being ineffective. The conscious shifting to a different *Core Values Strategy* puts the individual in full charge of his life energies. And since we are most effective when we are acting in fearless alignment with our most innate *Core Value Energies*, this is the ultimate key to human success.

Instead of being at the mercy of our old emotionally weighted behavior patterns that are not effective in our adult world, the adult person is now able to assume full ownership of his chosen strategies and to feel personally empowered to make a higher and better contribution of his deepest innate *Core Values Nature* to his society. We can learn to easily shift from a currently unsuccessful *Core Values Strategy* into one of our other strongly preferred strategies. This causes two important results:

- We avoid living in and acting out of fear, and
- We optimize our success and fulfillment because we can more continuously act in a positive, energized manner to fulfill our sense of meaning and purpose.

The alternative to learning adult *Core Values Consciousness* is to remain shackled by our survival instinct (ego) that never shuts down. It is always aware of all forms of attack or perceived attack. It is fear-based and ready to name almost any perceived threat as a legitimate reason for stimulation of a survival response. In social and business settings these perceived challenges come often. The responses driven by ego are never the best and are often destructive to our psyche and to our success.

As instinctual animals we often experience fear. Fear of failure or embarrassment. Fear of emotional hurts—rejection, disrespect, isolation (which connects to fear of starvation, freezing, loss of life through attack, all due to loss of group support). We are afraid of loss of emotional control, loss of mental utility, insanity, loss of social power and prestige, loss of mates, loss of jobs and professional status.

We make far too many decisions based upon anxiety and fear.

Being sentient creatures, we are able to rationalize and interpret any perceived social threat, no matter how innocuous, as a possible danger. A person's boss expresses disappointment in a small project. This offense is rationalized by the ego into a survival response. "I failed to satisfy the requirements. I will be passed over for a raise, possibly fired. If I am fired, I will lose the respect of my spouse and children. I may not be able to find another job. I will lose my family and my possessions. I will be out on the street, alone."

If we listen carefully to the tingling of our own unique set of fears in such moments of disapproval, we will find a similar string of internally verbalized rationalizations rattling around in our heads. Most of this is not usually brought into our conscious thoughts, but the reality of a buzzing adrenal gland or the sudden shutdown of capillaries in the brain causing a migraine, is all the proof one needs to identify this kind of fear reaction.

And most of us have experienced the after-the-fact mind mulling, in which mode we do hear ourselves thinking all of these self-justifying personality beliefs and attitudes that also tend to denigrate others.

We know through exploration of the use of our *Core Values Index*–based *Human Operating System* with thousands of individuals, that we are all able to bring all of this nonconscious, internal talking into consciousness. We are given specific types of anxiety to accompany each innate *Core Value Energy*. The purpose of this anxiety is two-fold: it serves to awaken us to our current ineffectiveness and to entice us to shift consciously to a different *Core Value Energy*, to be a different presence in the situation.

The anxiety, having awakened the conscious mind, provides a brief moment in which we can listen to the emotionally driven tapes of our fear-belief statements that come reeling into our mind. These fear-exciting phrases are a practiced mantra that reinforces the creative, survival instinct (ego) control.

Having been awakened enough to hear the phrases that roll through the brain on these occasions, we are provided a moment of conscious choice. We can choose once again to believe these emotionally weighted thought patterns, or we can choose to deny them. We can then incite our emotional rejection of these self-talk addictive phrases and break their hold on us.

We can then consciously shift into being a different *core value* presence, employing a different positive mode of action that aligns with our innate *Core Values Nature*, rather than relenting control of our behavior to our ego-driven personality.

We can easily attribute these reactions to the innocuous situation we are presently confronted with.

It is the ego's job to make certain we are conditioned to instantly react to such perceived threats at the survival level since at this level the response is pre-programmed and hardwired into the reticular receivers in our brain stem. This assures the quickest response with proof of survival success. It also works to keep us unconscious and therefore without the opportunity for choice.

Our survival instinct reacts to all forms of fear, internally or externally excited. We may find ourselves, as human creatures, in a rage or in a depression in direct response to a series of thoughts we are having *in private* (in a physically safe place, far away from any source of real danger) even when we are very distanced from such perceived threats by future time or past time.

Even then, our survival instinct still kicks in, exciting the need to respond to the fear, and searching for the most appropriate practiced response that will ensure our safety. This is the basis for anxiety disorders or for worrying something to death. In this process we completely forget our innate *core values*. We forget to make our values-compelled contribution.

Since we limit ourselves to proven strategies for safety, we are often necessarily functioning from a value set other than our dominant *core values*. We made the shift from being one *Core Value Energy* to another in childhood when we were unable to adequately meet situational requirements without being hurt or ignored and abandoned. These shifts have become part of our pattern of behavior, our personality, the way we are choosing to show up in the room.

This fear-trigger, ego-driven survival effect is built into us by all of the eons of human evolution. Edward O. Wilson, in his groundbreaking work, *Consilience, The Unity of Knowledge*, describes this mechanism:

"The human brain bears the stamps of 400 million years of trial and error, traceable by fossils and molecular homology in nearly unbroken sequence from fish to amphibian to reptile to primitive mammal to our immediate primate forerunners. In the final step the brain was catapulted to a radically new level, equipped for language and culture. Because of its ancient pedigree, however, it could not be planted like a new computer into an empty cranial space. The old being had to be jerry-rigged in steps within and around the old brain. Otherwise, the organism could not have survived generation by generation. The result was human nature: genius animated with animal craftiness and emotion, combining the passion of politics and art with rationality, to create a new instrument of survival."

This survival instinct, expanded over the centuries of evolution, is now fully and subtly integrated into and applied to all aspects of human existence even where actual physical survival risks are not at play. Each of our ego-driven personalities is a newly designed survival mechanism whose mission is overstated, and oversized, based upon our participation as adults in our current environmental and sociological systems.

We remain mostly asleep spiritually and psychologically as individuals and as a people. It feels safer to continue in our patterned responses than to take control and make conscious *choices* about what *Core Value Energy* might be best in a given situation. After all, we did survive this far without dying and with much less harm than would have occurred without our ego's protective guidance.

The universal purpose of human life is to come into an awareness of these mind-body factors and rise to our highest selves—spiritual beings living within and in control of physical bodies, including the intellect, emotions, and psychological natures of the physical self. Our universal purpose is to un-warp ourselves, to return to our real energy core, that unique blend of *power/faith, love/truth, wisdom/compassion, and knowledge/justice.* Our personal recipe of *core values* is what makes each of us the unique individual that we are.

It is this migration of the survival instinct into areas of emotional, psychological, and rational domains that makes the human animal different from all other creatures. This survival instinct, playing large in areas in which it was not originally designed to play, creates the human ego. Ego's enlarged domain, then, is the protection of the total self.

The total self is defined by all of the social and physical possessions or domains that are claimed by and identified with each person. We attach ourselves emotionally to the things around us, to our physical possessions, to our emotions, and to our perceived life framework. Any threat to any of these attachments is perceived as a threat to survival.

The ego's assignment is to see, anticipate, and design responses to all things and to all situations that by the lessons of experience are identified as fearful. Such situations are to be feared not just because our physical survival may be at stake, but feared because such situations may take away some abstract personal attachment or physical possession that is respected and deemed worthy of protection.

We believe at the personality ego level that we have the right and even the responsibility to protect everything we possess, including our emotions, ideas, and personality traits. Certainly such things as our jobs, the respect of others, money, our houses and cars, our children—everything that we have claimed as part of our life framework—all of this is subject now to the protection of our ego-driven, fear-based personality.

The subconscious mechanism ruled by the ego is perceived as being safer than the conscious choice of strategy—which *core value* is most needed at this moment. This is held to be true because the stimulus-response mechanism remains in place and allows for almost instantaneous reaction. Only one thought at a time is allowed to come into our consciousness. Why? To save us from confusion, and to speed the response time for maximum survival.

Notice we are not discussing ultimate social effectiveness here. We are talking about taking and getting, about defending our emotional attachments—not about making our highest and best contribution—not about being who we really are.

Each of us, if we look at our present adult life, can easily identify times in which we have not been effective, by our own judgment. These times are almost always driven by our protective ego and are often described as times when we were "just beside ourselves." This language is perfect. Our *Real Core Values Self* has been put aside and the personality has been brought forward by the ego, based upon our anxieties and fears.

Most of us would not consciously choose to behave in this manner. When we are "beside ourselves," we generally do not achieve the end result we are looking for as adults, and we usually have created some sort of a mess that we have to clean up later.

Making the choice to remain unconscious and to allow a fear-based shift to pre-programmed personality responses is a choice that keeps on giving. When this choice is made, those around us think they can now see the real person, the one they dislike and fear. They tend to believe more in the personality self that we have retreated into, than the *real self* that we were choosing to *be* just moments before. We have spoiled our chances to be effective with these people for the moment and possibly for all future moments.

Conscious choice requires a few brief moments for consideration. These moments of indecision in a life-threatening situation could be deadly. This is why the reticular receiver in the brain stem allows only one thought to come to consciousness at a time. It screens first for automatic, fear-based reactions.

If an urgent response message is received, there is a quick look-up in our brain for previous situations or patterns of circumstance. The goal is to decide instantly upon a response with a predictable outcome. Finding a pattern that closely matches the current urgent response message, an automatic trigger is sent to the hypothalamus and the appropriate mental, five senses, physical muscle response is triggered without conscious thought.

This personality-based stimulus-response mechanism is the reason we sometimes find ourselves acting in a manner that is embarrassing, or at least ineffective in adult situations. The phrase, "I was beside myself" is germane to this auto-response.

Because we attach ourselves to land and property, businesses and possessions, we make the protection of these things as vital to ourselves as is the freedom to take a breath or avoid physical harm. We attach ourselves to the image we want others to have of us. These attachments are driven by our own privately held low self-respect, which we seek to overcome through the creation of a material world around us, one that proves our worth.

The ego-constructed personality considers this self-constructed framework (job, relationships, beliefs and ideas, hobbies and activities, personality) part of the total self. The personality responds to any perceived threat to any of these things at the survival level, an instinctual, fear-filled protective position.

The selected strategic responses of the human animal are designed by the ego in accordance with innate animal reactions to physical threat, and in accordance with our practiced emotionally supported behavior strategies that are loosely aligned with one of our *core values—power*, *love*, *knowledge*, and *wisdom*.

The tactics that result from these *core values* are very different and result in hugely different effects—results. They are not fear-based so they do not tend to arouse fear in others. The actions have a *creative*, contributory agenda, so it is less likely that others will feel that something is being taken away from them.

Fear in me invokes fear in you. Clean agenda and congruence between *who I am*, and *what I am* choosing to do, causes people to trust, to want to cooperate and participate with us.

As the human animal learns to accommodate its adult social/cultural world, each learns to apply its unique mix of these innate *core values* in different ways based upon the results of past choices. In later chapters we will explore extensively the differences in strategies and tactics employed by persons attempting to honor their unique recipe of innate *core values*.

Wes's Story

Let's talk about a person who is doing the work of finding his place of highest and best contribution—and who has recently made a dramatic shift of occupations. I am thinking about Wes. And Wes is his real name. I know he will be honored to have us talk about him in this book. He deserves the acknowledgment. He is living a heroic life.

When I first met Wes he was working as an inside sales person for a mid-sized industrial equipment distributor/dealer in Seattle, Washington. Actually we didn't meet first face to face. We met via video conference call, a sales meeting for the entire sales department. I was the hired gun, asked to come into the company and stop its five-year decline into soon-to-be oblivion.

I liked Wes.

He was honest and straightforward. The sales manager and the newly anointed temporary company president—the fifth in three years—had already decided to fire Wes. This was ironic, since one of my greatest concerns was the inability of the senior management to make tough decisions and move things forward. Now they were completely set upon firing a person that struck me as a diamond in the rough. Or more like a golf ball in the rough—not in the fairway where it belongs.

A fluke of fate occurred.

Wes's teammate, the outside rep in his territory, resigned and went to the competition. It was decided that Wes would be kept on board temporarily to help cover the now vacant and valuable territory. This went against my grain, because his *Core Values Nature* was all wrong for the outside sales position.

Also, I liked him and felt I might be able to find a place for him on the team. I didn't want to spoil things by setting him up for failure.

Still, when a company is in survival mode, sometimes you have to just keep everyone bailing water a little longer to keep things afloat.

Needless to say, Wes did not make it as a sales rep for his company.

He floundered miserably within a few short weeks, and his employee neck was exposed a second time under my watch. But I was now getting my feet. The board of directors had given us carte blanche, and I had removed the poorly selected president and lost my sales manager in the process. This was not unexpected or life threatening.

The company would survive and a new sales manager (who is now serving as the president and CEO under our management) had already been found.

The changes were made.

One of the first assignments for our new sales executive was for her to figure out what to do with Wes. I told her that the decision was hers but that I wanted her to know I felt that Wes did not belong in field sales. He had a great attitude. I believed he had significant talents that the company could use. He had the right *Core Values Nature* for two other positions.

She heard the essence and went to work.

Before long I found Wes working back in Seattle at the home office as the operations coordinator. His high energy, great customer and team member relationships, and his quick-minded problem-solving, combined with his indomitable optimism, brought new energy and focus to our operations team.

His unique *Core Values Nature* was perfectly suited for the job he was now given, and he began to show his stuff.

Wes is now one of the most valued players in his company. He has been given broad operations responsibilities. This honor and respect is given to a person who had been written off as a sales loser.

Way to go, Wes.

And way to go, team.

Putting the right person in the right seat doing the right work is the single greatest accomplishment in business. Nothing else can make as much difference as quickly. And the mistakes that are made while attempting this feat from the usual subjective, ignorant position of most hiring managers, is often, if not always, the reason for any company's failure. Wes was educated in his understanding of his *Real Core Values Self.* He was coached to be clear about his place of highest and best contribution.

We can now ask: Wes, *who are you*?

And Wes's answer will be: I am a problem-solver and a fixer. I am a team creator and player coach. I am action and resolve and commitment. I am your energy to get things done. I have the talents and skills to make myself very useful to this company. I am a *power wisdom* person.

Now, this is getting a little closer to a good answer to our question, isn't it?

So, who are you?

Well, you are not your body, or your brain, or your skills, or your family name, or your personal name, or your occupational description, or your social role, or your talents, or your capabilities, or your style of clothes.

You are not your character or your personality or your reputation.

The list goes on.

None of these things that we have traditionally used to describe to others *who I am* are real indicators of *who we really are.* None of them point, any more than very generally, to any kind of occupation, work, or avocation. They only serve to provide others with a way to identify us through observable things—kind of like one dog getting comfortable with another by smelling his scent.

We, you and I, are so much more than this.

We are the *Core Value Energies* that comprise our *real self.*

We are a unique blend of these *core values*, housed in a body with certain capabilities.

We are not our capabilities. We are not the competencies we have reached by applying our talents.

We are the capacity of our person to *be* and to *contribute love, wisdom, knowledge*, and *power* to our social circumstances.

We are a unique blend of these intrinsic unchanging energies. We *are* the very contributions that we are here to make to our world.

We are each an individual that is different from every other individual on the planet. We are each different from every human alive now and forever before and from this time onward.

We have one life to live (as far as we know), one life within which to discover *who we are*—and one mission universal—to discover *who we are*, the *real self*, and to contribute this *real self* in the unique way inscribed within this self—to contribute our *real selves* to the world for as long as we live in it. We are each on a mission to find our place of highest and best contribution.

We are the *nature of our real self* and the *capacities* of that *real self* to be the delivered presence of the *core values* that make up our most central identity.

We are a consciousness that is alive and in control of a body and a mind.

We are the regulator of our own subconscious and conscious minds.

We are the seat of consciousness and the essence of our own contribution to the world.

Who we are is the contribution we are here to make to our world, through our work and through our activities within our society.

If you can't answer the question, Who Are You?, how can you possibly find the right place to work, the right work to do, the right job that is designed to allow the highest and best contribution of your unique self to your community?

7

Understanding Your CVI Score Better

To understand your *Core Values Index* (*CVI*™) score better, you simply look at the *core value* (*builder power*, or *banker knowledge*, etc.) with the highest score; let's say 22 points. That is your dominant *core value*. Next is a score of, say, 19, your secondary score, then a score of 16, your tertiary *core value*, and finally your minor *core value*, a score of 15, for a total of 72 points.

This *CVI* profile is the most common spread of scores. About 75% of all individuals have a similar spread of *core values* preferences with a 3-point, plus-or-minus, difference between values.

We know from the hundreds of thousands of persons that have taken the *CVI* that there is an important change of nature that happens when the difference between a person's primary *core value* score and the secondary score is three points or greater. We call this an *order of magnitude change*, because the nature of the person operates by shifting between *core values* in order to meet current circumstances effectively.

When there is a difference of only 1 or 2 points between scores, there is a preference for the dominant over the secondary, but the individual's ability to easily shift from the dominant to the secondary is high. When the difference is greater than 3, the ease of shifting out of a dominant into secondary operating mode is many times more difficult and the ability to continue to operate in the secondary *core value* motivation for any significant amount of time is greatly reduced.

We see a compounding of this effect when the difference between the dominant and secondary is greater than 6 points, and again, when it is greater than 9 points.

This same effect occurs when the score of the secondary is 3 or more points greater than the tertiary scores and also the difference between the tertiary and the minor scores.

It is very important, when attempting to understand how you operate at the conscious and the unconscious level, to study the relative scores of *all* of your *core values*. You will learn why it is so difficult for you to shift down into your tertiary *Core Value Energies* if the score in that *core value* is 4 points less than in your secondary and the secondary is 5 points less than your dominant. This builds a 9-point difference in preference between your dominant and tertiary values. These are several orders of magnitude preference making it difficult to shift to the tertiary strategy.

This simple little math exercise is the first thing each person should do when using the *CVI* to gain knowledge about one's self. It is also the first thing one should do with another person's *CVI* scores if one is using the *CVI* to coach or mentor others. Further, this is a wonderful starting point for two people to share their *CVI* scores and look at the relative mechanics of their individual scores.

This exercise dramatically reduces the tension between people, because they are able to quickly see why conflict often occurs, and the seeing of it this way depersonalizes the conflict. It's not about me versus you, it's about the preference for one *core value* over another, and the relative difference two people have in their preference for the same *core value*.

This same exercise can and should be replicated when looking at the preferences between the six *types of contribution*. Since there are now 72 points at play, the order of magnitude shifting number is 6.

The Way Our Core Values Work for Us

Our dominant *core value* is our preferred strategy, our preferred perspective, and almost always our preferred way of doing our work. The dominant *core value* is also our most essential sense of self. It is our primary contribution. It is our reason for being. It is the predominant energy of our human *being*.

So we attach meaning to any activity or work that requires us to operate in alignment with our dominant *core value*. We shift to our secondary *core value* when we determine that our dominant *Core Value Energy* is not working for us. But we will only shift to our secondary if we believe we can do so and not operate in opposition to our primary *core value*. The same applies when we shift to our third-level or our minor *core value*—except now the actions taken that are motivated by the minor value, must not undermine the tertiary value, or the secondary, and must serve to cause the dominant *core value* to be ultimately more successful. Otherwise we will not shift (consciously or unconsciously).

Build Your Personal Core Value Model

Here's how this works.

If the difference between your dominant *core value* score and your secondary score is less than 3, you can easily shift and do shift regularly between the two *Core Values Strategies*. And it's relatively easy for you to operate in alignment with your secondary *core value*—you have about the same amount of energy in your innate nature in both *core values*.

If the difference is 3 or more, then you have an order of magnitude more difficulty shifting from the first to the second *core value*, and it's many times harder to continue operating in the secondary *Core Values Strategy* for a sustained period of time. Your relative preference for being a certain type of energy in the room is strongly weighted toward your dominant *core value*.

If the difference between your first and second *core value* is greater than 5, the previous paragraph is amplified by several factors again, and so on. This same look at the relative preference you have in each *core value* should continue down through your minor *core value*, the one for which you hold the least preference.

8

Five Steps to Better Self-Knowledge

The fastest way to learn about your most innate unchanging nature (your *Real Core Values Self*) is to use the *CVI* information you have received after taking the *Core Values Index* and put yourself through a brief series of exercises, as follow.

Step One: Read your *CVI* reports and absorb any new insights. Ask your friends, coworkers, spouse, and family members to review these reports and to give you honest observations concerning the things they see about you as they read the information.

Step Two: Analyze your score. Use the 3-point order of magnitude rule and learn how hard or easy it is for you to shift from your dominant core value into your secondary, from your secondary into your third, and so on.

We have learned that the difference between each of your *core value* scores operates like the Richter scale related to earthquakes. Every 3-point difference causes a compounding magnitude of energy change, a compounding magnitude of intentionality in order to change. If my highest score is 7 points greater than my second score, this is two orders of magnitude difference in my capacity to be this lesser *Core Value Energy*.

This difference in capacity requires me to use specific amounts of energy to choose to shift out of my more dominant *core value* into my secondary *core value*. I must also apply specific amounts of energy to continue being my secondary *Core Value Energy* for any period of time. My operating system wants me to snap back into my highest innate energy as soon as possible. This reluctance to shift into my lowest capacity energy, and the urge to shift quickly back into the dominant is even more pronounced based upon the relative energy we have in our most dominance *Core Value Energy* and our most minor *Core Value Energy*. We are wired to be able to shift from any one of the *Core Value Energies* to any other at anytime. But most of us find much of this possible shifting to be only dimly possible.

If you have not taken the *CVI* please do so now.

www.taylorprotocols.com

Then complete the following exercise before continuing with this book.

Your Wired In Life Challenge

If your score for a **core value** in the **Core Values Index**™ is . . .

36 . . . You almost always operate in alignment with these *core values*. **26**
25 . . . You ordinarily and regularly operate in line with these *core values*, and you find it energizing. **19**
18 . . . You occasionally and with effort operate in line with these *core values*. **12**
11 . . . You almost never operate in line with these *core values* and you find it de-motivating. **1**

Write your four *core values* scores where each score fits on this ladder—i.e. **Power 33** then subtract your second highest score from your highest score to find the difference between each score.

____

____

____

____

____

____

____

____

____

____

____

____

____

Now you can see how you operate. You can see why it is easy or hard for you to shift from a *power* strategy to a *love* strategy, or why you can hardly imagine operating in the *wisdom* strategy at all.

Step Three: Take a look at the general shape of your *Core Values Nature.* This helps you visualize how you are balanced in your deepest *innate nature.* It helps you understand how you compare with others. For instance, if you are balanced in the most usual way, with clear dominant, secondary, tertiary, and minor *core values* that have only a few points between them, you operate in the most usual fashion, but with different *core values* as your preference for participation.

But if your scores are more extreme, either toward the almost perfect balance of 18-18-18-18, or with one or more highly profound scores above 25 points in any one *core value*, then you can see how uniquely you are wired and how unusual your mode of operating might be.

Let's work with a few examples to illustrate this.

EXAMPLE 1:

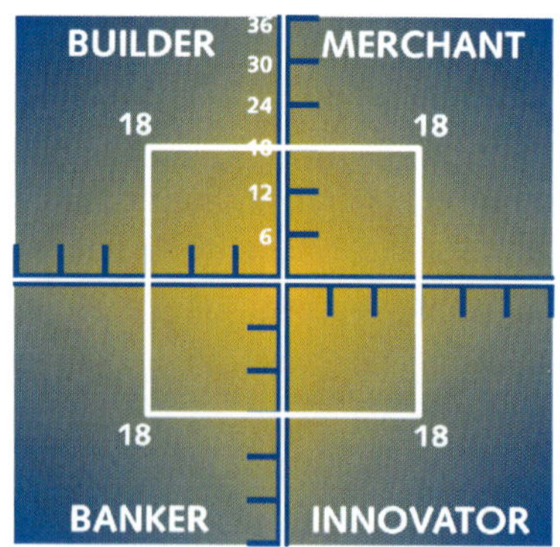

This shows the most perfectly balanced preference a person can have relative to the four *core values.* These scores also cause a balanced weighting of the six *Contributor Types*™.

This kind of person is wired to operate easily from each of the four *Core Values Strategies* and is also wired to make contributions that are balanced related to all six *types of contribution*: *creative* and *practical, intuitive* and *cognitive, community* and *independent.*

This type of person is highly flexible and adaptive. By default, this causes leadership to be difficult since they do not tend to stick with one *Core Values Strategy* long enough to cause others to accommodate their agenda.

EXAMPLE 2:

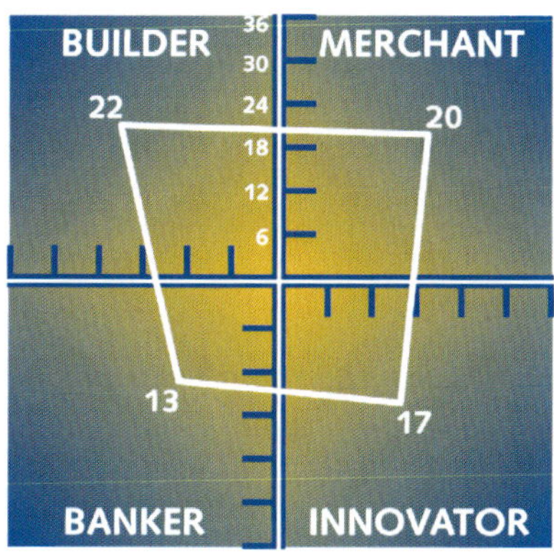

Most people have one *core value* that is the dominant, followed closely by a secondary *core value*, and then a third, with a clear minor value (one that is not a relevant part of their psyche).

This type of person is also geared to make certain *types of contribution* more than others. If you put this kind of person in a position that requires too much of the day doing tasks that are best done with his or her tertiary or minor *Core Values Strategies*, he or she will fail at the job or leave. The same is true for the *contribution type*. Putting a high *creative* in a highly *practical* position is a formula for frustration and failure for both the employee and his manager.

EXAMPLE 3:

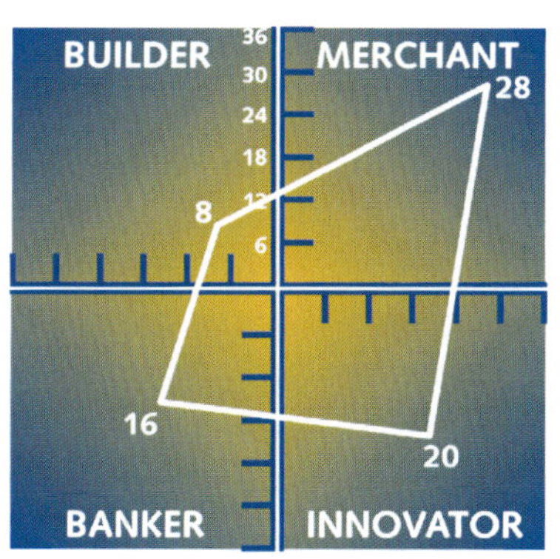

Here we see a profound score in one *core value*, the *merchant love* quadrant. We also see a highly spread distribution of points between the other three *core values*.

This type of person operates 80–90% of the time from the dominant *core value*, and that *core value* is their primary reason for existing on this planet. The other *Core Values Strategies* are utilized to support the agenda of the profoundly held *core value*.

Shifting down into one of the lesser *Core Value Energies* requires conscious effort or great stress, and operating from any one of the lesser energies can only be done for a brief period of time and not too often during the day. The more difference there is between the profound score and the lower scores, the greater the effort must be, and for a shorter period of time.

EXAMPLE 4:

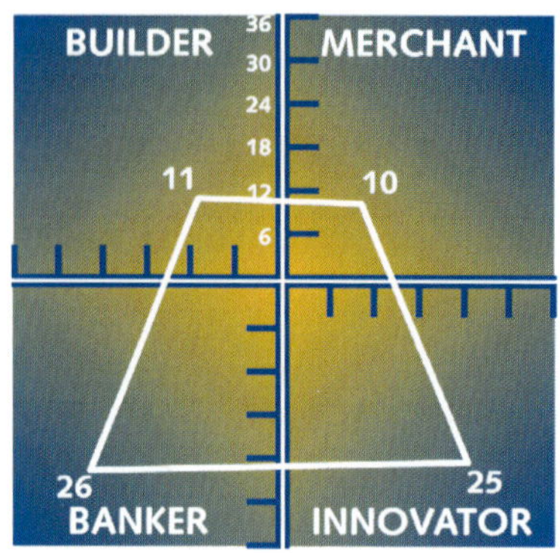

There are a few people, probably less than 1%, who have two profoundly held *core values*. Their innate nature is inherently wired to operate almost continually as one of the more dominant *Core Value Energies*. They are not likely to operate from either of the two minor *core values* unless under extreme duress.

This causes the person to be wired for one type of contribution, and one type only. In Example 4, the *cognitive* type of contribution will be the required activity, since the *banker* at 26 points, combined with the *innovator* at 25 points, creates a person with 51 points out of 72 focused on *cognitive* values.

EXAMPLE 5:

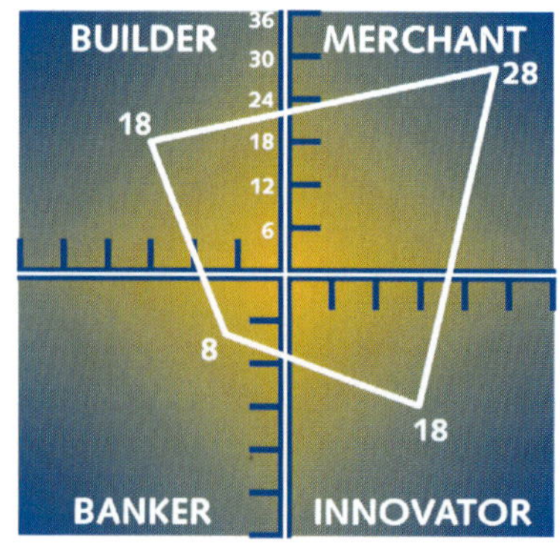

This profound *merchant (love)* individual is seen quite often among those persons with one profound *core value*. Notice that the secondary and tertiary are equal, with a distinctly minor *core value*.

This causes the person to operate with strong preference aligned as their most dominant *Core Value Energy*, but with a tendency to slip somewhat more easily into the two equally weighted secondary *core values*, oscillating back and forth between these two energies.

This person will shift from the dominant *Core Value Energy*, into the type of contribution that is composed of the two equal or nearly equal secondary values. In this particular example, the profound *merchant* will commonly but only occasionally slip into an independent mode of operation in support of the profound *merchant* agenda.

Step Four: Take a few minutes and write down the description of a situation in which you judge yourself to have been the most ineffective. Make it something that has occurred sometime in the past two or three years. Ask yourself this question: "What *core value* was I being when this situation began?" You will usually find that your most ineffective behavior occurs when you start a situation as your dominant *Core Value Energy*. This happens because you have become used to using that dominant strategy, even when it is not the most effective strategy to use. It also is true that you have more difficulty giving up on this strategy even when it's not working well for you at the present moment.

Look at your other most strongly held *core values* and ask yourself what might have happened differently had you switched to a different part of your *Core Values Nature* at the start of this subject situation.

Step Five: Ask your spouse or partner, or business peer, to give you feedback on a few important questions. Frame these in terms that anyone can understand without knowledge of the *Core Values Index* system.

First Question

Ask a team member, family member, friend, or spouse, "Which of the following would you say is my most important strategy for contributing to the world?"

Builder/Power	1. "Taking action and getting results."
Merchant/Love	2. "Creating strong relationships and inspiring others."
Innovator/Wisdom	3. "Making an assessment and finding solutions."
Banker/Knowledge	4. "Gathering information and conserving resources."

"Which is my strongest contribution?"
"Does one of the others pop out as my second strength?"
"How do you see this [repeat the description of the individual's first choice above] has helped me succeed in my business?"
"How has [repeat the description of the individual's same first

choice above] caused you frustrations and difficulty?"
Repeat this process for the second choice strategy above.

Second Question

"Which of the following conflict strategies is my most often used defense mechanism?"

Builder/Power	1. "*Intimidation.*"
Merchant/Love	2. "*Manipulation.*"
Innovator/Wisdom	3. "*Interrogation.*"
Banker/Knowledge	4. "*Aloof judgment.*"

"Which is my most common conflict strategy?"
"Does one of the others pop out as my second strategy?"
"How has [repeat the description of the individual's first choice above] caused you frustrations and difficulty?"
Repeat this process for the second choice conflict strategy above.

Third Question

"Which of the following decision strategies would you say is my most common approach?"

Builder/Power	1. "Intuition"
Merchant/Love	2. "Talk and listen."
Innovator/Wisdom	3. "Assess, brainstorm, and solve."
Banker/Knowledge	4. "Research and analyze."

"Which is my most common decision strategy?"
"Does one of the others pop out as my second strategy?"
"How has [repeat the description of the individual's first choice above] helped me succeed in my work?"
"How has [repeat the description of the individual's first choice above] caused you frustrations and difficulty?"
Repeat this process for the second decision strategy above.

Fourth Question

"Which of the following decision strategies would you say is the most important motivator for me?"

Builder/Power	1. "*Faith* in my gut instincts and personal power."
Merchant/Love	2. "Believing I can see the truth about the way things are."
Innovator/Wisdom	3. "Remaining *compassionate* regardless of the behaviors and emotions of others."
Banker/Knowledge	4. "Ensuring the *justice* in access, information, opportunity, and compensation."

"Which appears to be my strongest motivator?"
"Does one of the others pop out as my second strongest motivator?"
"How has [repeat the description of the individual's first choice above] helped me succeed?"
"How has [repeat the description of the individual's first choice above] caused you frustrations and difficulty?"
Repeat this process for the second choice motivator above.

Note: You will commonly see quickly that the individual answering these questions consistently selects options from the same one or two numbered options above. Sometimes there will be a switching back and forth between option one and option three, etc.

But at the end of this ten- to fifteen-minute discussion you will have strong evidence regarding the consistency with which you align yourself with your dominant and secondary *core values*, as witnessed and affirmed by others.

9

My Primary Core Values Strategies

You and I have chosen how we are going to compete with each other in a vast variety of circumstances and within the context of perceived safety or threat. We make these choices as children based upon two factors: 1) our natural propensity for reacting in certain ways, based upon our innate unchanging *Core Values Nature*, and 2) the relative effectiveness of these general propensities to keep us safe, warm, and loved, within the family and community environment into which we were born.

Our ego applies itself to all forms of social, emotional, psychological situations, working to make certain we do not make choices that lead to harm, especially those harms we have already faced in our original family situations. This ego-constructed personality takes on traits and behaviors that others notice and recognize as our personality (the way we are trained to show up).

There are four primary *core values* for action and competition that we as individuals rely on when we attempt to obtain what we have decided we want. These are the four capacities to *be* a certain kind of energy. These four capacities for *being*, held by each of us at different levels, comprise our *Core Values Nature*, that part of us that makes us a Human *Being*.

1. ***Power***: Pure energy applied for good. The drive to make a difference, to cause a lasting effect. The drive to take an *intuitive* action and get a desired result.

2. ***Love***: Nurturing the *core values* in self and in others. The drive to create and maintain strong, positive relationships with other people and things. The drive to create a vision and contribute to the creation of a possible future that is attractive to self and others.

3. ***Wisdom***: The drive to understand what the current situation is and to discern what to do about it. The drive to identify and solve problems and to create strategies and systems as part of the solutions.

4. ***Knowledge***: The drive to know essential information and to share this *knowledge* with others. The drive to conserve all resources for future use and to protect the community from failure and injustice.

From these *core values* all perceptions are derived, all choices are made, and all actions are driven. We each have a mixture of these four basic *core values* in our unique human nature. We mostly act from one or two of these *core values* either because these *Core Value Energies* are most natural to us or because we have been significantly warped into acting as an alternate *Core Value Energies.*

Early on we began making choices about which *Core Value Energy* to be with certain family members in certain situations. We become very adept at surviving and even succeeding in getting what we want within this family of origin construct.

This same reactive, balancing strategy that was effective when we were children no longer serves us consistently well within our adult society. In fact, it is our addictive dependency upon these early, adopted patterns of behavior that causes most of our disturbances in adulthood. They keep us from getting what we want from the current social environment we have constructed for ourselves.

Some of us become so committed to our childhood strategies that we unconditionally choose to reconstruct a close replica of our early family of origin in our adult relationships so we can play out the same dramas and interactions over and over again. We choose our friends from people who feel comfortable to us like brothers and sisters. We sometimes choose for a spouse a person who subconsciously reminds us of our mother or father.

This replica we have constructed may keep us from having to evolve as an adult being. After all, the strategies and tactics we learned in our original family did help us survive until now, so this reconstruction provides a known environment we can stay relatively safe in. This causes us to reinforce our personality beliefs and attitudes, by holding on to them even more strongly without any intention of letting them go.

We eventually have to let go of our personality stuff so that we can increase the amount of time we act consciously in alignment with our *Core Values Nature*. We become even more confident and skillful in being the presence of our stronger *core values* each time we choose this manner of participation in preference over the old stimulus-response personality behaviors.

If we choose to take the challenge, these very carefully constructed adult relationships provide a perfect means for working through the second stage of our spiritual development—conscious observation of our ego-constructed personality and greater consciousness of the unique *core values* person that sleeps within each of us, our unique innate recipe of *power*, *love*, *wisdom*, and *knowledge*.

The repeated interaction with people who have behavior patterns similar to the members of our family keeps our emotions churned up and keeps a sense of childish anger and disturbance near or at the surface. It is our choice whether we continue this drama or make different choices.

We tend to use unconsciously the replica environment to progress toward individuation and progress toward self-actualization, gaining the ability to drop our warped, fear-based personalities and make conscious choices. This process helps to get us back to *being* the *Core Values Nature* that we naturally *are*. We then can consciously choose which *Core Value Energy* will be most effective in a given situation, and shift consciously into being that *Core Value Energy*, instead of repeating old patterns of addictive personality behavior.

We tend to use unconsciously the replica environment to progress toward individuation and progress toward self-actualization, gaining the ability to drop our warped, fear-based personalities and make conscious choices. This process helps to get us back to *being* the *Core Values Nature* that we naturally *are*. We then can consciously choose which *Core Value Energy* will be most effective in a given situation, and shift consciously into being that *Core Value Energy*, instead of repeating old patterns of addictive personality behavior.

It is through this process of individuation and self-actualization that we find peace and contentment. It is also the way to find our place of highest and best use—that role in life from which we can make the contribution we were born to make.

Negative Emotions Are Road Signs for Spiritual/Psychological Discovery

It is through the experience of negative emotions that we most easily become aware of our "warping." When we find ourselves deeply fearful, depressed, or in a rage over seemingly insignificant situations, we must understand that these powerful reactions, usually beyond reasonable proportion to the situation, are pointers to beliefs, attitudes, and ideas—previous judgments—that we continue to hold as our truth. We can hear these patterns of thinking if we listen to our inner talk (self-talk). They are simple repetitions of childhood rationalizations. As children we used the best available logical reconstruction of events and explanations of other people's actions to justify ourselves. In other words, we shifted from our most comfortable and strongest part of our being to a lesser part, sometimes acting out through our *Negative Conflict Strategies*. In order to feel good about ourselves, we blamed the behavior on the actions and behaviors of parents or siblings.

When we could not discover a means to keep ourselves safe and warm within a current situation, when the gods of our life were more dangerous or less nurturing than we could effectively manage, we found some means to deflect the energy away from ourselves—to survive by any strategy required. And we explained this requirement to not *be* ourselves in terms of what we *had* to do in order to be safe or get what we wanted.

The behaviors of others that we could not understand or effectively manage at this early age, we could at least judge, blame, and shame, pushing responsibility toward someone else. Our negative emotions are most often caused by a replaying of these early tape recordings in our brains, setting off a repeat of the same dramatic scenes (our automatic strategic responses to situations) that we experienced in our childhood.

It is these childish patterns of perception, choice, and behavior that keep us from getting the fulfillment from life we so much desire. We each remain, to some degree, stuck in the repetition of unsatisfactory, unfulfilling personality patterns, struggling to find our unique spiritual path that will lead us to fulfillment.

The outward signs of the effect of these childhood patterns are: material insufficiency, failure to set and achieve goals, chemical and food addictions, poor posture, boring or frustrating careers, broken relationships, negative emotions, depression, extreme elation, anxiety, headaches, backaches, eye strain, teeth grinding, insomnia, and fatigue.

This nonconscious state of existence has us reacting without thought to words, body language, or other situations just as we used to respond to a parent's corrective statements or lack of acknowledgment. Because these patterns are basically defensive, designed to keep us safe, warm, and loved, we live much of our lives in a state of low-grade emotional, physical, and psychological pain.

We experience this as fear or anxiety, unhappiness or depression. Some of us replay conversations repeatedly in our heads, reassessing our effectiveness and making certain that our sense of things is true. Some of us work both sides of the emotional aisle, feeling anxiety when circumstances have been especially difficult and when they have been especially good.

My wife has observed my habit of feeling down or lonely after experiencing what can only be termed an extraordinarily wonderful family occasion. There is still a belief in me, engrained by decades of family training, followed by self-training, a belief that says when things get really good, you have to prepare for the worst.

The belief says that I don't deserve happiness and that I will likely be abandoned soon, so I had better not count on having this kind of wonderful experience again.

The belief also says that there must be a reason that I have been abandoned in the past. It must be that I am not as perfect as is required in order for me to be loved. The belief says that I have to be more perfect than most in order to be loved.

Welcome to my world.

At least now that I know these beliefs and fears, I can name them. By naming them as soon as I begin feeling the letdown after a great time with my boys, I am able to more quickly step out of the negative feelings and reengage in positive activity. This takes me immediately into a positive sense of self, and I feel more lovable and more loved. My fears of being abandoned and unloved melt into the background. I am then able to return to being the presence of *love* for others in my life.

I sometimes experience the added dynamic of feeling disappointed in small, mild love connections and working for constant feelings of being loved just like the feelings of being loved that happened in this recent experience. This one is a little more perplexing because it requires that I give up a deep desire that I know I can never have as an adult; the wonderful affirmations and expressions of love from my family cause me to want this all of the time. So I have to tell myself the truth: I really don't want to be surrounded by people who are constantly expressing love toward me. That would quickly become meaningless and irritating.

I am not adult enough to receive constant expressions of love without feeling a social requirement to respond in kind—having constant expressions of love then would seduce me into shift into acting like a loving person in order to keep love flowing my way. That's the shift from *being* and making a contribution, back into taking and getting—a personality-ego enterprise.

As adults it *feels safer* to continue these early life patterns, even though they may be deemed ineffective, than it does to wake up and make conscious choices. We instinctively know and fear that the people around us may not like our different responses, our new choices.

We know, and on some level we fear, that if we make different choices we will put our carefully constructed world at risk. We might lose the fragile balance we now have. We are not certain the alternative will be any better.

The call to wake up spiritually is a deep and constant call, hidden beneath our emotional fears and our intellectual rationalizations. But it *is* always there. The secret to *Core Values Consciousness* is to "Know Thyself."

We must start with self-observation and self-awareness. We must start working to understand and know who and what we are as individuals.

With our *Core Values Index*, you choose words that characterize you or describe most accurately *who you are* in your unique complexity of *being*. You use the *CVI* to paint a picture of your *real self*, for yourself. The *Core Values Index* assessment picture will help you observe yourself more objectively. Seeing the truth about yourself will begin to set you free from patterns that are destructive or obstructive in your life.

A positive picture of your *Real Core Values Self* will attract you toward full expression of that self and propel you toward completion of your life work—fulfillment of your passions and life mission. By understanding and working with this new picture of your *real self* you can find the courage to challenge one fear-based decision at a time.

We can test the merits of one choice after the other against these questions:

- Is this really an effective way to be my highest and best self?
- Will this chosen response get me the real results I want?
- Are there alternative choices that are more likely to bring me to fulfillment and happiness?
- What would happen if I chose to be more proactive and less reactive, if I decided to go directly after the life that I want to create?
- What difference would it make if I spent time and energy to develop a deep understanding of my purpose in life—a better understanding of those things that I must do in order to be fulfilled, in order to achieve a sense of meaning in my life?"

What would it be like . . . how would it feel . . . if you found yourself in a situation where what was needed from you was only that you be your *Real Core Values Self*, your unique being that consists of a special mixture of *power*, *love*, *wisdom*, and *knowledge*? This is the right seat of work, the right role at home, the real engagement of our *real self*.

Since the *core value* I have been choosing to be in this current situation is not getting me the results I want, the constant underlying choice is: Which *core value* in my *Core Values Nature* should I consciously choose to *be* in order to change my usual responses and therefore my results?

The desire for constant expressions of love works against my happiness—at the point when I feel the desire and in the moments when that desire feels gratified. But, you see, I already have something better than what I desire—I have my family and their love all of the time even when we are absent from each other. I have only to choose to remember this in order for the desire for expressions of love to loosen its hold on me.

I like these questions. They keep me open to a more exciting and more rewarding future. They remind me to honor my own life, to find the heart and passion of my life and value it. These simple questions, when framed in my newly realized *Real Core Values Self*, encourage me to explore different responses to personal challenges and to find new ways of responding.

How can I develop strategies in the other nondominant *core values* that I have within me, choosing the one that will be more effective in this kind of situation with the persons involved?

Eventually I begin to be proactive rather than reactive. I begin to take charge of my life and allow others their freedom to respond to the new energy and passion I am exuding in my quest for developing a complete life.

Note: If you deny negative emotions, refuse to consciously acknowledge them—if you are embarrassed by anger, envy, jealously, depression, or feelings of superiority, and will not allow others to know what you are feeling—you will be controlled by these feelings more absolutely than those persons who are willing to be seen venting these negative feelings in public.

By denying your emotions, your actions will likely be far more harmful and confusing to others than the actions of those you likely condemn for their display of childish negative feelings.

This is a primary trap for highly educated, highly intelligent persons; also for those who believe that the disclosure of the negative feelings they have will be an imposition where such feelings are not socially, politically, or economically allowed.

The emotions and feelings we tolerate least in others are usually the ones that lie just beneath the surface in ourselves. We judge these feelings so harshly that we are reluctant to show any sign that they may be part of us at anytime. This is a terrible indictment of our human emotions. Our human emotions are a natural function/*creative* element in each of us.

To deny and repress such emotions is to give them power over us.

To simply vent our emotions on others is to remain in the child's world of unconscious stimulus and response—and we can harm each other in the process. The only path that works is to truthfully acknowledge, within ourselves, that we are having strong negative emotions. Then we can name each emotion.

When we name our negative emotions we shift from feeling into thinking. Naming is a *cognitive* act. Just to say, "I am feeling very angry," causes an immediate break in the emotion. Then we can decide what to do about it. We cannot feel an emotion and talk about it at the same name.

Warning: Don't be confused by statements like "You really piss me off." This kind of statement is an expression of the emotion, not a naming of the emotion. When we blame someone else for what we are choosing to feel, we give the other person complete power over our life at that moment, and we become lost in feeling the emotion.

Two courses are generally effective:

1. See the negative emotion and name it (i.e., rage) within our own consciousness, which kills the power of the emotion, involves the conscious mind, and gives us a chance to select a different *core value* to *be* in a positive posture, or ...

2. See the negative emotion and name it openly for others—i.e., "I am feeling a deep sense of rage." This action also steals the thunder from our emotions and allows others to respond in a supportive way; instead of

venting our emotions on the people around us, we have taken full responsibility for them. Others are less fearful of us and more able to continue engaging with us in the circumstance.

When we step down on a sharp rock with bare feet, we grunt or yell from the pain. We lift the foot instantly from the point of pain and look around for sympathy and for a safe place to step down. Similarly, our negative emotions, when acknowledged (there is no requirement for public display), become a clear sign of internal distress.

If we follow the road signs that mark our inner spiritual journey, we will find the source of these feelings are always based in some fear. By acknowledging this fear, we have the opportunity to learn more about ourselves and to find a way to face the observed fear and make effective choices.

This act of naming the fear and the negative emotions it evokes helps us lift our foot off of the sharp rock of old experiences and emotionally held beliefs. We reduce the pain in our lives.

In our physical world we learn quickly to avoid sharp rocks. We watch for any that we may be approaching. This level of observation is also available to us in our inner world. There is no need to step on a sharp emotional rock over and over again.

High *wisdom* minds are often caught in an internal belief trap due to their ability to develop circling, looping, always thoughtfully constructed reasoning (rationalizations) around their negative emotions. Such persons often have a very elaborate personal psychology and philosophy carefully structured to create the appearance of *wisdom.*

This is just another avoidance strategy. They are forestalling the requirement to deal with embarrassing emotions and the beliefs that support them.

The parable of a camel trying to enter the eye of the needle is relevant here. It is easier for a camel to enter Jerusalem through the Eye of the Needle, than it is for a rich man to enter the Kingdom of Heaven. Whatever causes one person to feel rich causes that person to attach too much to that element of life, making it difficult to find his true calling through personal actualization and peak experiences.

These riches include innate energies such as *wisdom*, *power*, *love*, and *knowledge*. What we are rich in holds us back from learning about and being different kinds of participants in our lives. We get hooked on behaving a certain way, instead of being all of our essential natures as needed and making a real contribution to our society.

A person who is extraordinarily rich in education or in innate *wisdom* will likely rely on these riches to find the kingdom. They become lost in their own minds.

They are required to take the fearful step of shedding their intense logic and willpower and delve headlong into their negative emotions. This requires the non-logical *faith* that they may find greater happiness through this strategy than through the one they have so carefully constructed throughout their childhood and adulthood.

Those of us who are richest in *wisdom* often have the greatest difficulty in letting go of our carefully constructed personality behaviors. We tend to believe our own internal talk, and we can certainly help others understand how wrong they are about us.

The special challenge here is a willingness to occasionally put aside the primary *core value* of one's life during a period of growth, in order to find personal balance and happiness. This challenge exists for all people. Those who come from a position of *power* must explore the depths of *love*, *wisdom*, and *knowledge*. Those who rely on *love* must learn to work within and honor *power*-based decisions.

Who Wins?

Why we need to ask this question appears to be built into our psyches from birth.

We humans are like the animal kingdom in our competition for basic sustenance. We are more complex than the animals because we stretch this innate drive-to-compete into situations that are not survival-based. We compete for attention we don't need, for jobs we really don't want, for sex and other vices we wouldn't accept if we were more rational in our assessment of the likely consequences that tend to follow such behavioral choices.

In other words, our creature nature provides a basic set of life challenges just because we all have desires and built-in competitive energy.

It is natural, after all, to compete for the best mate. This is animal instinct at the most powerful level. It is also natural to gather sustenance and then to protect that sustenance from raids by others. The effective gathering of sustenance is proof of success as a human creature. Success makes one more attractive and therefore a more desirable mate.

As long as we are caught up in this instinctual drive to compete, we are focused on the material, social game and not on the inner state of our souls. Those who win the game of life may have many outward appearances of success or they may be seen as unsuccessful by social standards—generally measured by the degree of wealth, power and prestige, or fame.

When I choose to compete or give in to the pursuit of desires, I am choosing to *not* contribute. I am choosing to let my negative personality emotions show me how to get what I want. I am choosing this emotion-directed response as a substitution for being my *Real Core Values Self* and making a meaningful contribution.

The true winners of the game of life are those who learn to be conscious with all of their choices. They learn to allow their ego-designed personality to die slowly away while their true inner self, comprised of *power*, *wisdom*, *love*, and *knowledge*, grows steadily more vibrant and alive. They hone their creature skills and capabilities in order to better deliver their *Core Values Nature* to the world and make their highest and best contribution.

Choose to measure your own success by the effectiveness and quality of your contribution to others. This is the ultimate achievement of all people, to learn to be *who we are* and to make our highest and best contribution to the people who are on this planet with us and to those who will come after us.

The end game is to *be love*, or to *be power*, or to *be wisdom*, or to *be knowledge* in all of life's circumstances. The framework of our lives is important only in its value as a learning situation. We choose the course of our lives, consciously or unconsciously, in order to learn our next lesson. Each lesson is a letting go of some previous pattern of thinking, feeling, and acting—taking on a new, more conscious and effective strategy and behavior; choosing to be more *who we are* at this moment in order to continue making our highest and best contribution.

Wouldn't it be interesting if we decided to choose a life framework that also, simultaneously, afforded an opportunity for wealth, safety, comfort, and fulfillment?

Note: You will be more able to reach a deeper understanding of the information in ***Choices*** if you have taken the *CVI* assessment and read *The Core Values Handbook*. The *CVI* and *The Handbook* are available by logging onto the Web at www.taylorprotocols.com.

10

All Decisions Based Upon Fear Are Wrong Decisions

The First Core Values Law:

Personality patterns (stimulus-and-response mechanisms) are largely fear-based.

When we are participating from a mechanical stimulus/response position we are not making conscious choices about how we want to act. We are not consciously choosing how we want to participate. We are just responding in the way we have always responded. We are choosing to remain unconscious and to trust the old pattern.

The dichotomy is that we are choosing to be controlled by our fears. We are choosing to continue believing that to respond otherwise could cause us humiliation, loss, or harm. We are choosing to remain safe (comfortable) in our old patterns. They have gotten us this far. We are choosing to keep having the life we have right now.

We have survived.

This *might* be a reasonable strategy for life, if life were about survival. For most of us, it is not.

If we were simple creatures, unconscious survival mechanisms would be sufficient; survive long enough to propagate the species and then die. But human existence demands more, offers more. We are not comfortable at the survival level. In fact, if we allowed ourselves to believe that the only meaning in life is to propagate and die, we would all likely kill ourselves.

We cannot live with only this sense of existence and continuity. We must have a greater sense of connectedness, contribution, and meaning in our life. We are both *who we are* and *what we do*. We are *Core Values Nature* and creature.

Our fears keep us responding in the same pattern today as we did yesterday; they do more to us than simply restrict our level of success and fulfillment. Our fears, in fact, if given full sway over our lives, lead us to purely mechanical responses, survival and death without the passion of purpose and meaning. This kind of existence is what we should fear most.

Our fears of embarrassment, pain, disappointment, and humiliation are so packed with emotion and conviction that we cannot see the greater risk: the risk of losing or never claiming our own life, its purpose and its primary mission.

Adapted personality behaviors are based in fear. A person who is fearful, excites fear in others. When we choose to remain unconscious and autonomic (no thought or consciousness required) in our responses to others, we seduce them to do the same—our fears being the fear-based responses that bring out fear-based responses in others. When we choose this behavior, we don't get to experience their *Real Core Values Self*, only their adapted personality.

To make conscious choices continuously, as each moment may require, is to be fully alive. This is the fundamental requirement for those who are willing to seek, find, and fulfill their personal mission in life.

The Second Core Values Law:

It is not possible to be happy as a human being as long as we continue living our lives unconsciously.

I clearly remember a time in my college life when I became deeply aware of my propensity for being more demonstrative, more expressive, more attention-seeking than was effective and comfortable for me.

My father made one simple suggestion that I decided to practice. He said, "Shut up, sit back, listen and observe, and let other people take the lead. Do this until you see some simple easy thing to say or do. Say or do it, then shut up, sit back, listen and observe, and let other people take the lead."

I shifted into this gear for several months, consciously withholding myself, keeping my usual demonstrative high-charged dynamo in check, withholding my questions and ideas. I did this effectively enough that several professors asked whether I was okay: "Why aren't you participating anymore?" I just shrugged and took note inside. I didn't tell them that what I was learning was more valuable than any lesson in History or English.

I had always been afraid that in order to be loved I had to perform. I thought I had to always be emotionally *up and out in front*, to be emotive and dramatic. I felt like a well-trained performing seal that gets its supper based upon its daily performance—on-stage and on-demand. The supper I was seeking was to be loved.

Because I performed so hard, with so much commitment to obtain the love and approval I received, I discounted all love and attention, thinking to myself: "You don't love me. You love the person on stage. You don't know me. Why did I have to work so hard and be so special in order for you to love me?"

The harder I worked to gain love, the less love I felt. The more love expressed toward me, the harder I discounted it for fear of being fooled and disappointed. I believed secretly that if I quit performing, all the love would go away. This was not a fun world to participate in.

When I finally held back and just watched, letting love come easily and gently to me without performance or high acclaim, I became grounded in a more real world and began to participate from a more real and effective position.

My desire now is to *be* the *love* in the room. Do you agree that this might be a better motivation for participation?

I know that the fears I faced, as I willfully withheld myself, sat back, and observed, were as difficult to conquer as the fears others experience when they are called upon to climb up out of their comfort zones and get on the stage. We are all required occasionally to take a visible position, be more affectionate, be more demonstrative or verbal than ever before.

Or we may be required to sit back, be patient, reserve our opinions and judgments. We all have to cross those comfort zone boundaries. It's the life on the other side of those seemingly death-threatening walls that we each want.

The Third Core Values Law:

The life on the other side of my fears and ego-driven personality beliefs and attitudes is my *real* life. The only barrier is a wall of childish beliefs and attitudes that justify my personality.

The difference between those who live an extraordinary, fulfilled, and meaningful life and those who feel dragged down and disappointed in life, is the pace and level of consciousness at which decisions are made; decisions that take each person through the walls of fear and into possession of a conscious, purposeful life.

We have to see, accept, and act against the fears in our lives in order to participate in a manner that will give us fulfillment and a sense of joy.

So, take stock right now. Identify those fear-based choices you are making unconsciously now.

The Fourth Core Values Law:

Each person's deepest fear is that they are the opposite or antithesis of their most dominant *core value.*

The deepest fear of people is that we are not our dominant *core value*; that we are truly the opposite of this positive energy, or void of this dominant *Core Value Energy.*

We see the *core values* conflict mechanism clearly in the pairing of each *core value* with a supportive *Catalytic Value*. A catalyst causes elements (metals, molecules, chemicals) to join together or break apart—to change in nature. The *Catalytic Values* associated with each *core value* also cause these reactions—this change in nature.

For each *core value*, its *Catalytic Value* sits in the person's subconscious, acting like a dimmer switch for the chandelier in our dining room. The lower the energy in the *Catalytic Value*, the greater the dimming of the *Core Value Energy* flowing into the room.

My highest capacity of *Core Value Energy* is *love*. My deepest fear is that there is no *love* in me, that I truly love no one, nothing, not even myself.

What is your deepest fear?

Remember the times when you wished you had been more assertive, or less reactive, more gregarious and friendly, or more reserved and quiet. Resolve to become more conscious and aware of these situations in the future, and to make new choices when faced with these options. This is not a new brand of behavioral modification. We will help you in this book to become more conscious about ineffective behaviors, not so you can control yourself, but so you can wake up and choose which *Core Value Energy* you want to be at any given moment.

Once you shift from a dominant *Core Value Energy* into a different energy that is also an important part of your innate nature, you don't have to worry about misbehaving. The behavior will be guided naturally by the new underlying *Core Value Energy*. You see, it is not a matter of stopping foolish or ineffective behavior. We are about helping you reclaim your deepest more innate *Core Values Nature*, then being true to that nature.

Make a list of the kinds of people, circumstances, work challenges that cause you the greatest concern. Make a list of the fears that seem to be at play in these circumstances. Write a good description of each fear and use the words that feel truthful to you.

However you think of God or a higher power, say to that presence, "Help me see my next opportunity to face my fears. Show me my fears. Help me acknowledge and take responsibility for each of my fears."

This single commitment, if made on a daily basis, will ensure that you are faced with a few of your most pressing fears in the near future. You will see the fears and be able to acknowledge that you have fear. And an amazing life key will be instantly available to you.

The Fifth Core Values Law: Name that FEAR!!!

An ancient Chinese Proverb:

A young boy is sleeping in the room next to his father.

The boy begins to have a nightmare. He is walking through a dense forest that is growing darker and darker and more and more dense. He hears sounds that make him feel that there is something big coming up behind him.

The boy wakes up screaming. His father goes to see what's happening. The boy tells his father about the dream. And the father says simply, "Go back to sleep. Whatever is in your dream can't hurt you."

The next night the boy has the same dream. He stays in the dream even when the noise gets louder and louder behind him in the dense, dark forest, until he feels a hot moist breath on his neck. He wakes up screaming.

After listening to his son's dream, the father again says, "Go back to sleep. Whatever is in your dream won't hurt you."

The next night the boy dreams that he is again walking in the dark forest. The sounds come again and the hot breath hits his neck. He begins to run, terrified. The forest itself is hitting him in the face and cutting his arms. He wakes up thrashing and screaming.

His father, after listening to his son's dream, says, "Go back to sleep.

Whatever you dream won't hurt you, but this time, when you hear the first frightening sound, turn around and see what's there."

That same night, the young boy walks into his father's room and stands quietly by the bed. He nudges his father's arm to wake him.

"What do you want, son?"

"It was a tiger, father. When I turned around, I said, 'you are a tiger'; and the tiger lay down in the forest."

So: **Name That FEAR!!!**

Face that fear. Obliterate that fear. Shift to a different *Core Value Energy*. Decide to be that different energy every time the named fear comes into your dreams or into your reality. As adults we choose not to stay asleep but to see and name our fears. From this fearless position we can decide which of our strongest *Core Value Energies* to be. This allows the shift out of personality and into self—out of narcissistic desires and fear and into contribution.

Through our experiences with more than 250,000 people who have taken the *Core Values Index*, we have learned how the conscious and subconscious mind works in people. We have been shown how anxiety triggers consciousness, and how shifting from being one of the *Core Value Energies* into a different *Core Value Energy* is the skill used unconsciously by children to form their personalities. We have also learned that this unconscious skill in children is available to adults in their conscious and subconscious mind. The anxiety triggers provide a wake-up call that allows us to learn to shift consciously between *Core Values Natures* for improved effectiveness as human adults.

Once you understand how your internal operating system works, you will be able to observe your anxieties, identify the *Core Value Energy* you have currently chosen to *be* (unconsciously), then decide which *core value* to shift into.

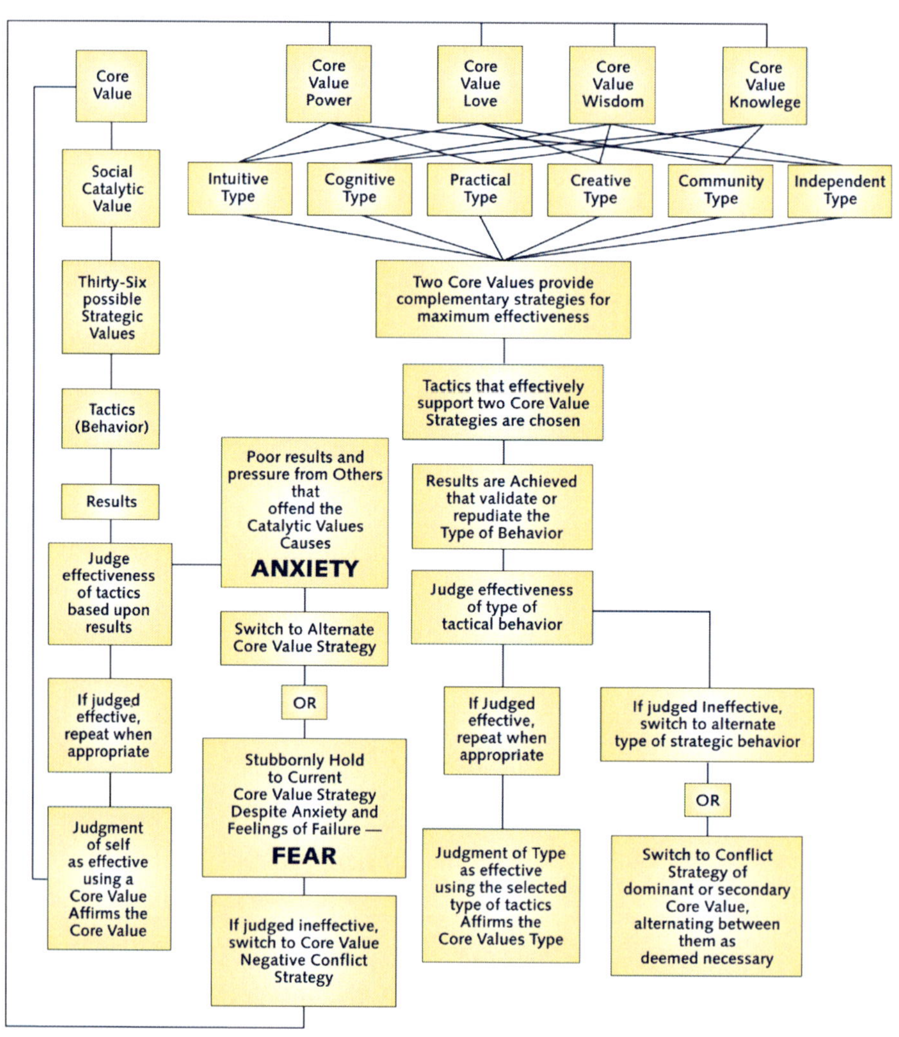
Core Values Assessment
Human Operating System™
Core Value
Core Value Power
Core Value Love
Core Value Wisdom
Core Value Knowlege
Social Catalytic Value
Intuitive Type
Cognitive Type
Practical Type
Creative Type
Community Type
Independent Type
Thirty-Six possible Strategic Values
Two Core Values provide complementary strategies for maximum effectiveness
Tactics (Behavior)
Tactics that effectively support two Core Value Strategies are chosen
Results
Poor results and pressure from Others that offend the Catalytic Values Causes
ANXIETY
Results are Achieved that validate or repudiate the Type of Behavior
Judge effectiveness of tactics based upon results
Switch to Alternate Core Value Strategy
Judge effectiveness of type of tactical behavior
OR
If judged effective, repeat when appropriate
Stubbornly Hold to Current Core Value Strategy Despite Anxiety and Feelings of Failure —
FEAR
If Judged effective, repeat when appropriate
If judged Ineffective, switch to alternate type of strategic behavior
OR
Judgment of self as effective using a Core Value Affirms the Core Value
If judged ineffective, switch to Core Value Negative Conflict Strategy
Judgment of Type as effective using the selected type of tactics Affirms the Core Values Type
Switch to Conflict Strategy of dominant or secondary Core Value, alternating between them as deemed necessary

Core Values Shifting Scenarios

Power shifting into *knowledge*

A dominant *power* person may find himself feeling anxious about his team of workers. He has given clear directions and expectations, but is often disappointed in their results.

He finally decides to try something new. He expresses his concerns to a friend. In that process he clearly states what he thinks is happening . . . "I just know that when my back is turned they are not working as hard as they need to be."

The next step in the *Core Values Consciousness* process is to name his fears.

"I am afraid that I am powerless to change their behavior. That I will never get these people to do the things I want them to do."

This being said, he realizes he is operating as the presence of *power* in this situation, and that he is feeling anxious about how effective his *power* energy is. He then decides to shift into his second strongest *core value—knowledge.*

In this operating mode, he does not turn his back.

He checks in a few minutes later to ask what is happening, measures the productivity briefly, and proves to himself that things are going well or not going well. If not going well, he asks for a report on progress. This is the presence of his *knowledge* energy. His team members see that they have not responded well and that they are being measured.

The performance improves for the next period, during which the *power*-based leader is doing something powerful somewhere else, until he shifts back into his *knowledge* energy and shows up again unannounced to measure progress of the now better performing team.

There is nothing more impotent than a person who is continuing to be the *power* in a situation when what is most needed is *knowledge, love,* or *wisdom.*

Power shifting into *love*

A dominant *power* person may find himself feeling anxious about his team of workers. He has given clear directions and expectations, but is often disappointed in their results.

He finally decides to try something new. He expresses his concerns to a friend. In that process he clearly states what he thinks is happening . . . "I just know that when my back is turned they are not working as hard as they need to be."

The next step in the *Core Values Consciousness* process is to name his fears.

"I am afraid that I am powerless to change their behavior, that I will never get these people to do the things I want them to do."

This being said, he realizes he is operating as the presence of *power* in this situation. He then decides to shift into his second strongest *core value—love.*

In this operating mode . . .

He checks in a few minutes later to ask if anyone needs help or a clarification about their job. He encourages them and reminds them that he respects and appreciates their efforts. He asks them how things are going and hears that things are going well or not going well. If not going well, he asks what is getting in their way, how he can help. His team members see that they have not responded well and that they are letting him down.

The performance improves for the next period, during which the *power*-based leader is doing something powerful somewhere else, until he shifts back into his *love* energy and shows up again unannounced to measure progress of the now better performing team.

There is nothing more impotent than a person who is continuing to be the *power* in the situation when what is most needed is *love, wisdom,* or *knowledge.*

Power shifting into *wisdom*

A dominant *power* person may find himself feeling anxious about his team of workers. He has given clear directions and expectations, but is often disappointed in their results.

He finally decides to try something new. He expresses his concerns to a friend. In that process he clearly states what he thinks is happening . . . "I just know that when my back is turned they are not working as hard as they need to be."

The next step in the *Core Values Consciousness* process is to name his fears.

"I am afraid that I am powerless to change their behavior, that I will never get these people to do the things I want them to do."

This being said, he realizes he is operating as the presence of *power* in this situation. He then decides to shift into his second strongest *core value—wisdom.*

In this operating mode . . .

He checks in sometime later to ask what is happening. He discovers what is working well and what isn't. He brings everyone together for a brainstorming session, hears their problems, and together they develop better strategies. His team members see that they have not been achieving the desired results and that they are not working as intelligently as they are able.

The performance improves for the next period, during which the *power*-based leader is doing something powerful somewhere else, until he shifts back into his *wisdom* energy and shows up again to coach, mentor, and guide the strategies of the now better performing team.

There is nothing more impotent than a person who is continuing to be the *power* in the situation when what is most needed is *wisdom*, *knowledge*, or *love*.

Knowledge shifting into power

A dominant *knowledge* person may find himself feeling anxious about his team of workers. He has provided written instructions, processes, and procedures for every person, but is often disappointed in their results.

He finally decides to try something new. He expresses his concerns to a friend. In that process he clearly states what he thinks is happening . . . "I just know that when my back is turned they are not working as efficiently as they need to be, wasting time and resources, and setting us up to fail . . ."

The next step in the *Core Values Consciousness* process is to name his fears.

"I am afraid that my instructions are being ignored. That they are not able or willing to change their behavior. That I will never get these people to do the things I want them to do."

This being said, he realizes he is operating as the presence of *knowledge* in this situation. He then decides to shift into his second strongest *core value—power*.

In this operating mode, he steps back into the situation and . . .

He instinctively knows what is needed. He gets everyone focused on their most important tasks. He shows them how to do things, and states his expectations for successful results. He doesn't pull back until he is convinced that things are going well. His team members see that they have not responded well to the written directions and that they are now being directed individually how to do things . . .

The performance improves for the next period, during which the *knowledge*-based leader is providing facts and written information somewhere else, until he shifts back into his *power* energy and shows up again unannounced to energize and refocus the team with clear expectations and increased requirements to perform.

There is nothing more ignorant than a person who is continuing to be the *knowledge* in the situation when what is most needed is *power*, *love*, or *wisdom*.

Knowledge shifting into *love*

A dominant *knowledge* person may find himself feeling anxious about his team of workers. He has provided written instructions, processes, and procedures for every person, but is often disappointed in their results.

He finally decides to try something new. He expresses his concerns to a friend. In that process he clearly states what he thinks is happening . . . "I just know that when my back is turned they are not working as efficiently as they need to be, wasting time and resources, and setting us up to fail . . ."

The next step in the *Core Values Consciousness* process is to name his fears.

"I am afraid that my information and instructions are being ignored. That they need more information and guidance. That I will never get these people to do the things we need them to do."

This being said, he realizes he is operating as the presence of *knowledge* in this situation. He then decides to shift into his second strongest *core value—love*.

In this operating mode . . .

He checks in sometime later to ask how everyone feels about the work processes and learns whether they believe that things are going well or not going well. If not going well, he asks them to try harder, and spends time reminding them of the importance of their corporate mission and how much he is counting on each person. His team members see that they have not responded well and that they are disappointing him.

The performance improves for the next period, during which the *knowledge*-based leader is providing facts and written information somewhere else, until he shifts back into his *love* energy and shows up again to inspire, motivate, and challenge the team to do their best.

There is nothing more ignorant than a person who is continuing to be the *knowledge* in the situation when what is most needed is *love*, *wisdom*, or *power*.

Knowledge shifting into *wisdom*

A dominant *knowledge* person may find himself feeling anxious about his team of workers. He has provided written clear instruction and processes and procedures for every person, but he is often disappointed in their results.

He finally decides to try something new. He expresses his concerns to a friend. In that process he clearly states what he is afraid of . . . "I just know that when my back is turned they are not working as efficiently as they need to be, wasting time and resources, and setting us up to fail . . ."

The next step in the *Core Values Consciousness* process is to name his fears.

"I am afraid that my information and instructions are being ignored. That they need more information and guidance. That I will never get these people to do the things we need them to do."

This being said, he realizes he is operating as the presence of *knowledge* in this situation. He then decides to shift into his second strongest *core value—wisdom*.

In this operating mode . . .

He checks in sometime later to ask what is happening. He discovers what is working well and what isn't. For what is not going well, he brings everyone together for a brainstorming session, hears their problems, and together they develop better strategies. His team members see that they have not been achieving the desired results and that they are not working as intelligently as they are able.

The performance improves for the next period, during which the *knowledge*-based leader is providing facts and written information somewhere else, until he shifts back into his *wisdom* energy and shows up again to inspire, motivate, and challenge the team to do their best.

There is nothing more ignorant than a person who is continuing to be the *knowledge* in the situation when what is most needed is *wisdom*, *love*, or *power*.

Wisdom shifting into power

A dominant *wisdom* person may find himself feeling anxious about his team of workers. He has assessed the situation and developed brilliant strategies, but is often disappointed in their results.

He finally decides to try something new. He expresses his concerns to a friend. In that process he clearly states what he is afraid of . . . "I just know that when my back is turned they are not working as smart as they need to be . . ."

The next step in the *Core Values Consciousness* process is to name his fears.

"I am afraid that my strategies are not understood. That I am helpless to change their behavior. That I will never get these people to do things the way they should be done. Why can't they think for themselves?"

This being said, he realizes he is operating as the presence of *wisdom* in this situation. He then decides to shift into his second strongest *core value—power.*

In this operating mode, he does not turn his back.

Instinctively, he knows what is needed. He gets everyone focused on their most important tasks. He shows them how to do things, and states his expectations for successful results. He doesn't pull back until he is convinced that things are going well. His team members see that they have not responded well to the written directions or coaching about processes and that they are now being directed individually how to do things.

The performance improves for the next period, during which the *wisdom*-based leader is providing facts and written information somewhere else, until he shifts back into his *power* energy and shows up again unannounced to energize and refocus the team with clear expectations and increased requirements to perform.

There is nothing more ignorant than a person who is continuing to be the *wisdom* in the situation when what is most needed is *power, love,* or *knowledge.*

Wisdom shifting into *love*

A dominant *wisdom* person may find himself feeling anxious about his team of workers. He has given clear directions and expectations, but is often disappointed in their results.

He finally decides to try something new. He expresses his concerns to a friend. In that process he clearly states what he is afraid of . . . "I just know that when my back is turned they are not working as smart as they need to be . . ."

The next step in the *Core Values Consciousness* process is to name his fears.

"I am afraid that my strategies are not understood. That I am helpless to change their behavior. That I will never get these people to do things the way they should be done."

This being said, he realizes he is operating as the presence of *wisdom* in this situation. He then decides to shift into his second strongest *core value—love.*

In this operating mode . . .

He checks in sometime later to ask how everyone feels about the work processes and learns whether they believe that things are going well or not going well. If not going well, he asks them to try harder and spends time reminding them of the importance of their corporate mission and how much he is counting on each person. His team members see that they have not responded well and that they are disappointing him.

The performance improves for the next period, during which the *wisdom*-based leader is providing facts and written information somewhere else, until he shifts back into his *love* energy and shows up again to inspire, motivate, and challenge the team to do their best.

There is nothing more ignorant than a person who is continuing to be the *wisdom* in the situation when what is most needed is *love*, *power*, or *knowledge*.

Wisdom shifting into *knowledge*

A dominant *wisdom* person may find himself feeling anxious about his team of workers. He has given clear directions and expectations, but is often disappointed in their results.

He finally decides to try something new. He expresses his concerns to a friend. In that process he clearly states what he is afraid of . . . "I just know that when my back is turned they are not working as smart as they need to be . . ."

The next step in the *Core Values Consciousness* process is to name his fears.

"I am afraid that my strategies are not understood. That I am helpless to change their behavior. That I will never get these people to do things the way they should be done."

This being said, he realizes he is operating as the presence of *wisdom* in this situation. He then decides to shift into his second strongest *core value—knowledge*.

In this operating mode . . .

He checks in sometime later to ask how everyone feels about the work processes and learns whether they believe that things are going well or not going well. If not going well, he asks them to try harder and spends time reminding them of the importance of their corporate mission and how much he is counting on each person. His team members see that they have not responded well and that they are disappointing him.

The performance improves for the next period, during which the *wisdom*-based leader is providing facts and written information somewhere else, until he shifts back into his *knowledge* energy and shows up again to inspire, motivate, and challenge the team to do their best.

There is nothing more ignorant than a person who is continuing to be the *wisdom* in the situation when what is most needed is *knowledge, love,* or *power.*

Love shifting into *power*

A dominant *love* person may find himself feeling anxious about his team of workers. He has provided an exciting vision with great opportunities for everyone to help create a great success, but is often disappointed in their results.

He finally decides to try something new. He expresses his concerns to a friend. In that process he clearly states what he is afraid of . . . "I just know that when I leave the room they are not doing the things that will make us successful . . ."

The next step in the *Core Values Consciousness* process is to name his fears.

"I am afraid they don't take me seriously. That they don't respect me and disregard what I ask them to do. That I am helpless to change their behavior. That I will never get these people to do the things I want them to do."

This being said, he realizes he is operating as the presence of *love* in this situation. He then decides to shift into his second strongest *core value—power.*

In this operating mode . . .

He calls a meeting and clearly states his expectations of performance of tasks, deadlines, and requirements for individual success. He remains engaged with the team and gives them clear directions. He reminds each one of his or her goals and requirements, and makes certain things are going well before he leaves the situation.

The performance improves for the next period, during which the *love*-based leader is doing some relationship building somewhere else, until he shifts back into his *power* energy and shows up again unannounced to reinforce urgency and recharge the now better performing team with his personal energy.

There is nothing more unloving than a person who is continuing to be the *love* in the situation when what is most needed is *power*, *knowledge*, or *wisdom*.

Love shifting into *wisdom*

A dominant *love* person may find himself feeling anxious about his team of workers. He has provided an exciting vision with great opportunities for everyone to help create a great success, but is often disappointed in their results.

He finally decides to try something new. He expresses his concerns to a friend. In that process he clearly states what he is afraid of . . . "I just know that when my back is turned they are not working as hard as they need to be . . ."

The next step in the *Core Values Consciousness* process is to name his fears.

"I am afraid they don't take me seriously. That they don't respect me and disregard what I ask them to do. That I am helpless to change their behavior. That I will never get these people to do the things I want them to do."

This being said, he realizes he is operating as the presence of *love* in this situation. He then decides to shift into his second strongest *core value*—*wisdom*.

In this operating mode . . .

He calls a meeting and clearly states his expectations of performance of tasks, deadlines, and requirements for individual success. He remains engaged with the team and gives them clear directions. He reminds each one of his or her goals and requirements, and makes certain things are going well before he leaves the situation

The performance improves for the next period, during which the *love*-based leader is doing some relationship building somewhere else, until he shifts back into his *wisdom* energy and shows up again unannounced to reinforce urgency and recharge the now better performing team with his personal energy.

There is nothing more unloving than a person who is continuing to be the *love* in the situation when what is most needed is *wisdom*, *power*, or *knowledge*.

Love shifting into *knowledge*

A dominant *love* person may find himself feeling anxious about his team of workers. He has provided an exciting vision with great opportunities for everyone to help create a great success, but is often disappointed in their results.

He finally decides to try something new. He expresses his concerns to a friend. In that process he clearly states what he is afraid of . . . "I just know that when my back is turned they are not working as hard as they need to be . . ."

The next step in the *Core Values Consciousness* process is to name his fears.

"I am afraid they don't take me seriously. That they don't respect me and disregard what I ask them to do. That I am helpless to change their behavior. That I will never get these people to do the things I want them to do."

This being said, he realizes he is operating as the presence of *love* in this situation. He then decides to shift into his second strongest *core value*—*knowledge*.

In this operating mode . . .

He calls a meeting and clearly states his expectations of performance of tasks, deadlines, and requirements for individual success. He remains engaged with the team and gives them clear directions. He reminds each one of his or her goals and requirements, and makes certain things are going well before he leaves the situation

The performance improves for the next period, during which the *love*-based leader is doing some relationship building somewhere else, until he shifts back into his *knowledge* energy and shows up again unannounced to reinforce urgency and recharge the now better performing team with his personal energy.

There is nothing more unloving than a person who is continuing to be the *love* in the situation when what is most needed is *knowledge*, *wisdom*, or *power*.

????????????????????????

There is a secret key I use that you may want to learn. It is this . . .

Fear is an emotion.

When we are feeling fearful, we cannot think, we can only feel fear. We cannot be psychologically conscious, we can only react out of fear.

The opposite is also true.

When we are thinking, being cognitive instead of emotive, we cannot have or experience any feelings. When we say the name of a fear, we have shifted completely out of feeling the fear and into naming the fear. We are being cognitive, so the feeling cannot continue to exist. You can't have a conscious thought and feel an emotion at the same time.

Whatever fears you still have in your life, are things and possible situations you dreamed up in your childhood experiences. Whatever fear you have in this dream-like world of your nonconscious personality cannot really hurt you.

The secret is to simply turn around and look at your fears, one by one, and name each fear. Whenever you think the name of those fears in the future, these fears will have lost much of their power over you. You cannot feel those fears as long as you keep acknowledging them and saying their name. When you say to yourself, "I am feeling anger toward my spouse," the anger is put on hold because you are naming the fear. Continue to name the fear without venting or rationalizing (these also are fear- and emotion-driven responses). You will kill your own ability to hold onto the anger.

You also cannot have the same fears that you are now experiencing if you shift to a different part of your *Core Values Nature*. Your motivation will be different. Your perceptions will be different. The range of available and trusted strategies will be different. And, in addition to all of that, you will be living consciously, and fear is not part of the conscious mind.

Oh, you can think about things that are dangerous and think consciously about possible negative outcomes. But all of this conscious thinking about a given fear keeps that fear itself from coming into your emotional psyche. You have shifted from feeling fearful into being thoughtful about possible ramifications of certain actions and cognitively attempting to determine risk reward. This is not giving into the fear. This is transition of the fear to thoughtful process.

When you say to God, "Show me my fear," you are setting a switch in your unconscious mind, asking the unconscious mind to report to your conscious mind the next time you are about to feel that fear.

When you have the courage to turn around, like the small boy in the tiger story, you see the fear clearly enough to name it. When you name it, it will disappear—for that moment, at least. From that point on, you can say to your higher power, "When I feel that fear again, please give me the courage to face the fear and say its name."

This is the first step to conscious living, the secret key. Begin using your fears and negative emotions and anxieties as wake-up calls to your conscious mind. From this posture of just being awake, you cannot hold onto your unconsciously aroused fears and feelings.

The wonderful life-changing human operating mechanism here is the presence of the fear, negative emotions, and anxieties.

They are there for what purpose?

To wake us up. To cause us to stop what we are doing and decide consciously *who we want to be*, which aspect of our *Core Values Nature* we want to be: *power*, *love*, *wisdom*, or *knowledge*.

These mechanisms are alarms, designed to make us look at the current fear and emotion, and decide whether we want to act in response to them, or to shift to a different *Core Value Energy* and remain in the contribution mode of *being*.

They invite us to take an adult view of the childhood fear and give it a name; take away its power over us. This gives us a moment to consciously choose *who* we want to *be* in this current situation. This is the key to conscious living. This is the key to *Core Values Consciousness*.

The Sixth Core Values Law:

All fears and negative emotions are wake-up calls to our *Core Values Nature*. Learning to shift out of *being* our currently chosen *Core Value Energy* and into one of our other preferred *core values* will automatically cause things to be different—usually better.

Once we are able to name our fears and lift ourselves out of our unconscious stimulus/fear–based response operating mode. We are able to ask the simple question, "Which *Core Value Energy in* me will be the most effective at this moment?"

We can shift into being the presence of *love*, *wisdom*, *power*, or *knowledge*. We can trust that we will know what to do, based upon our conscious decision to operate in alignment with, to *be* the new consciously selected *core value* instead of continuing to operate in response to your fears, resolve to:

- Face your fears and to go through your fears.
- Name your fears, no matter what the price may be.
- Choose to participate now, more fully, and more adventurously, more consciously than ever before.

For those of you who are adventurous in outward activities (highly *intuitive* in *power* and *love* energy), this may mean commitment to your *wisdom* energy, in which quiet study, delegation of authority to others, holding back, asking for more information and evidence before taking action—these are the comfortable and easily maintained operating tactics. Why? Because you have shifted into a different *core value* and that *core value* naturally drives completely different strategies and different tactics. The behaviors change without effort, after you consciously shift into a different *core value*.

What are the new fears that may be excited by this decision to sit back? Make a list.

For those of you who are more reserved and observational, the adventure of shifting to different *Core Value Energies* within your *Core Values Nature* goes in the opposite direction. The thrill of conquering your fears is just as great. The effect in tangible results is awesome. What are the fears that may come up if you take a more assertive action, or make a decision before you have perfect information, from an *intuitive* motivation? Make a list.

Reclaim your Real Life that exists for you on the other side of these walls.

To do this feels like swimming up from the bottom of a cold lake, lungs bursting for want of air, body aching, a sense of pending disaster, holding on, holding everything in. When at last the swimmer breaks the water's surface, sees the clear sky, white clouds, and suddenly draws in fresh, redeeming air with an uncontrolled gasp—there is nothing better in life than these moments.

The young boy who decides to turn around in his dream and face the dangerous creature behind him, sees the tiger and names it "Tiger." He can go back to sleep fearlessly.

He may never have that dream again, but if he does, he knows the Tiger and knows that by turning around and naming the Tiger, he is able to enter the dense and dark forests of his life fearlessly. He may even lose the need to go back into that dense dark forest where the Tiger lives.

When we shift from one *Core Value Energy* in which we are experiencing fear and employing ineffective behaviors, into another aspect of our innate *Core Values Nature*, we are rising up out of deep water into our *real self*—into our *Real Life*.

The Seventh Core Values Law:

All choices are made unconsciously until we consciously choose to make our choices consciously—one choice at a time.

All choices made by infants, toddlers, and young children are in response to the environment around them, as perceived through foggy eyes, inexperienced hearing, and sensations of falling, heat or cold, physical pain, hunger and thirst. Through the monitoring of these basic evidences of normalcy or jeopardy, the infant/toddler decides to be content or to cry out.

As the child develops and becomes more complex in his learning, these choices are driven more and more by need for acceptance and approval, desires for comfort and freedom of activity. These choices are driven by fears also, but they are not life-threatening fears, at the first level. They are social fears about acceptance and approval that wash back through the psyche to connect with possible exile, rejection, and therefore back to starvation or death through freezing, etc.

This choice to cry or not cry in any of these cases is not made consciously.

It is a built-in mechanism designed to ensure the child's survival; it is a creature mechanism, not an adult consciousness of human nature.

As we discussed earlier, this survival instinct causes each of us to evolve over time into our personality ego. Ego expands these unconscious survival mechanisms into not-physical realms. The ego directs the construction of a personality, loosely based upon our unique *Core Values Nature* and other genetic dispensations such as intelligence, physical skills, innate interests, and passions.

The strategies accompanying these basic traits are all adopted instinctively and unconsciously by the ego as the protector of the child.

As we begin to enter adulthood between the ages of 8 and 12 years, we are each given the opportunity to begin the process of becoming more and more conscious about our choices, to take more and more accountability for our own lives.

For some, this process is encouraged by parents, teachers, and other authorities. For others, this process is severely squelched. Regardless, of the situation there is a built-in urge to become more conscious of alternative responses to our varied individual circumstances. This is the urge to become fully individuated, as described by Dr. Carl Jung.

In *Core Values Consciousness* language, this is the natural progression of all humans toward being *who we are*, and making our highest and best contribution.

We choose either to become more and more conscious of alternative strategies and responses, or we choose to continue responding in an unconscious automatic, emotionally, and psychologically addictive fashion.

In either case, all of our responses as adults fall into one of two categories: 1) a contribution—action I have consciously decided to take, or 2) taking and getting—a response that I unconsciously allow myself to take without consideration of ramifications or alternatives.

11

Self-Knowledge

There Are Several Important Questions That Are Beneficial To Hold In One's Mind.

It is not important to have a *fixed* answer for these questions. But it is critical to have a workable answer to these questions at all times. It is important to hold these questions constantly in our minds so we may continuously be given new understanding.

Question One:

Why am I here on this planet? Why am I here in this situation? What is my life's next learning opportunity?

Question Two:

What do I want?

Question Three:

What passions, desires, fears, ideas, attitudes, and beliefs affect my getting what I want?

Question Four:

How effective am I at getting what I want? Where am I most ineffective? Where am I least effective? What *Core Value Energies* in me are contributing to this result?

Question Five:

What are my beliefs related to the things I want? Do I believe I deserve the things I want? Do I believe I have the skills, talents, personality to get the things I want? Do I know what habits, lack of discipline, or other issues are blocking my access to the things I want?

Question Six:

In situations where I feel "beside myself"—what am I afraid of? What do I believe or think will happen if I choose a response that is different from my learned personality behaviors?

People with similar *core values* tend to have common beliefs that support their personalities. Remember, personalities are founded on fear, whereas our *Core Values Nature* is the foundation of our innate *Real Core Values Self.* Our *real self* has no fear. It is separate from our created personality. You have a personality, self-designed by you as a child, refined in adulthood—and this personality must die—you are meant to be actualized as the *Real Core Values Nature* that you are.

One of the primary skills of life is the ability to observe ourselves as we bring our learned belief systems into play in a given circumstance, a belief system that supports our stimulus/response mechanisms and encourages us to continue to behave as we have always behaved.

This skill is founded on our willingness to see our personality issues as they take over our lives for periods of time. This is the ability to be conscious about *who we are* and about what aspect of our ego-driven personality we are choosing to behave like at any moment.

The personality works like the cocoon of a butterfly—it protects the vulnerable real nature it surrounds—and when the *Real Core Values Self* is invited forward into full actualization, the personality cocoon falls away.

This skill is simply to hear or be conscious of our inner talking, the repetition of negative or positive feelings, the beliefs that are driving our fears, and the reasons we reiterate to ourselves and sometimes to others that support a personality behavior.

Once a personal belief is identified, it is easier to see the fear that underlies each belief. Here are some of the common undermining beliefs that tend to be held by persons with each of the *Core Values Natures*.

Builders: *Core Value—Power* supported by *faith*

I have to make things happen in order to get the things I want.
I told him/her/them to do it, so it will be done.
I feel the importance of this decision now, so it's time to act.
This system (process) may be a good one, but I have to go around it for now.
They may think I'm too demanding and become angry with me, but I can fix that later.
I'll respond to this person when I have the time.
If I don't do it, it won't get done.
Intimacy and chit-chat just slow me down.
If it (she, he, they) doesn't move the first time I push, I'll have to push harder.
If you can't watch what I'm doing and learn from that, you have little value to me.
Don't ask a lot of questions. Just do it.

Merchants: *Core Value—Love* supported by *truth*

If I don't take care of this relationship, nothing will happen.
Conflict in a relationship is a bad thing.
Development of relationships is the best approach to almost everything.
The future will be better than the present.
New opportunities are exciting—the spice of life.
People should treat each other with respect and courtesy at all times.
There's no excuse for rudeness.
I don't need to be told what to do. Just ask.
Teams are more powerful and useful than individual effort.
Development of consensus is the best way to accomplish group goals.
Intimacy is the primary ingredient of a good life.

Innovators: *Core Value—Wisdom* supported by *compassion*

There is always a better way.
I can solve any problem, change any person.
Why settle for a quick fix when you can have the best solution available?
When all else fails, ask another question.
The answer is easy. I shouldn't have to explain it.
People should be reasonable and think things through.
It's important to observe things for a while before jumping in.
It's better to be late than to be foolish.

Bankers: *Core Value—Knowledge* supported by *justice*

Always have the right answer or no answer at all.
Ideas, without facts and empirical proof, are a fool's opiate.
If you can't prove it, don't do it.
History repeats itself and is a good indicator of present and future outcomes.
You can't know the answer unless you do the math yourself.
It only takes one good *banker* to keep a hundred *builders*, *merchants*, and *innovators* from hurting themselves.
Standing solid against the pressures of popular beliefs is a primary contribution.
When I find myself alone against the masses, I am fulfilling my highest mission.
A bird in the hand is better than two in the bush.
Hold onto what you have. Sooner or later someone will run out of theirs.
I can't trust responsibility for these resources to anyone.
If I weren't here, everything would go into chaos and wastefulness.
Nobody cares about the facts.
I am the only one who really knows.
Organization and law and order are the glues that hold society together.

You can see by reflecting briefly on each of the above-stated beliefs held by people with the various *Core Values Natures*, that there is some truth in each statement. There are many situations in which the belief may be reasonable. But that is the difficulty: overreliance upon a belief that tends to state the truth much—but not all—of the time.

We all tend to continue believing our trusted beliefs even when the circumstances call for a very different strategy. It is hard to act against long-held beliefs, beliefs that have kept us safe or provided us with successes in the past. So we put ourselves and others in little boxes of beliefs and fears that supposedly keep us safe and enable us to get the things we want without too much danger.

Some of the most valuable, powerful information available for business management is obtained through effective individual and team assessments.

People are the most important assets of any corporation. The effective deployment, motivation, measurement, and development of people are the greatest challenges for business. This is also where the greatest gains can be made in any company's performance.

We have learned through working with hundreds of companies and tens of thousands of individuals, that most businesses operate at about 33% human capital efficiency. This simply means that most companies have three times as many people as they actually need in order to make the same productivity contribution.

We agree with the Gallup study that found that about 26% of all American workers are significantly engaged in their work. This means that most of us are not significantly engaged in our work.

We *know* why this is true.

Most of us are in the wrong seat. We are not assigned a job that asks us to make the right contribution or to perform the right functions. We are investing our life energy in tasks that do not arise naturally out of our innate *Core Values Nature*.

When a person is put in a position in which the contribution, the functions, and the tasks of the job do not align with his *Core Values Nature*, he will: fail, redesign the position, disrupt, or leave. Some do all of the above. The people who leave are the people who still have some modicum of self-respect. The people who remain in a wrong position have low self-respect or a desperate need to survive.

The Meaning in Real Work

A person's real work is not always fun, seldom easy, always engaging, often provocative to his spirit and to his person. Real work challenges and rewards at the soul level. Real work makes the maximum contribution each is called to make, delivering all of one's Core Values Nature to society; a natural and pure expression of who I am, requiring a constant refinement of all of the talents and skills that comprise what I am, an integral part of my mission, and my sense of purpose on earth.

My real work causes my presence on earth to be useful, positive, and of significant value to those around me.

The secret is not to learn how to have fun and joy at work; the secret is to do work that is naturally engaging to who you are and what you are, so you know that you are making your highest and best contribution. This allows you to experience real joy as part of your work life. Sometimes this makes the right job downright fun.

The Grass IS Greener, Lynn E. Taylor

The *Core Values Index* assessment created by *Taylor Protocols, Inc.* is the most useful, accurate, and reliable instrument for business today. As hundreds of businesses continue to employ this important tool, there is little resistance. The only limitations appear to be: 1) lack of awareness of the power of the *Core Values Index* within any given business, and 2) the occasionally expressed fear of being "put in a box."

People are openly curious and eager for information about themselves and about those around them. There is occasionally some reticence about providing a full disclosure of oneself to others. "I don't want to be put in a box," is the common expression of this fear, so let's deal with that fear head on.

Everyone around you has already put you into a box. Everyone's box, defined by them for you, is different. This provides you with tremendous challenges daily. Many of these challenges you know about. Many more are hidden from you.

One person, for instance, experiences you as being difficult to work with, not based necessarily upon any negative attributes of yours, but based upon this person's previous experiences with someone else, or with many people, you remind them of. This person is intolerant of your personality, due to his judgments of other similar personalities like yours and based upon the relative difficulty he has dealing with what he believes to be your *kind of person.* You are in this person's "Rejects Box."

Another of your business associates has decided that you provide little or no value to them, or maybe even to the business, and they are therefore unwilling to invest any time and effort in a relationship with you. Likely, they are cordial and act appropriately with you when situations draw you together, but based upon their value judgments, you are in their "Junk Box."

Another person sees you as their mentor and savior. They seek you out for support, answers, strategies, and interference with others on their behalf when things get sticky. They have you in their "Hero Box." Their expectation is that you will not let them down and that they can take some of your time anytime they desire it.

Another individual seems always to take a position in opposition to yours. Their agenda is always counter to yours, and they are effective in arguing their point. They see you as a dangerous or worthy adversary, and they are constantly working to make certain you do not gain inappropriate power in the company. They have you in their "Eat-or-be-Eaten Box."

You, on the other hand, also have people in little boxes.

Something about them raises the hair of fear on the back of your neck.

Or, the way one person looks away when trying to formulate an answer to an important question makes you distrust his answers.

You felt hopeful and open to these people when you first met them, but over time, an act of rudeness, disregard, stubborn resistance, or other behavior you judged to be negative, showed you their "real" nature. Now you presume to know *who they are*. You are now more reserved and sometimes even avoid them. You have all these people in one of your boxes.

When we as individuals on a team use an accurate reliable assessment instrument that clearly reveals our inner core, our *Real Core Values Self*, we do not put ourselves and others in a box. The opposite is true. We take down the walls of the boxes in which we are all currently dwelling and are confined. We stand more clearly seen and understood with our desired contributions known and appreciated.

This process depersonalizes character traits and allows people to see beyond their psychological or sociological projections regarding *who you are.*

We simultaneously provide clues regarding the manner in which we like to be treated and the approach with us that is most likely to elicit a positive response. Given these clues, most people choose to utilize them, not to manipulate or abuse, but to optimize our usefulness to them and for the good of the team.

When we are each given a clear picture of the other person, the unfair nature of the boxes we have put them in becomes very clear to us. We are able to see past our fears and discomforts and strive toward a productive and mutually beneficial relationship. The inverse is also true, the people looking your way are able to drop their fear-based judgments about you and begin seeing you for the wonderful, contributing human being you are.

So the next time you hear someone say, "I just don't want anyone to put me in a box," say simply: "That's already happened. You are in a box prescribed by the people around you. Let's show them what's inside the box, a unique and valuable blend of *wisdom*, *knowledge*, *power*, and *love*, so they will know how to work with you and help you to make your important contributions."

All of the strategies chosen by individuals are based either in fear or in *core values.*

We respond to each the same way. We observe a situation, feel a fear, or select a *Core Value Energy* to be, then act in accordance with the dictates of that fear or the basic *core value* that drives a given strategy. These kinds of automatic responses are performed at the subconscious level much as driving a vehicle becomes subconscious after a few hours on the road.

All actions taken in response to fear are harmful to our well-being.

Actions taken in response to fear are generally less harmful (at the moment) than the perceived (expected) losses or hurts that excited the fear to begin with. Once our conditioned responses have proven to cause us less harm than the harm we believe will come if we do not react, we allow our conscious mind to pay attention to other things while we simply react.

At these times we are not looking for ultimate effectiveness or making our positive contribution. We are simply modulating the amount of harm we risk having inflicted upon our self and others versus the restriction of future fulfillment and success if we choose a fearless response.

In the adult situations in our lives this auto-response mechanism sets us up for repeated conflicts with persons who have no clue about our chosen course of action—why we are reacting the way we are.

We often surprise ourselves by our overly strong reactions to a person's tone of voice, or to someone's constructive criticism. These reactions are set up by fear and belief patterns so ingrained in us, that we no longer check out the situations consciously. When this happens our responses are seen by others as being out of context, out of character, or exaggerated relative to the situation.

We appear to be out of control to some degree, and indeed, we are. We have placed the control of our actions into the past, refusing to receive new information, choosing to go with responses/actions that have been previously approved by our ego, but are currently inappropriate, or at least ineffective.

It is easier to trust these proven safety measures than it is to observe ourselves, consider alternative reactions, and take a proactive step forward. It is easier to shift into our usual victim-response mode of action; it feels safer and there is no work involved. We simply let our auto-pilot continue to control us. The problem is, this sets up a fear-based response in others . . .

Fear in one excites fear in others.

Fear-based responses are always wrong responses (wrong being a descriptor of effectiveness, not morality). We can say this in the absolute, because a fear-based response does not allow for thorough review of a situation, does not look for alternatives beyond the trusted stimulus-response mechanism, and therefore does not look for a positive alternative or modification of previously chosen actions.

Fear-based responses assume that everything today is the same as it was when we learned the particular response. This is transference at work. We forget that most of our responses were developed in childhood when we had no power in our relationships and little experience to give us ideas for different, more effective responses.

A fear-based response by definition precludes a proactive *core values*–driven strategy or tactic. The fear has excited instantaneous response, so it is already too late to take a positive step forward by the time we decide we do not like the results of our fear-based actions.

We fail to recognize that every fear-based response elicits fear in others and that others tend to also react in a stimulus-response mode, seeking safety first. We get into these fear-based cycles with people and spin our wheels constantly in this mud without any forward motion. Our fears control not only our present actions and reactions, but also set up future reactive requirements because we stimulate fear in others.

12

How Can I Make More Conscious Choices?

This question is central to all human spiritual, emotional, social, and psychological development. It is important to know a few basic methods for becoming more conscious in our daily lives.

We of course start with the secret key mentioned previously: fear is an emotion. We begin by observing our fears, anxieties, and negative and positive emotions. This allows us to not decide from a position of fear or anxiety, or when we are feeling emotions.

We learn to shift into consciousness and decide first which *Core Value Energy* to *become* at this moment in time.

A good next step is a search for answers to the following questions.

First Question:

What situations in my life are causing me the most pain, embarrassment, physical jeopardy, or loss of respect or opportunity?

By answering this question, we can easily see the areas of our life in which we are still choosing to remain unconscious and are continuing to rely on old childhood strategies; choices that are being made without adult thinking and without hesitation. Having answered this question, we are prepared to ask the next.

Second Question:

What *Core Value Energy* (*power, love, wisdom, knowledge*) am I choosing too often to continue *being* (relying on unconsciously) to get me through?

When we are learning to cope with the world around us, our survival-based egos look to our trained and programmed personality which has been constructed loosely on our unique mixture of *core values*, but warped by childhood experiences. We are all a unique blend of the four *Core Value Energies* and tend to have greater capacity in some more than others. We tend to over-use the *Core Value Energy* of our higher capacity *core values.*

As discussed previously, these personality structures cause us to make judgments about our circumstances, and then we tend to unconsciously make decisions and take actions based upon these judgments.

The Eighth Core Values Law:

In every situation the strategies inherent in one of the *Core Value Energies* will be most effective.

Knowing what *core value* my unconscious response is based upon is an essential step in making a better (more effective) conscious choice.

In any given situation one of the *core values* is the best choice for an effective response. In situations that are causing me pain or embarrassment, the best response is not likely the learned unconscious response.

And the most effective strategy cannot be built upon the same judgments and actions that arise easily out of my usually selected dominant or secondary *Core Value Energy.*

Ask yourself what would be the impact if you increased your conscious use of your most minor *core value.* How great would the impact on your life be if you employed that *Core Value Energy* just 10% more than you now choose to do?

Third Question:

So how do I clearly identify the *core value* that drives my current response?

First, I look at my negative emotions in a fear-filled situation—my most obvious reactions. These usually show up as one of the following: *intimidation, manipulation, interrogation*, or *aloof judgment*. These are the *Negative Conflict Strategies* that are part of our *Human Operating System*. When feeling fearful; *power* becomes *intimidation, love* becomes *manipulation, wisdom* becomes *interrogation*, and *knowledge* becomes *aloof judgment*.

When I see myself interrupting others, raising my voice, possibly standing up and moving toward people that I feel are resisting me, I know that I am trying to protect my sense of personal *power*. I am afraid of being powerless and vulnerable. So I pretend to be the awesome power I now believe I am not.

When I experience embarrassment or anger because I am being criticized, and I begin to exaggerate statements or to get overly friendly and charming in a negative situation; when I smile while I am feeling angry, or say yes when I mean, Hell no!!—I know I am trying to regain the sense of being *loved* through *manipulation*. I am trying to get back to being the *love* in the room. I am afraid that I am not a loving person.

When I feel that people are not willing to listen to my sound ideas or that they are pushing me to make decisions and finish projects before I feel ready, I may find myself: harshly questioning the people around me, redirecting the discussion to different issues, or undermining another person's argument through harsh *interrogation*. I know then that I am trying to regain my sense of *wisdom*. I am afraid I may actually be a fool.

When I see people treating me or others unjustly, or when I *judge* that my carefully constructed reports and information are not being valued, I may see myself shutting down, leaving the room, or just going cold, unapproachable. From this position I may openly or secretly *judge* people harshly. I know then that I am trying to reclaim my sense of being the *knowledge* in the room and restoring my sense of *justice*. I am afraid that I may be ignorant after all or that my expertise is insufficient.

As we learn to distinguish the *core value* that we are currently operating in, we can decide whether to continue in that mode or to shift to another more effective strategy. The best way to make such a shift is to ask yourself the question, "What would *knowledge* do?" Or, "How would *love* respond?"

When the *core value* you are exploring is not the one you were aligned with when you started being ineffective, you are consciously awaking to make a better decision about a more effective action. The answer to this question may surprise you with a simple and effective obvious solution to the current disruptive dilemma.

Luckily, we all have some capacity to be even our lowest *Core Value Energy*, providing us the opportunity to shift our response strategy from an automatic *power*-based response, for instance, to a position based upon *knowledge* and conservation of energy. Remember when you took the *CVI* assessment: you had to select two of the *core value* words over two others. This was the case even for the *core value* words related to your lowest capacity *core value.*

In short, the *core value* words you selected in your lowest *core values* are just as important to you as those you selected in your dominant and secondary *core values.* You had to reject *strategic* and *tactical values* from other *Core Value Energies* in order to include the strategies and tactics of your minor *core value.* You are willing and you want to live according to these *core values*, but you are so used to acting unconsciously in accordance with your more dominant *Core Value Energy*, you forget to honor other *core values* that would serve you better in many instances.

If my answer to the first question (What situation is causing me the most pain?) is: Being criticized and ridiculed in public causes me the most pain and discomfort in my life,

My answer to the second question (What *Core Values Strategy* (*power*, *love*, *wisdom*, or *knowledge*) am I relying on unconsciously to get me through?) is:

Love. When I am not feeling *love* I resort to *manipulation*, cajoling, and whining—clinging to others who agree with me. This is not a particularly *lovable* response, so I continue to feel *unlovable and unloving.* This is a negative trap, and one I can lose myself in.

Then, I know it is important for me to shift to another *Core Value Energy—wisdom*, for instance—since my *love* strategy is not supporting me in getting what I want in this type of situation. The *wisdom* energy requires that I remain open and observant, collecting information out of pure curiosity, until I understand the situation and derive an effective, *wise* response.

When the answer to the above question is *wisdom*, the need may be to shift into being the *wisdom* in the room. The shift from trying unsuccessfully to be the *love* in the room, to being the *wisdom* in the room is a provocative, effective, influential shift. This feels very risky for a person who is more *love*-based than *wisdom*-based.

We can learn by pursuing these questions what kind of events trigger our most painful or ineffective experiences, when we tend to act out, manipulate others, maybe exaggerate and lie a little—all to win back the approval of others. These efforts are made to get us back to feeling *loved* or admired or respected, etc. We are lost in our getting taking behavior, we are completely out of our highest and best contribution role.

Since this strategy to hold compulsively to my dominant *Core Values Strategy* causes me pain, and I have identified my unconscious choices, I am now ready to move to the fourth question.

Fourth Question:

What are my alternatives?

Since my response to the above circumstance tends to be a negative reaction from the *love*-based *core value*, I know that I am not likely to succeed in making a different choice based on the *love* strategy. At least I have been ineffective at developing a positive strategy to meet the current painful situations. So, it seems reasonable to choose one of the other *Core Value Energies* to *be*:

> **A *power* response**: An immediate reaction declaring my lack of appreciation for the criticism and ridicule, clearly stating whether and why I disagree with the judgments being made. There is no anger in this *power* response. *Power* can also fearlessly hear the real criticism and simply accept it.

> **A *wisdom* response**: Remain open by asking questions in an attempt to understand what is being said, by whom, and whether the criticism is valid. Ask what kind of behavior the criticizing person would have preferred. *Wisdom* is able to hear its criticism and declare honestly, "I will take a look at that."
>
> **A *knowledge* response**: Stand my ground based upon evidence of facts, history, logic, or statistics. Remain dispassionate and quietly observant of all information being offered, judging the accuracy of the criticism for myself. *Knowledge* is able to fearlessly accept the facts of a criticism and acknowledge the validity.
>
> **A *love* response**: As a general rule, there is a reasonable and effective response to any situation based upon any of the *Core Value Strategies*. In the above criticism/embarrassment situation, it is possible to remain open to criticism. Criticism can be a high form of *love*. So *love*, for a person who has not lost composure or fallen victim to feelings of not being loved—this still vibrant *love* energy is able to ask for more clarity and thank the criticizer for the courage and care being offered.

The risk taken by one who criticizes is anger and rejection from the one being criticized. I value friends that risk criticizing me. A *love*-based response is to openly acknowledge and thank the person for the criticism and expect (trust) the "public" around you to be mature enough to see all of you, not just the part being criticized.

For those of you who pride yourselves in taking the hard road, go ahead, try to remain the presence of *love* in the above situation. For the rest of us, it is more effective to choose an alternative strategy, to shift into being a different *Core Value Energy*.

Once I am able to see the ineffectiveness of my current response, I can identify the *core value* that is the basis for current strategies. The next step is to pause long enough to make my choice concerning which alternative *Core Value Energy* might be best, and to consider how to make this chosen *core value* effective.

13

Choosing What to Think and Believe

What Are My Core Beliefs and Ideas That Control Most of My Life's Decisions?

When addressing this question, it is important to learn how to distinguish between primary *core values* biases (basic beliefs that are aligned with our *Core Values Nature*), and those beliefs, attitudes, and ideas that justify and rationalize our personality behaviors. The latter are our personal truths that exist due to childhood experiences and later adult circumstances that incite the transference of these beliefs into the adult world from the child world.

These personality beliefs serve to keep us out of alignment with our *Core Values Nature*. They also cause us to have an exaggerated, emotionally based attachment to the beliefs and attitudes that are aligned with one of our primary *core values*. In other words, our ego-driven personality will often talk like and sound like our *Real Core Values Self*, but the agenda is one of taking control and protecting one's self, not one of making a contribution.

The simplest test of integrity regarding motivation is to ask yourself whether you are motivated by personal desires and fears or by a desire to make a positive contribution. Be careful here. Most of us have some pretty slick ways to rationalizing fear-based decisions and activities. We are able to present to ourselves and to others some wonderful-sounding arguments that

This ground is slippery. The person operating in integrity is only concerned about making a contribution and is therefore operating free of fear, free of ulterior motive, and free of negative emotions.

The agenda of the *Real Core Values Self* is always to contribute the energy of one *core value* or another into the present situation, without concern about control or personal safety and comfort.

To clarify—we each become somewhat warped away from our most *intuitive*, organic self, our *Real Core Values Self*, by our childhood experiences. When we are in this personality mode, we are acting robotically in response to our ego's directive. It is impossible to make a contribution of our *Real Core Values Self* when in this personality mode.

We each have some areas in our worldview (personal belief system) that are warped into too much reliance upon the strategies and tactics of one *core value* over another. This is almost always experienced as too much comfort operating in our most dominant *core value* or sometimes the secondary. This preference tends to continue irrationally even when it is not in our best interest, a compulsion to act in accordance with this *core value* at each moment in time. This degrades what may have started out as a motivation to contribute.

When we continue to be our most comfortable *core value*, even in situations that call for something completely different, we begin to fail, and we tend to just try harder without shifting to a different aspect of our innate nature, until the motivation to get control or to be appreciated takes over. This creates anxiety and then fear, and causes the shift into negative conflict and personality strategies.

It is ordinary to have an exaggerated preference for the strategies, tactics, and behaviors that are aligned with our dominant and secondary *core values*. These are the value structures that we are designed to operate within most often, the presence we are most designed *to be*. We are most comfortable, we feel the most secure, and we develop the most self-respect when we are operating in alignment with our dominant *core values*.

We tend to try a dominant core value response in every situation first.

When this gets a reasonable result for us, we tend to use the same response over and over again in the same or similar situations. Since we try most often to use our dominant *Core Value Energy* first, we give those strategies the most opportunity to create success for ourselves, building a greater trust, an inordinate level of trust in this value structure, and the actions or behaviors that most commonly deliver this energy to society.

This causes us to put our lesser *Core Value Energies* on hold more often than we are wired by nature to do.

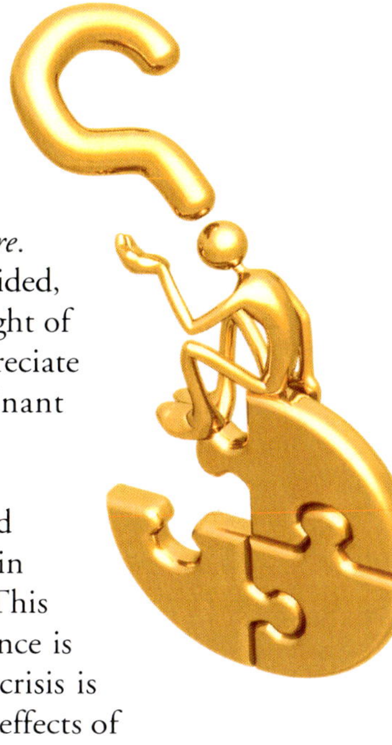

This results in a natural warping away from our uniquely balanced *Core Values Nature.* We become more and more one-sided or two-sided, until quite often, people see us only in the light of those preferred strategies. They cannot appreciate our deeper commitment to our less-dominant values.

We rely upon our dominant *core values*, and we are emotionally committed to continue in this habit toward our dominant *core values*. This natural warping away from our organic balance is not avoidable. The often discussed mid-life crisis is the period of time when most people see the effects of this natural process in terms of lack of success in areas of life they deem to be important.

If a person follows the natural comfortable course of life, the mid-life crisis will result naturally in the reclamation of some of our lost and least used *Core Value Energies* and an increase in effectiveness. We raise the value of our participation and contribution in this process.

We need not wait until we are in crisis in order to claim our own life and begin to rise to our highest potential. This can begin right now, for you. It requires only a commitment to wake up and observe negative emotions, anxieties, and fear. This is only effective when driven by a desire to make your highest and best contribution, not by a desire to achieve success and gain fame and fortune.

All of this brings us to the first question of this chapter:

What are my core beliefs and ideas that control most of my life's decisions?

We start with a willingness to observe ourselves in situations in which we judge ourselves to be least effective—times when we are "beside ourselves." We are able to hear inner talking (internal rationalizations of our actions). We can also sit back in our conscious minds and observe our actual arguments with others in which our negatively derived beliefs, attitudes, and ideas are being put to work.

We can watch ourselves rationalizing why it is okay to act as we are now acting and to feel the way we now feel. We can hear our patterned phrases (inner talking) that justify our need to take control or act defensively. To act otherwise, we believe and remind ourselves silently, might put us in harm's way and cause us to lose something we are emotionally attached to.
A few examples of this kind of inner talking might be . . .

He made me so angry that I . . .
People can't be trusted to . . .
There is never enough time for me to . . .
If I don't tell him what to do . . .

You will notice that the universal theme of these internally recorded phrases is to relieve you from responsibility for your current feelings and attitudes and lay the responsibility on someone or something else. This is generally followed by a restatement of the same rationalization when the consequences of our choices for reaction are suddenly upon us. These rephrased beliefs tend to begin with, "If he hadn't made me so angry, then I wouldn't have had to . . ."

When we are willing to hear these emotionally loaded beliefs and challenge them from an adult position, we are able to see the falseness or lack of necessity of many of these personal beliefs.

Challenge and deny the old personality beliefs.

Once we see the futility or inappropriateness of these beliefs and we begin to build emotional commitment to giving up certain childish actions, we are able to make conscious decisions to act in accordance with the *core value* that is most needed at the moment.

The greater opportunity exists in becoming more and more clear about *who I am* so my desire to be *who I am* begins to take more precedence in my life. I am more willing to let go of fear-based reactions in preference for making a positive contribution.

This opportunity and willingness to make conscious choices in the moment automatically results in a more successful life.

Remember all choices that are backed by the above-described rationalization are based upon fear. We earlier discussed the fact that ***all decisions based in fear are wrong (ineffective) decisions.***

We are all attempting to live a life that is fulfilling and meaningful. We are challenged with the necessity of learning how to build emotional and psychological muscle in the *Core Value Energies* that we have left somewhat dormant because of our preference for our more dominant values.

The attempt here is not to become perfectly balanced in our *core value* preference and usage, but to learn when it is in our best (most effective) interest to act in alignment with, to *be* one of our lesser values in order to obtain greater results in our lives.

The attempt is to build sufficient muscle in each *Core Values Strategy*, so that we are able to consciously decide to operate in alignment with a lesser *core value* for a period of time and in certain instances.

We all have some of each of the four *core values* in us. We all have certain different levels of capacity to *be power*, *love*, *wisdom*, and *knowledge* at any moment.

We have never had anyone score a zero in any *core value*, nor has anyone chosen all 36 strategic and tactical values that the *Core Values Index* used to discover your innate *Core Values Nature.*

So there is always some aspect, some *Core Value Energy* that we don't know how to access easily or put into good use on demand. The intentional use of a seldom-used *Core Value Energy* builds emotional, psychological, social, and spiritual muscle related to that *core value.*

Each individual unconsciously chooses life situations that give him or her an opportunity to build this muscle. Often for extended periods of each fully individuating life, we find ourselves attempting to learn to operate more often than our natural balance, in alignment with one or more of our lesser values.

Example: My *Core Values Nature* is structured with a dominant preference (capacity) for the *love* strategy. This means I have a greater innate capacity to *be* the *love* in the room—more capacity than for the other three *core values.* This is followed closely my next highest capacity, *wisdom.*

There is a significant difference between my preference and capacity for the *wisdom* strategy and my third-level *core value*, *power.* In my childhood home I was given far too much praise for *love*-aligned actions and almost totally discouraged from acting in alignment with the *power* strategies. My mother didn't tolerate well my choice to be the *power* in the room (the room she was in).

This resulted in a preference for and dependence upon the *love* strategy even beyond the normal warping that comes from frequent use of a dominant *Core Value Energy.*

I was profoundly warped into extreme dependence upon the *love* strategy. By the time I was a teenager, my *power Core Value Energy* was completely foreign to me, and my *power* muscle almost totally atrophied. I judged through my *love*-biased filters, that all *power*-based actions were offensive, especially to women—therefore, also unacceptable for me to utilize.

This was not a formula for success as a consultant specializing in mentoring and coaching powerful CEOs.

In my mid-forties, the results of this warping became more apparent and also more intolerable. I have always felt a *calling* to lead a meaningful existence and to make a strong contribution in business. I found myself in a role, turning around failing businesses, in which the need for power was extraordinary.

I quickly (by galactic time) learned that I was often going to fail with certain kinds of people (are you surprised that this would mostly be *power*-based people?). In many situations the *power* strategy was essential if I was going to save a given business. *Power*-based people were not going to even hear me speak, let alone be influenced by me, unless I learned to develop my intrinsic *power* muscles.

Over a period of fifteen years I have built up my *power* muscles so that I can call on this strategy whenever consciously required; I can choose consciously to be the *power* in the situation. This does not mean that I have changed my *Core Values Nature*. It means that I have learned to use *power* more naturally, in service of my *wisdom* and *love core value* drivers. Sometimes I even decide to be the *power* in the room just because that is what is so clearly needed. *Power* has become natural enough for me that I often feel compelled to *be power* for people for the sake of making a powerful contribution. My natural wiring would normally have me shift into *power* in order to make my contributions of *love* and *wisdom* more effective.

The process has helped me reclaim the natural balance of *core values* in me—*power* being my third-level *core value*, but with enough capacity for being the *power* in the room, that I should be able to access my *power* energy easily, in its relative capacity with my stronger *core values*.

The goal here is to learn how to be all of *who I am*, in my most natural balance. Then I can put myself in a role in which *who I am* is what is needed all day long. I can make my highest and best contribution.

I now often operate *intuitively*, naturally in alignment with the *power* strategy, without having to think about it. Since my business position required an inordinate amount of reliance upon the *power*-based strategies, I have been able, over the period of a decade and a half, to bring my alignment and appreciation for the *power* strategy into balance, my natural balance, with *love* leading the way, supported by *wisdom*, and now fully supported by *power* as required.

I can now see clearly that for the next decade or so, I must focus on bringing my capacity for *knowledge* more to life in me in order for me to gain ultimate balance. This will allow me to complete my life mission. When all of my energies are accessible upon demand, at the level for which I am designed to operate, I will be able to make my full contribution. I will feel fulfilled and meaningful in the process.

I propose that it is not possible to make a full contribution to this world without regaining a significant amount of our innate, unchanging *core values* balance. This is, after all, what we are here to contribute to this world. We are each a unique mixture of *love*, *power*, *wisdom*, and *knowledge*, and this, delivered through our chosen roles in life by our native talents and learned skills, allows us to make our highest and best contribution.

14

On the Other Side

The Ninth Core Values Law:

Success in life is greatly enhanced when you claim your deepest *core values* and make your choices in alignment with those values.

The second level of development is obtained through making conscious choices to shift into tertiary and minor *Core Value Energies* (those you hold at a lower level than your dominant and secondary values).

These second-level development shifts also occur between our dominant and secondary contribution type value structures, i.e., shifting from a preferred *cognitive* posture to the utilization of one's *intuitive* value structure when life circumstances call for such a shift.

Finding the Balance Between Cognitive and Intuitive Choices

Getting out of your head and into your life

There is a difficult challenge for a person who is strongly weighted in his preference toward *cognitive* processing and *intuitive* choices.

When we are designed to operate more naturally in the *cognitive* mode than in the *intuitive* mode of decision-making, we tend to rely upon the *cognitive* in almost every situation. The more often we choose to make decisions from a *cognitive* posture and view of life, the more we gain *cognitive* skills, the more comfortable we become.

Having gained more skills in the *cognitive* decision process, and being naturally prone to use *cognitive* processing to make decisions, it is not likely that a person will *easily* shift to an *intuitive* process when difficulties arise.

When things are relatively nonstressful, the easiest mode of operation is generally taken without much consternation. When situations are challenging or stressful we almost always shift into our worst dominant type of participation causing us to be more likely to shift into the *Negative Conflict Strategies* of our dominant and secondary values.

So the more strongly weighted we are in our value structure toward the *cognitive* side, the more we use *cognition* as a primary mode of operation, the more practiced and skilled we become, deepening our sense of comfort and reliance upon *cognition* as *the* way to be.

For *cognitive* people the most profound improvement in the increase of success and effectiveness in life comes from consciously watching for situations in which we would be better served by an *intuitive* leap to understanding; *intuitive* choice rather than our usual stepping back into the *cognitive* reasoning processes.

This also teaches us to respect the choice processes of others who are *intuitive* individuals.

Example: We hired a gentleman to work as one of our consultants years ago. He was used to making more than $300,000 per year providing consulting services to large corporations, and he came highly recommended. He was a highly reasonable and *practical* person with good people skills and a professional appearance and presence.

After significant training in our rapidly paced turn-around processes and clear guidance in the creation of a twelve-month business improvement plan, we felt confident that "Jack" would hit the street running. We believed, as he believed, that he would be able to make tough decisions and cause the changes necessary to first preserve our client's company, and then cause dramatic growth and structural, operational development.

After ninety days we met with three clients that Jack had been working with in order to review the results. There were no positive results.

Not one of the changes that the business plan clearly required had been made. Jack and the client spent two hours rationalizing why the changes had not been made, spelling out the decision process that was in place to bring them to consensus and cause the changes to be made.

They had designed a process that would take another three months to make the decisions and effect the changes. They had spent their time redesigning the plan and re-strategizing how to implement the plan.

In the meantime, this small $3-million company was burning $40,000 of losses per month, and the bank, which had already called the line of credit before our involvement, was now pursuing payment and a complete cash-out with a vengeance.

Our highly experienced and professional consultant had allowed our client to lose another $120,000 and had set up a process to ensure yet another $120,000 in losses before any changes would be realized. He was stuck in his process of *cognitive* decision-making, frozen from action by a need to have a perfect strategy and a full consensus among all parties before action could be taken.

This was the result of a simple oversight on our part. We put a highly *cognitive* person into a position of leadership with a highly *cognitive* client. Together they were stuck in the cycle of increasing complexity, expanding the change process into a wholly unmanageable program and sinking the business in the process.

What was needed was a *power/love* strategy—the *intuitive* duo of *core values* that trust instinct. *Intuitive* people do not wait and re-rationalize something that is *intuitively* known. The decisions in this case had already been made, yet no actions were taking place.

Within two weeks of taking over this account, my partner and I had the company running at a nominal $4,000 per month profit, with increases in sales and decreases in costs that yielded $30,000 per month profit in the next month. This was an increase in profit of more than $800,000, per year in a $3-million company that had been on the brink of bankruptcy. We also were able to get more time from the bank, having shown our ability and willingness to effect important changes in the company.

By moving quickly out of our *cognitive* heads and into our *intuitive* value structure, we were able to accomplish in a matter of weeks what would likely have never been accomplished by Jack and our client.

They were committed to a continuation of *cognitive* brainstorming, complexity-creating machinations. They were two very intelligent and knowledgeable people who were unable (unwilling) to shift into an *intuitive* mode of operation and set essential changes into motion.

There is nothing more foolish than a *wisdom* person who does not recognize when *wisdom* is no longer the necessary *core value* in a situation.

Getting into your mind and out of spontaneous combustion

The challenge for people on the other side of the *intuitive/cognitive* fence is equally great.

When the heart of a person is tuned to the *intuitive*, spontaneous, gut-level—instinctive—mode of decision-making, choosing to slow things down is difficult. It feels impossible and weak to allow more rational processing time, to seek additional information in order to obtain a greater rational basis for making decisions:

Why slow things down? I know in my gut what to do.

The invitation of others into the process and the acceptance of an extended thought-fest into the decision process feels like a direct offense against the *intuitive* spirit.

The greater the self-respect of an *intuitively* weighted person, the more difficult it is for him to see times when the shifting into a *cognitive*, reasoning mode might be more effective. After all, the same preferred strategy patterning process described above for *cognitive* persons is at work in everyone who is weighted in their *Real Core Values Self* toward the *intuitive* side.

The more I rely on my *intuition*, the better I get at setting things up to make *intuitive* choices effectively. By making the *intuitive* process more effective more often, I further tune myself toward reliance upon the *intuitive* and get away with less *cognitive* processing than is needed by others. I learn to use *intuitive* processes even in situations where *cognitive* processing would be significantly more effective.

I become skilled in tuning into my *intuitive* mind. I open myself to *instinctive* insights and inspired activities. People around me reinforce my commitment to the *intuitive* by complimenting me on my ability to make quick decisions and cause dramatic changes around me.

Example: It is not difficult to come up with numerous examples of this need for *intuitive* to *cognitive* shifting. One of our most profound examples of an *intuitive* leader is the president of a regional construction services company with a balance of smaller projects ($50,000 to $250,000) and site work projects ($500,000 to $3,000,000 and more).

Historically, this company had been able to generate gross margins in the 25% range on the smaller projects and had lost money on almost all larger jobs. Since the larger projects were bid at lower margins (under 15%) in order to close these sales, the likelihood of not generating good margins is predetermined.

Still, with the rational reporting of results from an outside objective source and the recommendation to shift sales toward a mix of projects that is 80% smaller projects and less than 20% larger contracts, is a recommendation that was completely unacceptable to our overly *intuitive* clerks. "I know we can make money on these large projects."

"But you haven't made money on such projects so far."

"We haven't had good project managers."

"What is going to be different now? We don't have the project managers on board."

"I know that we can find them."

You can see the difficulty of trying to shift this president into a *cognitive* mode.

His *intuitive* passions were aroused by the suggestion that he might not be able to be successful in the larger projects. His *intuitive* energy is so strong, so tuned by a lifetime of getting by without high *cognitive* skills, that the interjection of a requirement to slow things down and expend energy in a *cognitive* process even from a respected and well-paid advisor was not acceptable.

This person happens to have a highly profound *intuitive Core Values Nature*—making his challenge of shifting to the *cognitive* difficult for him naturally. This, combined with years of nearly sole reliance upon the *intuitive*, plus his emotional addiction to nearly constant *intuitive* decision-making, work together to set up a blind spot—one that nearly destroyed his fifteen-year-old company.

We have witnessed this before in the construction services industry, many times. Even our sharing of the stories of others was not sufficient to pull this strong-minded *intuitive* person over to the *cognitive* side. In the end, we could only stand to the side and watch.

The sadness of this is sometimes overpowering.

I have to personally gird myself for the future bad news and detach from my sense of caring for this person's business success; I cannot, however, pull away completely.

We are working to link this president with a former president of a similar company, trying to encourage a partnering with a more *cognitive* president. If we succeed, the company will thrive. If we fail, sadly, the not-too-far-in-the-distance-failure of the company is almost a sure thing.

If you are a strongly *intuitive* individual, you might be well served to ask yourself and others around you, especially a highly *cognitive* person, where your blind spots are. Ask them where they see that you may be headed for a collision with your unique set of *intuitive* choice addictions.

Finding the Balance Between Creative and Practical Modes of Operation

Crossing over from creative into practical tactics

Persons who are designed to be a *creative* presence on this earth have a powerful urge to visualize what is possible and to make assessments, seek solutions, and to come up with *creative* responses to life's challenges and difficulties. The *cognitive/intuitive* shifting described above is equally important for *creative*-type individuals. They must learn to shift occasionally to the *practical* type of contribution.

The anathema of *love*- and *wisdom*-based *creative* people against shifting into a strongly *practical* mode of operation for more than a few moments (hours) of time is intense. The need to do this is real.

Most *creative* people know that they make life harder for themselves occasionally (or often), by not paying enough attention to *practical* issues. We are not talking about paintbrushes and watercolors, or even architectural design, although these are creative pursuits. The *creative* energy in humans is driven by the ability to envision how things can be made better, how things can be changed, and the nature of processes and procedures that might deliver better results.

Still, the *creative type of contributor* feels compelled to be involved in participation in *creating* something new and doing something different rather than repeating the same tasks, making the same decisions, fulfilling decisions, and implementing plans that have already been made.

To desert the development of new relationships or to set aside the instinctive requirement to make certain every decision is wisely derived and not foolish—the *creative Core Values Nature* finds it difficult to allow time for purely *practical* activity, redundant tasks, or measurement of past and current results.

These kinds of essential issues are readily acknowledged to be important, but often not sufficiently important to cause the setting aside of *creativity*, which, after all, is the *core value* that these individuals are primarily here on earth to deliver into their society.

Example: I personally am weighted in my *core value* preferences toward the *creative* side. The relative weighting is significant: 45 points out of 72 toward *creative* and 27 points of *practical* energy. We have discovered in the processing of hundreds of thousands of *Core Values Index* assessments that the numerical percentage of weighting becomes further magnified toward the dominant *core value* due to consistent overreliance upon the dominant type of operation, and the steady use of skills and attributes that align with and are routinely used in support of the dominant *core value.*

This normal skewing or warping of preference toward the dominant type is significant and becomes more and more irresistible when the individual preference scores are above the 25 out of 36 *core values* scores and above 50 out of 72 type scores. These people become profoundly committed to using these overly dominant values, almost incapable of even respecting the opposite type of participation.

Due to economic pressures in the general U.S. market since the 2001 dot-com bubble burst and the 9-11 terrorist trauma, my own company had to face its own challenges of survival.

We found business owners so fearful that, even in the face of possible business failure, they were frozen into inactivity. The overwhelming sense of hopelessness—that nothing I can do will make a difference—was so pervasive that even our business turn-around practice did not attract many new clients.

This presented me with the personal requirement to do what I have had to coach many client owners to do. I had to shift from my usual *creative* mode—providing innovative and resourceful guidance to leaders under financial and business duress—into a more *practical* mode.

I found it necessary at one point to make a commitment to myself that I would not allow myself to use any emotional, mental, or psychic energy in *creative* pursuits until I had mastered the practical demands of my business and caused it to survive and stabilize.

This period of strong self-management lasted for twenty-six months, until my business and the businesses of our company clients had shifted into sufficient positive cash flow that I could allow myself to once again return to writing this book, writing poetry for my fourth published collection, and creating new bonsai for my personal collection.

I have yet to bring back into my life framework the composition of music, voice lessons, and completion of a novel and other business books I have started. This book is sufficiently *creative* for me to feel a deep sense of satisfaction in the composition of it, yet closely supportive of my company's business objectives and therefore *practical* enough in nature so this activity represents a nicely balanced expression and contribution of *practical* and *creative core values.*

Crossing over from *practical* into *creative* practices

It is no less difficult for the strongly *practical* type of person to put aside the sense of urgency for action, requirement for keeping things steady and organized, getting things done, and measuring results.

This setting aside of *core values* tactics and strategies that align with *practical values* in preference for *creativity* feels soft and fluffy, nonproductive, wasting energy and time, wasting resources for unknown value received, in replacement for keeping the head down, shoulder to the wheel, all energy pouring into proven mechanisms that cause known, concrete, and essential results.

The primary urge is to take an action, get results, measure results, drive efficiency, derive knowledge, and information for future improvement—survival and success. How does a person who is strongly weighted in their preference for these critical, *real* issues, cast these aside in lieu of setting up a *creative* process that involves open-ended brainstorming, relationship development with nebulous long-term value, and the processing of emotions, dreams, and visions and unproven ideas and strategies?

This challenge feels even more overbearing when faced with a time of crisis or of extraordinary productivity. The urge to become even more *practical*, even more focused and action-oriented is highly seductive. Yet it is at these times, the *practical* person, by ignoring the need for a new strategy or a *creative* modulation of tactics, is most likely to self-destruct and take the team or organization down with him.

Example: A project supervisor in a large regional home-building company was one of the more educated and broadly experienced supervisors in his company. He was used to managing half a dozen projects with leads in the field and support from project engineers and purchasing/expediting people in support positions. When he made the move to a smaller company he was asked to make a similar number of projects run smoothly.

He was used to relying on a support team for the paper processing, and on project engineers and the sales/estimating staff to set things up effectively. The limited skills and limited time allotment from these kinds of support people in his new company left him floundering in a sea of missed delivery dates, forgotten communications, and dropped balls.

He was profoundly *practical* in his makeup, so his tendency, since the small company could not afford more employees, was to work harder and faster. He needed to work smarter, to be *creative* about how to develop personnel and team systems to catch things up. He was not able to complete tasks and details to the 90% level. He was compulsive about being perfect, so almost nothing was being completed.

He found himself being unsuccessful for the first time in his life.

His response, being a very strong *practical* nature with a powerful *builder* energy and an almost equal *banker knowledge* value, was to put his shoulder down, push ahead, drive others, fix everything personally, give up any trust of others, and take control of all aspects down to the last nail.

His inability to step up and design a new process, or to ask others to help him in different ways after they had failed in their support of him in the past caused him to flounder. When confronted with his own growing failure and the out-of-control status of his projects, the criticism to him appeared wholly unfair.

It was, after all, the failure of others in their lack of support for him and his customers that were the cause of the current failed status.

Even when shown his micro-management Achilles' heel and given the opportunity to make a shift toward more teamwork, he could not see the light on the other side of *creative* processes.

Some creative re-planning and adjustments to his schedules and staffing plans were needed. He was unwilling to make the shift. To do so would have been tantamount to admitting that the poor status of his projects was, to some significant degree, his sole responsibility.

This was proven, not to him directly, but to the management team of this company when we hired another supervisor to take over his failing projects.

The new supervisor was also weighted toward the *practical* in his *Core Values Nature,* but not so strongly. He was able to shift fluidly between his *practical* and *creative* type tactics, and within a few short weeks had things back on track and the limited support structure pulling more of the load and working with him as a team.

Finding the Balance Between Community and Independent Values

Moving out of *Community* into *Independent* Action

For a person who is strongly weighted in the *community* value structure, the concept of operating *independently* is a distant vision. They believe that a person gains strength and influence when surrounded with a good team—that corporate power comes from focusing on organization, structure, consistency, and the motivation of people toward a common goal.

These beliefs are valid and made evident to anyone who is willing to witness companies and organizations that are particularly gifted in the creation and maintenance of a strong *community*: the internal community of each company, and the community of companies, customers, and vendors that surround each business.

Independence, hours alone traveling from one place to another. No one to share new ideas with, no time to gather a group together for brainstorming, no requirement for support structures. Just me and my great ideas and pure *power* against the obstacles in the world. These are wonderful challenging obstacles that exist for an *independent* person on his road to success.

Many *independent* individuals find a home with a strong community. If they are utilized to their highest potential, these *independent* individuals find a role in which they act very autonomously, without a lot of oversight, and with sufficient authority to make and implement decisions.

For the *community* participant, this sounds like a negative perspective on the desirability of the *independent* mode of operation. He has difficulty seeing the benefits of this *independent* mode of work. This negative attitude toward *independent* strategies defeats any inclination to set off in an *independent* mode and to be self-reliant and solitary in work or play.

For a *community* person to get into the skin of a truly *independent* person is next to impossible. The two approaches to life appear to be in conflict and not complementary in nature. This mistaken perspective is caused by the innate nature of the person that prefers one strategic response to life over the other. Conquering this limiting belief requires that the *community* person learn to build more emotional muscle and better skills in *independent* tactics.

The goal here is not to learn to be perfectly balanced in these kinds of preferential wiring.

We learn instead to use all of the energies we have in us, in roughly the balance that these *core values* are hardwired into us. We learn to consciously choose to shift from *community* to *independent* strategies when the consciously chosen type of contribution will likely created better results—when and where they might cause us to make a better contribution.

Then we put ourselves with conscious effort and *core value*–based choices into roles in life in which *who we are* at this deep innate nature level, is what is needed. The approximate balance of *Core Value Energies* that we *are* is what will make the best contribution in the role. If the functions and tasks of the job require us to use all of our innate nature, in approximately the same levels that these capacities exist in us, the chosen job contributions to mature us into a more fully actualized version of our *Real Core Values Self.*

If a person is so highly weighted in preference of *community* over *independent* contribution that he cannot easily see even the potential benefit of *independent* operating modes, he needs to hire or find a partner who has this opposite energy. Then give this new person support and acknowledgment for their very different contribution.

The person with highly dominant *community* values needs to seek a role in which autonomous and independent activity is seldom if ever required.

It is much harder for some to switch from one favored type of behavior to a behavior that honors a completely different set of values. Some are wired almost equally between value structures. Others have profound preference for one over another.

Example: A young man I know is highly energetic and skilled at gathering people around him for any one event, adventure, project, service, or performance. He is constantly surrounded by attractive, interesting, and fun-loving people.

He is musically talented and when not surrounded by friends, tends to sit down at any keyboard he can find and light it up with incredible jazz riffs, adding a resonate and lyrical vocal rendition of a well-known or self-composed song into the mix.

This activity also draws people to him.

He has been repeatedly honored for his management skill in the college food service center where he served as manager of all student managers, basically running the daily operations and driving excellent customer service.

Everything about this young man is *community*-oriented, to a profound degree.

Yet, when he graduated from college, he set off from his home in Seattle and landed in Washington, D.C., with no job, very little money, and no circle of friends. He left his parents, with whom he had a warm and open relationship. "I have nothing to escape home for," he has often said, "nothing that I can complain to friends about."

He could easily have stayed in Seattle, near his parents' home, gotten a job in the area, and settled into a prolonged extension of friendships with people he knew and loved. But the desire to explore himself in the unexplored world was strong. He bought a plane ticket—one way—sold his car, landed in Washington, D.C., and began looking for a job.

This adventure, he knows now, was important to him—to disconnect from comfortable roots, to establish himself in an area where he was not known. To start fresh, putting a new face on his life, experiencing himself without a sense of being observed by family and friends—his wilderness adventure, his spiritual journey into the void.

It was also strongly about learning to develop his *independent* contribution muscle.

He wanted to learn how to operate in the *independent* mode. For him it took a fairly drastic decision, moving him across a continent in order to explore the other side of his inner universe.

Having accomplished much, and learned much, he is having renewed success in a job that requires significant *community* energy, while requiring a daily, conscious shift into the *independent* mode of working for maximum success.

As I hear him tell about his experiences and see his development, I enjoy seeing him settling into his own spiritual and physical skin. I can see and understand the incredible importance of his independent adventure.

He can bring so much more into his communities, into his life framework, because he knows the *independent* path just a little more now than before. He can stand his ground within his community, fearlessly, knowing that if required he is able to take up his life and walk into a new life if the call should come.

Most important, he is able to consciously shift confidently into his *independent* nature whenever needed in his work and private life. This capacity to play from the less-dominant side of his nature gives him an incredible range of strategic options to maximize his contribution.

Moving out of Independence into Community Activities

For the individual who is strongly bent on living an *independent* life, free from too much scrutiny, void of tight management and restrictions, subject only to self-monitoring, self-motivation, and self-constraint—the invitations to join into *community* activities that are centered around group meetings, committee work, consensus management, cooperative, interdependent efforts—all sound like an invitation to voluntarily inflict himself with a straitjacket, and to put himself under the watchful eye of a night nurse.

Independent values thrive when a very loose structure exists; when the way I spend my day is subject only to my own judgment of what should be done. I figure out what to do and I do it. My problem-solving and assessment of situations is a *wisdom* activity that I thrive upon. I instinctively know this is a prime contribution of mine to my society.

I also *decide and do.* I take action and get results. I act on the *faith* that I know *intuitively* what to do. After I take this *intuitive* action, I will know what to do next. I am the presence of *powerful wisdom*, or *wise power* at any given moment.

I am a change agent, not governed by rules and structure imposed by others. I act in the manner I deem to be appropriate, and the opinion of others regarding my actions is insignificant by comparison to my own judgment of my worth and potency.

How could I possibly find any benefit in subjugating myself to a *community* with rules and restrictions and constant compromise, limitations on decisions and actions I am allowed to make?

Example: A nationally respected minister of a fundamental Christian denomination held beliefs that were largely discomforting if not completely unacceptable to the majority of his fellow ministers in his chosen denomination.

This gentle man was very charismatic and much loved by his congregation. Those who sharply disagreed with his teaching had long since moved on, and those remaining were intensely supportive.

It would have been easy for this man, with an independent mind and a free will, to lead his congregation in a separation from the parent church. Many others have done so in the two hundred years of its history.

Then a vote came that declared doctrine (dogma) to the world and the church's membership that gay individuals could not be ministers in this denomination. Although this devout minister was not gay and was happily married, a strong part of his leadership had been directed toward the population immediately surrounding the old downtown church.

This population had gay and lesbian couples, homeless people, alcoholics, and many poor families in it, along with a strong aging group of upper-middle-class, conservative members who had supported the minister and had wholly adopted his strong belief that all people should find an equal acceptance in their church community.

A powerful movement within the congregation coalesced and went to the minister to express their support of separating from the mother church.

They believed because of his many sermons about the inappropriateness of discriminating against the socially outcast, that the minister would welcome their assertion of loyalty and willingness to separate from the denomination of which they had always been a part.

To their surprise, the minister rejected their entreaties, and instead of joining in the mutiny, declared that he would only leave the denomination if chased out, and then only after a defiant and prolonged battle. He would not leave the community in the hands of intolerant and wrong-minded people.

Despite all his years of leading an independent pastoral role, working at the far edges of the community, despite all of the times he had found himself standing alone against dogma that he believed was destructive to his ministry and destructive to the church . . . Even with all of this history of independence, his inner guidance caused him to put this independence aside and to drive headlong into the center of the church's legislative community heart.

He set out to affect the church from within, rather than abandon it just because some were trying to control the community in a manner that was almost unbearable.

Years later the denomination amended its position making it possible for gay individuals to be ordained as ministers within the church.

He had been willing to put his own comfort and success aside and work to change the nature of the larger community.

This *independent* man, by shifting into a strong *community* posture for a long period of time caused changes in hundreds of church congregations around the world and even affected other denominations.

He successfully shifted his focus and attention from his *independent* values into a focus on *community*, and in doing so had a much greater impact on the world during his time.

15

The Unconscious Choice of Our Negative Strategies

The Effective Negative Strategies for Taking Control Are:

Power shifts to *intimidation.*
Knowledge shifts to *aloof judgment.*
Love shifts to *manipulation.*
Wisdom shifts to *interrogation.*

The Art of Intimidation

(Prompted by the fear of not being *power*, of being vulnerable or not powerful enough.)

When *power*-based people feel anxious worries that they cannot trust their *intuitive* instincts, or that their *power* is insufficient for the circumstances, they unconsciously shift into *intimidation* the *Negative Conflict Strategy* that is associated with *power*.

Intimidation is an effective defense mechanism because it catches people off guard, makes them feel overwhelmed and threatened. The energy coming from the *intimidator* is an order of magnitude greater that what is normally expected in a given situation—especially for persons whose *power core value* is relatively low.

Intimidation tends to work immediately.

Then it comes back to haunt the *intimidator*, because others harbor ill will and use their alternative defense mechanisms to defuse the *intimidation* strategy. Also, *intimidation* works best when people are face to face—*intimidating* over the phone is secondarily most effective, followed by written *intimidation* as least effective.

Once people have the ability to hang up the phone, tear up the letter, or delete the e-mail, the strategic advantages of *intimidation* are made somewhat impotent.

Part of the potency of *intimidation* comes from an overt use of shame and blame toward others. The *power*-based person who is resorting to *intimidation* will try to make his behavior completely justifiable by pointing the shame and blame finger at others.

This is the nature of the *power* person's victim position. The victim posture is another social strategy that is owned by all four *Core Values Strategies*. They each put a different face on their victim persona. For the *power*-based person, the victim script goes like this: "I wouldn't have to be like this if you just did your job," or, "If you would just stop doubting me, I won't have to be so assertive," Or, "You really make me crazy."

Another price paid by a person who occasionally or commonly uses *intimidation* is the loss of the ability to use clean, appropriate *power* strategies in social and work situations. People will become convinced that even the more appropriate *power* strategies employed by the *intimidator* are *intimidating* behaviors. Since *intimidation* is a fear-based *power* strategy, persons who have been the target of a certain person's *intimidation* or have witnessed his use of *intimidation* with others, will hold back, avoid confrontation, and avoid close proximity with the *intimidator*. These witnesses of the intimidator in action will avoid getting into a situation where they might become the target.

At this point, every act of *power* may be interpreted by others as part of the *intimidator's* arsenal of attack. Many people begin to resist, avoid, and redirect and resist the *power*-based person's efforts to put his/her personal energy into work and cause others to work hard with or for him.

On the other side of the ineffectiveness curve is this truth: once *intimidation* has been exercised in a group with any frequency, others begin to see that the *intimidation* is not all that fearful. People begin to assume, at the subconscious level, that they don't need to respond to directives, commands, or stated expectations until the *power*-based person escalates into the *intimidation* mode.

Everyone jumps to attention and works furiously—until the *intimidator* leaves. Then everyone sags back into a slightly less productive mode than existed before this latest round of *intimidation.*

People who do not use *intimidation* as a strategy are often at a loss about how to deal with someone who is using *intimidation.* That's why it works—*intimidation* comes as a surprise, and the level of emotional, psychological (and sometimes physical) energy is so great it causes people to instinctively back away and give in.

Many people are suckers for accepting blame and shame from others. Some are willing to accept the anger and hostility of *intimidation*, because they continue to believe that they may have been the legitimate cause of the other person's emotional outburst. They accept the shame and the blame.

Effective strategies for defusing the *intimidation* strategy

To defuse the *intimidation* strategy, allow the individual to feel powerful and respected without allowing them to take control or get their way when they have chosen to become intimidating.

Meet *intimidation* with real *power*. If you are a *power*-based person (as a first or second dominant *core value*), you may use a counter-punch approach: meeting *intimidating power* with *fearless power*. It is very important to understand that you will not be able to deal with this person effectively if you allow yourself to become fearful and move into *intimidation* behaviors yourself.

Unless, of course, you are truly more *powerful* and more willing to give up self-control and allow your *intimidating* behaviors to win "no matter what." Otherwise, an *intimidating* response to *intimidation* is only good for escalating things into a more destructive conflict.

If you have a position of authority that is superior to the *intimidating* person, the assertion of this authority will usually cause the person to back down, or cause them at least to keep their behavior within reasonable (socially tolerable) bounds.

If you are wired with a greater capacity for being the presence of *power*, significantly more *power*-oriented than others, if you are physically stronger, richer, smarter, or better connected, or just simply more self-assured—whatever the source of *power*, the *power*-based person makes an *intuitive* estimate of any opponent's *power* and chooses whether to escalate into higher conflict. Real personal *power* can work occasionally to back down a person who is trying to *intimidate*. Why? Because *intimidation* is based in fear while real *power* emanates from the *real self* and is not threatening; real *power* does not intimidate as a tactic, so *intimidations* can actually relax and disarm their *intimidating* strategies. They sense the real nonthreatening *power* just as we will sense the fear in the intimidator and know to be wary.

Distract the intimidator with honest questions. By shifting from the *power* strategy to the *wisdom* mode of operation, the tactic for defusing an attempt by another person to *intimidate* you requires you to remain passive and calm. Ask a pointed, honest question in a quiet voice, with a willingness to leave the situation if this tactic fails.

When you ask an important question calmly, the *intimidator* is taken off guard. There is no returned threat or identifiable strategy to overpower or to harm. The need for *intimidation* begins to dissipate immediately, held onto only by the depth of the fear the *intimidator* is feeling, or an egotistical need to appear more *powerful* in front of others and self.

The assertion of intelligent questions into an emotional situation causes everyone involved to shift from the *intuitive*-type behavior to a more *cognitive* behavior. This shift into the conscious *cognitive* mode of operation automatically causes a loss of energy and a reduction of the rage and fear that was driving the *intimidation* strategy.

You cannot be *cognitive* and fearful at the same moment.

Defuse *intimidation* by asserting the value of the friendship/relationship.

The shift to a *love* strategy also requires a calm exterior. Remain seated, arms open and nonprotective, and face relaxed and peaceful. In this unintimidating posture say the person's first name several times until there is a break in their shouting and make one of the following assertions:

"I don't want to fight with you and I am unwilling to stay here with you while you are 'shouting' and 'threatening.'"

"I value our relationship and will be happy to talk again at another time."

Then leave.

Note: If someone gets into an intimidating posture with you and refuses to leave your office, it is time for a restroom or coffee break. Leave your own room if that's what it takes to defuse the situation. This is not a time for giving in to the ego's concerns about appearances in front of others or negative judgments you might make of yourself.

Contrary to common belief, this act of leaving is a powerful deflector and may cause the *intimidator* to try to follow you around in order to continue the conflict. If so, simply find someone else to start talking to, ignoring the *intimidator*. If the person is reasonably socially acceptable, and not violent or neurotic, the inappropriateness of their escalated intimidating behavior will cause them to back out of the situation.

Remain emotionless and in a fixed position. The *knowledge* strategy is equally effective against *intimidation*. This generally involves continuing to remain seated or standing in a fixed position, not speaking moving, or even looking in the *intimidator's* eyes; basically, ignoring the individual who is deemed to be inappropriately *intimidating*.

This refusal to become emotional, and to consciously disengage from the situation while remaining quiet and nonresponsive, can cause another escalation of shouting and even physically threatening postures (standing over, forming a fist, going nose to nose). The lack of forceful response, however, causes most *intimidating* individuals to defuse quickly and to try another tactic. After all, the intent of *intimidation* is to cause the *intimidator's* opponent to run or fight. The *banker* strategy provides nothing to aim at, nothing to fight.

The Art of Manipulation

(Pretending to be loving while being destructive and selfishly motivated.)

When *love*-based people feel they are not being treated well, disregarded, and unloved, they begin to doubt that their preferred strategy, to be the *love* in the room, is not going to be safe or effective. They begin to feel anxious, but still want to be a loving person. And at this ego level they want to be loved.

They are most comfortable with relationship strategies. When they start to feel angry and unloving toward others, they begin to fear that they may not be a loving person after all. This is true at that moment. They are not being loving toward themselves or others. This is a dark place for *love*-based people to be. This causes them to shift into *manipulation*.

The *manipulation* strategy is effective because most people assume that the people around them have a good degree of integrity. The expectation is that what another person says is basically true and that what a person appears to be wanting or trying to do is the whole recognizable agenda.

It also works because people generally like to be liked, enjoy being an accepted part of a group. *Love*-based people who have shifted into the *manipulation* defense mechanism may appear very much like a *love*-based person who is happy, fearless, and simply being an effective relationship-building and relationship-nurturing individual. This is the art of *manipulation*—to fool others into believing that the *love*-based person is continuing to act in a *loving* fashion, even when feeling fearful and angry.

Another side of *manipulation* is to claim the victim posture and cause people around you to see someone else as the cause of conflict and hurt feelings. This still keeps the *manipulating* person from appearing unloving, only wounded and undeserving of such disregard and abuse.

The strategic objectives of the *manipulation* strategy are many and varied, making them difficult to understand, track, and defuse. When you are the target of a person who is on the defensive and using *manipulation* to regain composure and to get what he wants in an indirect fashion, you may find yourself feeling confused. Some people talk about "being slimed," or flattered and used, or "suckered" by a story that has worked to deflect conflict, criticism, and disapproval to others.

Finally, the *love*-based person may find himself talking about the past or the future, thus avoiding talk about any criticism, measurement of performance, or reality of the current situation.

Part of the *manipulator's* quiver of strategy arrows consists of exaggeration (lying) and high-energy, emotionally based attempts to excite people into compliance with the *manipulator's* agenda. All of this is done to make certain the world sees the *manipulator* as free from faults, free from accountability, free from any failure—a person who is innocent beyond the scope of measurement or responsibility for anything deemed by others to be negative in any way. The founding belief of this functioning personality is that . . . "I will not be loved if I am not perfectly lovable."

Once in the mode of *manipulation*, the *manipulator's* use of others through emotional *manipulation* is ordinary and effective—getting others to fight their battles, the *manipulator* can remain outside the fray, while appearing to be a good, happy, and wonderful person.

Once a leader has used *manipulative* tactics within a group with any kind of regularity, his word is no longer trusted. Hopeful statements are guessed to be exaggerations and not based in fact, and the recipient devalues displays of overt emotion and compliments. In short, the *love*-based person is not seen as a caring person, but a user, a liar, and a fake.

The ability to make the primary contributions of a *love*-based person is diminished.

People are reluctant to be inspired by the leader's vision and goals when the trust in the relationship has been broken. As a result, the expected ingredients of success—team spirit, interdependence, and sharing—have been cut off or reduced in magnitude by the *manipulative* acts of a *love*-based person who is experiencing fear and acting out old childhood scenarios in a now adult world.

Others then skeptically view the positive, inspirational, motivational, and *creative* vision of the *love*-based person as just a part of another kind of *manipulation*. The leader's ability to excite his team, inspire, and set new initiatives into motion is dramatically reduced, sometimes totally defeated. It takes a long time for trust to be reestablished in a group.

Once the *love*-based person believes he is not being *loved*, is being unfairly treated, disregarded, left out, blamed for failures, the people who are seen as the unfair, blaming, and unaccepting individuals are judged to be unloving and not very good people (at this moment, or forever).

Since these perpetrators of unkindness are being unfair and attacking a "wonderful" *love*-based person who is trying to be a loving presence on this planet, these perpetrators must be *not good*—a judgment that allows the *love*-based person to employ *manipulation* freely until the sense of being *loved* and appreciated returns to him.

We, as individuals, no matter what our *Core Values Nature*, do not appreciate being seen as *not* good. The message that we should always be a *good girl* or *good boy* has been drilled into almost every child (appropriately or inappropriately). The judgment that I am *not* good sets off an alarm deep within each person that causes them to unconsciously consider using their defense mechanism to defeat this deep threat that is aimed at the soul, not just at today's activity.

Merchants, people whose dominant *core value* is *love*, are generally the most forgiving type of person—but once slighted, offended, disregarded to an unacceptable level, a little too often—once they have lost their sense of *truth* in the situation—these people become the least forgiving, least trusting. Once cut off by a *merchant*, the likelihood of recovering that relationship is low.

Extreme acts of humility, words of apology, expressions of caring are required to begin to earn the chance to get back on their good side.

Note: It is important to separate the concept of a forgiving attitude from a long-suffering, tolerant attitude. *Love*-based people are generally not long-suffering and often are quite intolerant of even perceived slights. They tend to forgive easily at the surface, but may hold in their minds a count of wounds and afflictions caused by any other individuals. This roster of perceived offenses is used for two important purposes:

1. As a tool to justify their own negative shaming attack and as proof of the badness of the perpetrator when yet another offense is received. This justifies and makes right the *manipulation* response—at the ego-personality level only, of course.

2. As evidence of reasons for distrust that are aimed at the protection of the *love*-based person. Protection from being too trusting, being fooled again, and hurt by the actions and words of others whom the *love*-based person has allowed to hurt him.

One of the most effective tactics of the defensive—in the *manipulation* mode—*love*-based person is the rage-filled listing of the offenses perpetrated by the "bad" person in the past. A diatribe of past offenses often hits the present offender with enough force to cause them to back off or attempt to get forgiveness (overtly or covertly) from the *merchant*. The table is turned.

The individual who is now under attack from the *love*-based person may also be willing to use rage to *manipulate*, *interrogate*, *intimidate*, or use *aloof judgment* to gain compliance or relief from abuse. The reacting individual acquires sufficient evidence that they are under attack, making the *love*-based attacker appear "bad" as well.

Anxiety and fear begin to take over both individuals who are now in the defense/attack mode, using their most practiced weapons of strategic defense to disarm, defuse, or destroy the other.

Counter-*manipulation.* "Oh, what a web we weave, when first we practice to deceive."

My unconscious decision to use *manipulation* causes any other *love*-based person to mistrust me. It gives them the proof that I am not the good person I represent myself to be. Like a good debater, they now have yet another strong argument for their position; that I cannot be trusted, that I am not worthy of being *loved. Manipulation* of me, a bad person, is no longer a crime against *love.*

Effective strategies for defusing the manipulation strategy

Help the individual feel loved and appreciated for his loving ways, while refusing to give him control or freedom from accountability in response to his *manipulation.*

Meet *manipulation* with assurance of *love*. You are not being advised to be permissive, or to let *manipulation* achieve its goals. This strategy is the affirmation of *love* and acceptance—expressions of how much you value your relationship with the person currently stuck in his *manipulative* strategy. It is an intentional validation of the worth of this individual, a direct and earnest honoring of the *Core Values Nature* of this person.

It offers the *manipulator* the opportunity to decrease his emotions and opens the possibility for a continued good relationship—basically you are allowing him a chance to let go of the need to defend himself. Even a relatively immature *love*-based person may be able to shift out of the *manipulative* posture and into a workable, effective listening and sharing mode if you honor his deepest *core value—love.*

End the situation. This *power*-based response *intuitive*ly judges the current situation as being potentially destructive and assumes the right to call an end to the engagement. Try the statement, "I am not willing to continue with this now." This is followed by the commitment to try again at a specific time—far enough into the future to allow the defensive *love*-based person the chance to relax away from the need to *manipulate*, but soon enough that he does not feel pushed aside.

The *love*-based person will feel respected and honored and will have difficulty maintaining any commitment to his negative emotions. Acts of *power* can be received as validation of *love*, as long as there is no threat or *intimidation*, or disregard of the person. *Power*-based language that does not yield to *manipulation* but also does not overpower or dismiss the *love*-based individual is what is needed.

Example: "I want to have more effective communication with you than we are having. I am willing to take this up again tomorrow morning." These are strong, assertive, powerful statements that can easily be interpreted by the *love*-based (now fearful and *manipulative*) person as statements of commitment to a good relationship. This provides the opportunity to say yes or no to the chance to work things out in the morning. *Love* is honored, but the *manipulation* is not allowed to have any influence.

Give a chance to share a positive accomplishment. *Wisdom* sits back and watches a person who is in the throes of *manipulation*, and wonders, what is going on? Why is this person so agitated? The *wisdom* person can look past the emotion, whether it is whining or rage, and remain curious about the source of discomfort. The wise person, may, however, more easily see the *manipulation*—especially if he allows himself to begin questioning the *love*-based person who is in the *manipulation* mode.

But great care must be taken not to ask questions that feel like *interrogation*, or that require a disclosure of uncomfortable *truth*, when the *love*-based person is already feeling embarrassed, *judged*, unloved, and unappreciated.

Wisdom, then, looks for an honest question that can be answered with a sure, positive statement of accomplishment, success, or simply the claiming of good skills or attributes. This re-founds the *manipulator* in self-respect and offers them the chance to defuse the negative emotions. This may allow the *love*-based person to be willing to stay in an uncomfortable situation without resorting to *manipulation* for survival.

Example: Ask the *manipulator*: "What was the strongest part of your efforts before now? Who did you most trust to help you create your success? Who could have been most helpful if you had called him in earlier? What value can we create from this current circumstance?"

Once the person who is resorting to *manipulation* relaxes a little, he may begin to feel that a simple conversation may be okay. The sense of criticism and potential rejection or shame is relieved, so this person who was embarrassing himself by lying, or whining, or rage, will be able to sit quietly and explore the possibilities for improvement.

The first requirement is to honor this person's *core value* of *love* and establish a talking and listening environment that promotes continued relationship.

Report to others this individual's previous personal successes. In order to establish a frame of reference, a buildup of previous successes creates the sense of longevity and consistent contribution. The reporting of a *love*-based person's successes needs to have more than hard facts. There needs to be an enumeration of personal attributes, relationships that have been established by him, and the value that these relationships have brought to the team or group, or company. The best effect is achieved when this is done in front of a group that is important to the *love*-based individual.

With a reasonable basis of facts in place, the person should be able to return to an open posture of integrity. If not, a second, closely related strategy is recommended.

Ask for a written report about the current circumstance that has created an embarrassment for this individual. Allow a cooling-off period. A day or two to write things down will allow him to find the good and bad about his performance for himself. It is much easier for a *love*-based person to tell his own foibles quietly to one person in private. Give this person a chance to do just that; but not under duress, and in front of the masses, and not while he is exhibiting his worst self through *manipulative* tactics.

The Art of Interrogation

(Asking questions that are designed to tear down arguments of others, reveal their foolishness, and illustrate the interrogator's intelligence and his ability to take control when necessary.)

Interrogation is the *Negative Conflict Strategy* of a *wisdom*-based person. It is a very effective ploy since it catches others off guard, reveals their ignorance or lack of ability to respond glibly. The art of *interrogation* is designed to use *wisdom*-like strategies to strip away any reasonableness from anyone else's argument, revealing ignorance in others and making others appear to be fools. It is also a very assertive way to take control and to remain in control.

Using cutting, vindictive questions, the *interrogator* causes observers to keep their distance and remain quiet for fear of undergoing a similar *interrogation* themselves. This tactic also establishes the superiority of the *interrogator's* logic and reasoning skills enhancing the *interrogator's* sense of being in control.

Note: This is not the same thing as having people respect and value one's *wisdom*. But the acknowledgment of reasoning skills and questioning talent by others is often sufficient to allow the *wisdom*-based person to relax away from *interrogation* and slowly return to the *wisdom* process.

The weakness of this tactic is that often when talking about ideas, a *wisdom*-based person will become quite excited about the ideas he is expressing. He may enjoy the parry and jab of logical argumentation, getting juice from this mental sport—a form of brainstorming that often causes another level of thinking to be reached.

But others, having witnessed or been themselves targets of this person's *interrogation*, tend now to hear this positive *wisdom*-based strategy as part of the same cruel, offensive *interrogation* tactic. They will tend to hold back, not venture the expression of any but the soundest ideas in open brainstorming sessions. The *wisdom* person is thus cut off from the interactive best thinking of others that he needs to fuel his inquiring mind.

Like the other *Negative Conflict Strategies*, *interrogation* invites others to become fearful. So the *interrogator* often excites *manipulation* in *love*-based persons, *intimidation* in the *power*-based people, and *aloof judgment* in *knowledge*-based people. *Wisdom*-based people who resort to *interrogation* invite emotional and cruel *interrogation* by other *wisdom*-based persons.

They find themselves occasionally revealed as the *fool* they are so afraid they just might be. This incitement of counter-*interrogation* causes an escalation of the intensity and a deepening of the negative, destructive intent. The counter-punching war of two or more *interrogating* persons is an interesting battle to watch—from a safe distance.

Effective strategies for defusing *interrogation*:

Acknowledge the individual's *wisdom* while refusing to be *interrogated.* Ask a question driven by true curiosity, that helps the *interrogator* give up his impulse to take control and get his own way through *interrogation*.

Ask an honest question about the intent of the *interrogator*. When a *wisdom*-based individual (*innovator*) slips hard into *interrogation*, it is in defense of a perceived attack. He perceives a judgment that his ideas are not being respected or put to good use, a belief that some people may be viewing the *interrogator* as a *fool.*

This incites the deeper fear that maybe "I *am* a *fool.*" So the act of *interrogation* is a deflection, throwing the weight of intellect into tearing someone down through *interrogation* rather than providing strategic guidance, solid solutions, essential *wisdom*.

Ask a question about the intent of the *interrogator's* question(s): "What is the most important thing that needs to happen right now?" This kind of question will not necessarily stop the *interrogation*, but whatever integrity remains in the person underneath his fear of being seen as a *fool*, wants to stop and respond to an honest question. It is *calling* for his true *wisdom* to return and reengage. You are calling out his *compassion*, which is the cornerstone of his *wisdom* strategy.

This kind of question is a surprise. What an *interrogator* expects is to catch you off guard, put you on the defensive, and cause you to do and say *foolish* things, sharpening another round of *interrogative* questions. When you refuse to be led around by the nose by his *interrogation* yet refused also to become an interrogator yourself, this is a moment during which the interrogator is being replaced in the situation by the presence of *wisdom*.

This is a wonderful irreversible invitation for the *wisdom* person who is still reachable at the *Real Core Values Self* level.

Other examples: "Are you trying to hurt me with that question?" This question offers the chance for the *interrogator* to show leniency and mercy, and, if asked with sincerity, can break through to the deeper person who is hiding behind the *interrogative* strategy. After all, it looks foolish for a knight in armor to raise his sword against his page who is holding the reins of the knight's horse. Like using an atomic bomb against people shooting arrows, the *interrogative* bomber wants to have his *interrogation* appear to be a reasonable and justifiable response to the offender's actions. Since the goal of the *interrogator* is to make others look and feel foolish, this tactic of asking about the degree of intent disarms the *interrogator* if only for a moment.

"Do you really want an answer to that question?" The fact is, the only answer the *interrogator* is looking for is a foolish one. If you remain reasonable and calm, showing that you have no intention of becoming defensive, hysterical, or interrogative yourself, the *interrogator* is hard pressed not to answer a reasonable question with a reasonable response. To do otherwise would illustrate the foolishness of the *interrogative* strategy and ruin its intended destructiveness.

Return facts and information for abusive *interrogation*. This *knowledge*-based strategy is effective because the supply of facts and information is a neutral, non-emotional, nonthreatening response. This offers a real break in fear-based *interrogation*, calling the person to become a cognitive presence. This call if answered destroys the fear that was fueling the *interrogation*. This can only be seen as peaceful and noninciting by anyone watching and listening. Since the accepted legitimate purpose of any question is to obtain information or to excite new ideas, the provision of details and facts defuses the *interrogator's* strategy.

The *wisdom*-based person feeds his drive to be a *wise* person with information and ideas the seduction of new information is quite often sufficient to allow him to return to his tasks of observing and asking questions that come from a place of curiosity, not hostility.

It also works to sit quietly and refuse to answer.

Look the person in the eye without hostility, or any emotion. Like the *innovator's* innocent question about the intent of the *interrogator*, this nonresponse, emotionless, nonthreatening posture provides no new fuel for the *interrogative* battle. Without a silly response to incite a further query, the *interrogator* now must run on his own *creative* steam just to keep the questions pounding. If the pounding is producing no effect—the goal being to illustrate your *foolishness*—the strategy will be forsaken.

Wisdom-based people are amazingly tenacious and resourceful. They are adept at coming up with new ideas, one type being new *interrogative* questions. They will resort to all kinds of circular logic, recall of long-forgotten mistakes of others—anything that may evoke a defensive response from others.

So in the event either of these two strategies fail, turn and walk quietly away. This either ends the *interrogation* due to lack of proximity, or causes the *interrogator* to shift to a different conflict strategy, making him look and feel *foolish* in his pursuit of you as you exit the room.

Acknowledge the interrogator's usual *wisdom*. It should be unnecessary at this point in this book to remind you that this only works if you speak with integrity—but there, consider yourself unnecessarily reminded. Assert your need for the *interrogator's wise* counsel. Now more than ever, the acknowledgment of his *wisdom* will defuse the need to defend his *wisdom*. This destroys his need to make you look *foolish* by comparison.

This *merchant* strategy, then, is eloquently effective. The statements might be: "I was hoping that you would give me some good advice about that as always. I'm counting on that from you." Or, "Maybe we can talk later, because I really need to hear your opinions and ideas."

Granted, this evasion of answering the *interrogator's* questions and substitution of positive affirmations is difficult to accomplish and will not easily be trusted by the *interrogator*. After all, if he quits his *interrogation* because you are using some *manipulative* ploy, he will look more *foolish* than he feels now.

So you have to sell this posture of acceptance and respect. This happens naturally if you are without emotion and earnest in your communication. Selling is meant here to be understood as asserting the integrity and unavoidable presence of *love*.

If the *interrogation* continues, wait for a pause, respond to the last question with a statement something like this: "I don't believe you want an answer. I believe you want to fight and make me look *foolish*. I'm not interested in continuing this. Please come back later because I do need your advice and ideas."

This strategy is difficult for a *merchant*, *love*-based person to use effectively.

It is counter-*intuitive* for the *love*-based person to be the first to call a time-out, or to walk away, or separate from another person. *Merchants* might often be seen pursuing another person in order to continue whatever ineffective communication is happening, with the hope that a resolution can be reached now, so we can feel good together again—right now.

The *love*-based person must learn to convert childish beliefs about what *love* looks like, and see the situation from an adult perspective. What is the likelihood that a person who is resorting to *interrogation* is not feeling good about himself right now? He is feeling fearful and attacked. The *loving* thing to do is to give this person space.

The *innovator wisdom* person often seeks a quiet space so they can work things out in their own mind before continuing. It is an act of *love* and respect to set things up so your *interrogator* opponent is able to calm himself down. He will get back to a reasonable posture and try again later to achieve an effective communication with you.

Power-based persons can be very effective at defusing the *interrogative* strategy. They must however, not use an *intimidating* tone, posture, or look when effecting their counter-*interrogative* response.

Speak with a clear, unequivocal voice. Delivering a message this way is often effective: "You are trying to *interrogate* me. I am not interested in continuing this." Then turn and leave—even if you have to leave your own room. Have a place to go, a meeting to attend: "I have to meet John for a sales conference. Try me again later."

Wisdom-based people are reluctant to get into open conflict.

That's why the *interrogation* strategy works so well for them.

They appear to be simply asking questions, ducking and parrying without overt *power* or attack. When confronted with real *power* that is not *intimidating*—just clean and difficult to resist—they are hesitant to continue the *interrogation*. To do so would be to show a willingness to go into open conflict. This is not the art of *interrogation*. Situation defused.

I envy *power*-based people sometimes.

The Art of Aloof Judgment

(The ability to be completely detached from the situation even while remaining physically in the room. Being without emotion, without intellectual engagement, without resistance or compliance—completely unavailable—judging others to be unworthy of the *knowledge* person's participation.)

Oh, the wicked, wonderful, enigmatic strategy that *knowledge*-based people have when feeling fearful and under attack. Their response is so off-setting, so uncomfortable to fight against—in fact, there is nothing in their strategy to do battle with. All other *Core Value Energies* are baffled by the *knowledge*-based person's use of *aloof judgment.*

Let's take a look at how and why the posture of *aloof judgment* puts the *knowledge*-based person in control of the situation. Let's take a look at how it effectively defends against slights about his *knowledge*, his information, his expertise, his responsible conservative actions and work.

First, most of us are painfully aware of our own inadequate supply of real *knowledge*, or hard facts, or expertise, or ready information. When another individual demonstrates that he has *knowledge* and expertise that we do not have, we develop instant respect and begin to rely upon this person's judgments and facts.

When in conflict, the first reaction of the *knowledge*-based person is to pull back and become aloof, inaccessible emotionally, mentally, and physically. The first reaction of others is to pursue the aloof *knowledge* person to try to keep them engaged. This failing, the *knowledge*-based person withholds his *knowledge.*

This negative strategy is further enhanced by the reality that the *knowledge*-based person is convinced that he has the right facts and answers, that there is injustice in the current situation, and that the pronouncement of this *judgment* is needed to bring others to their senses.

This declaration of the wrong of others and the right (correctness, not goodness) of the *knowledge*-based person causes others to step back, secretly reviewing the situation to see if they are in the wrong.

This momentary focus away from the *aloof judge* provides time and conserves emotional and psychic energy. Since the *aloofness* works to stop interaction and reduce the required energy of the *aloof* person, he can outlast all of the other strategies. The *aloof judge* can wait silently, while *builders* shout, *merchants* pout, and *innovators* re-route. *Knowledge* people quietly back out.

The longer a *knowledge*-based person withholds his *knowledge* and remains aloof, the more desperate the others on the team become. They instinctively begin seeking him out, asking for his expertise and *knowledge*—mission accomplished.

This tactic also serves the desire to avoid conflict and sets up a passive-aggressive tactic that can be even more effective when in full bloom. The *knowledge*-based person works in the background, presenting the truth, as he sees it—providing proof he is right and gathering the forces in a politically astute, low visibility fashion.

Often the mature *knowledge* person, even when in the negative conflict mode, is able to enlist *merchants* to whine or sell the *banker's* point of view. He may encourage *builders* to begin taking action, believing the *power*-based person will self destruct. Or the *power*-based person may be encouraged to force results that align with the *knowledge* person's view. He may concurrently encourage *innovators* to develop tactics and processes that will honor the *knowledge.*

What often backfires for the *aloof judge* is that a feeling of resentment develops in other team members. Since the withholding of information and the *judging* of others as being wrong only happens under a stressful situation, it may become commonly accepted that the *knowledge*-based person who resorts to the *aloof judgment* tactic cannot be counted on in a time of crisis.

Others also resent being judged and made to seem wrong. They instinctively look for faults in the one who has chosen to be, even if only momentarily, the *aloof judge*. So the severe judgment that the *banker* uses in times of fear and duress can become the commonly held *judgment* of others toward him. "He is not worthy of my participation with him."

Effective strategies for defusing *Aloof Judgment*:

Refer to the *knowledge*-based person's information, analysis, or results of conservation information or strategies initiated by him. Commit to use the requested knowledge to make decisions that are beneficial to the entire community. Notice but choose to ignore the *aloof judgment*, and assume in public the just response from the *knowledge*-based person and their willingness to help make things right.

Meet accusations and withdrawal with a request for information. This *banker* response to another *knowledge*-based person's *aloof judgment* tactic is very effective. As the *aloof judge* exits, or withholds information, judging others around him to be wrong, the composed *banker* team member simply acknowledges that this person has been correct in the past, then requests that the exiting person "please leave your information so I can review it and understand your position."

Even though the intent of the *aloof judge* is to withhold information and avoid the conflict, this invitation to prove himself right with others (honoring his *core value* of *knowledge*) is compelling and squelches the urge to exit as rapidly and completely as previously intended. The need of the *banker* to be always seen as being appropriate causes the *aloof judge* to hesitate and to be enticed into delivering his *knowledge* as requested.

If he withholds his information after being acknowledged as someone who is often right, and after being told his information will be used to determine what is right in the situation, it is almost impossible for the *aloof judge* to continue his chosen fear-induced strategy.

Also, since the request is coming from a like spirit, another *knowledge*-based person who generally acts appropriately and avoids open conflict, there is nothing to fight against in the acknowledgment and request. There is an opportunity to develop a political ally in defense of the *aloof judge's* position. A bravura performance for the quietly perceptive fellow *banker*.

Include reliance upon *knowledge* as a key to obtaining the team vision. The effective *merchant*, working from a *love*-based position, will enjoy acknowledging the importance of a conservative, *knowledgeable* team member and will paint a positive picture about the current *aloof judge* as a reliable contributor to the team.

The essential nature of the *knowledge*-based person's participation will develop a base for the *aloof judge* to let go of his need to withhold information and withdraw.

This act of acknowledgment must not be emotional or have any scent of exaggeration. There can be no urge to act or seduction to change thinking. The exchange has to be above reproach, with high integrity—done in this manner, with the real desire to connect with the *knowledge*-based person's most dominant innate *core value*—the need to resort to *aloof judgment* will be eradicated.

Any vision put up as worthy of the *knowledge* person's expertise and information must, by its nature, include the creation of a just and fair organization, with all people respected and worthy of the gift of *knowledge*. There should also be a clear picture of the mission of the team and of the essential materials, supplies, and resources that will make the mission a success.

The magnitude of the mission, the availability and importance of the resources, provide the *knowledge*-based person with the motivation to invest their life energy in conservation of resources and guidance of the team with the *knowledge* in this leader's possession.

Lastly, but with immeasurable importance, is the requirement that the mission and the team will by their nature, and in the normal course of fulfillment of their purpose, generate significant new information, new expertise for the *knowledge*-based person—new *knowledge* that can be put to use in an even greater mission.

Attract *knowledge* with a declaration of ignorance. A truly wise *innovator* instinctively knows that a poignant question is a seduction impossible to resist for a strong *knowledge*-based person. A question well expressed will offer the *ignorance* of the questioner as a real opportunity for the *aloof judge* to make a contribution. The urge to fill the *ignorance* void with personal *knowledge* will be so great that the ego-driven requirement to withdraw and disengage and withhold *knowledge* will evaporate.

Combine this honest provocative question with a stated problem—the scarcity and critical nature of the essential resources—and you will add to the attractiveness of ignorance in others, the *knowledge* person's natural conservative passions—so strong that he will have little motive for remaining in his *aloof judgment* mode. He will rise to the call for expert guidance through a difficult time.

The *knowledge* person's self-respect is not based in the *knowledge* he has; it is substantiated by the magnitude of the mission of his team, the level of importance of the preservation of resources, and the clarity of his responsibility to provide essential *knowledge* and to preserve the resources.

When his *knowledge* is requested, analyzed, and applied correctly to make better decisions, when the results are better because his *knowledge* was used appropriately, the *knowledge*-based person is fulfilled—only then.

Put the responsibility for survival and success on the *knowledge* person's shoulders. The *builder's* response is naturally a *power*-based tactic. That's what makes him a *builder*. So the application of *power* into the effort to defuse *aloof judgment* must simultaneously honor the *core value* of the *knowledge*-based person. This is done while also staying true to the *core value—power*. This is not difficult, once understood.

The *builder* response cannot be a threat or a command. It must be a statement of fact: "I can't do this thing without someone watching my back, protecting our resources, and keeping me on track." This acknowledgment of the *power*-based person's need for expertise, *knowledge*, and a responsible keeper of the resources is a strong seduction to give up the *aloof judgment* tactic.

The call to deliver support to a *powerful* person who is going to cause significant things to happen is what the *knowledge* person wants—my *knowledge* and expertise put to good use.

Again, the integrity of this statement must be absolute.

The *power*-based person cannot be perceived as commanding or intimidating the *knowledge*-based person into compliance. So there needs to be a pause that allows the *aloof judge* to put down his defenses on his own and take up the responsibilities being put forth. The call to action can be a clear statement of requirement: "John, I need that report first thing in the morning." But with the added information: "Whatever I have in front of me then will be the basis of my decision and the reason for the actions I take."

If presented, not as a command, but as a clear acknowledgment of requirement for the *knowledge*-based person's contribution and with the promise that the information will be used to make an important decision—even if some hard personal feelings still remain—this call to put information to good use is too pure and clear to ignore.

The Positive Core Value Conflict Strategies

The effective positive strategies for assuming leadership or making a strong contribution are:

Power asserts *intuitive knowledge* and forceful action and a commanding presence. *Power* takes action and causes change and makes a new circumstance for everyone to focus on.

Knowledge proves right thinking and judgment and expects compliance with rules and judgments, conserving everything possible, while gathering and analyzing information. *Knowledge* provides information that is compelling and lets it fight the battles.

Wisdom asserts solid strategies and tactics and convinces others with reason, making astute assessments and developing good solutions and systems. *Wisdom* asks intelligent and provocative questions from a position of curiosity. The one who asks the best questions is in leadership.

Love persuades morally right action, team spirit, positive vision, and inspiration, building on the inclination of people to work together. *Love* asserts by expressing a passionate position, a strongly inspirational viewpoint, a commitment to others.

When we look at the *core value types of contribution*, we see an amazing elaboration of conflict strategies that can be employed, both for positive results and for fear-based defense and taking control.

Intuitive-type Strategies

The *intuitive*-type person relies upon either *loving power* or *powerful love* when working to make a positive contribution.

This shifts to *manipulative intimidation* or *intimidating manipulation* when the person has shifted to old fear-based responses in order to take control.

When a positive contribution is the aim, this strategic value-based response to situations will appear as inspired *intuitive* action that includes and honors the near-term and long-term good of the group—***Inspired Initiation***. When anxiety and fear cause control to be the aim, these strategies may translate into desperate shouting, assertions of being right and good, charges that others are wrong and bad, followed by pouting and whining about disregard and threats of force or dominance—a demand for immediate obedience or surrender.

Cognitive-type Strategies

The *cognitive*-type person relies upon either *knowledgeable wisdom* or *wise knowledge* when seeking to make a positive contribution.

When these persons shift to their old fear-based responses they will demonstrate their ability to take control through *judgmental interrogation* or *interrogative judgment*. When a positive contribution is the aim, this strategic value-based response to situations will likely appear as careful planning and brainstorming, curiosity, and research supported by a *compassionate* attitude and commitment to *justice*—***Reasoned Response***.

When control is the aim, these strategies revert to cold, emotionless questioning, repetition of facts, withholding of information, and denial of any responsibility for the future, and accusations of injustice, ignorance, and foolishness on the part of others.

Practical-type Strategies

The *practical*-type person relies upon *powerful knowledge* or *knowledgeable power* to make positive contributions.

To take control, they utilize *judgmental intimidation* or *intimidating judgment.* When a positive contribution is the aim, this strategic value-based response to situations will appear as appropriately expressed demands to review the *practical* person's information and to take immediate action based upon the facts—***Right Action and Organization.***

When control is the aim, these strategies devolve to shouted *intimidation,* shame and blame, and *aloof judgment,* interruption, then abandonment.

Creative-type Strategies

Creative-type people rely upon their *loving wisdom* or their *wise love* to make positive contributions.

When seeking to take control, they use *manipulative interrogation* or *interrogative manipulation.* When a positive contribution is the aim, this strategic *core value*–based response will appear as resourceful exploration of ideas, invention, and strategic thinking, supported by *truth* about the present and past and *compassion* for others—***Strategic Vision.***

When control is the aim, these strategies revert to whining isolation, letters, e-mails, and faxes about the wrong being done, attacks on the reputations of others, and accusations of falseness and foolishness on the part of others.

Independent-type Strategies

The *independent*-type person uses *powerful wisdom* or *wise power* to make a positive contribution. They revert to *intimidating interrogation* or *interrogative intimidation* to take control.

When a positive contribution is the aim, this strategic value-based response to situations will appear as strategic thinking and directed brainstorming, combined with immediate actions that yield measurable results and new ideas for new actions—***Focused Inventive Action***.

When control is the aim, these positive strategies transmogrify into shouted autocratic decisions, desperate invention, confusion, exaggerated crises, and foolish off-focus activity.

Community-type Strategies

Community-type people use their *loving knowledge* or their *knowledgeable love* to contribute to their society.

When taking control, they revert to manipulative *aloof judgment* or *aloof judgmental manipulation*.

When a positive contribution is the aim, this strategic *core values*–based response to situations will appear as development of rules, publishing of policies, informative reports and meetings, and constant team-building activities—***Collective Resourcefulness***.

When control is the aim, these strategies revert to whining and passive aggression, politicking behind the scenes, accusations of injustice/unfairness, shaming and blaming others, and denial of culpability for anything that is wrong or bad.

16

Your Deepest Fears and Conflict Strategies

Builder Power/Faith Conflict Mechanism

The *Catalytic Value* of *faith* is that I know what to do now. I have sufficient power to succeed. I will know what to do after I take this action. This socially translating value, when open and strong, allows the *power* person to act freely, *intuitively,* and without fear. If this same *power*-based person is repeatedly restricted from taking action, slowed down by bureaucracy, overwhelmed by too much chaos, or otherwise made to feel wrong or inadequate—the *faith* dimmer switch gets turned down.

This dimming of *faith* causes the *power*-based person to feel anxious, self-doubting, and uncertain about trusting his *intuitive* prowess. As the *faith* dimmer switch continues to be turned down, the anxiety devolves to fear. At the fear line, the dimmer switch is off, fear takes over, and there is no longer any capacity for the *power* person to act from a sense of personal *power.* He can no longer *be* the positive contributing *power* he was born to *be.*

He freezes momentarily, feels the powerlessness of the situation, and shifts from the positive contributory drive to take an action and obtain a desired result into a strategy of survival—a fearful response.

The nature of the *power*-based person is changed from one of positive *intuitive* forceful action into *intimidation. Intimidation* is the pretense of overwhelming *power*. Its purpose is to back others down, to force submission, to take control, even if "I am wrong." All desire to make a positive contribution is lost. The drive is now to eliminate the fear of being overwhelmed—the feeling of being impotent—without *power*. Nothing is more devastating to a *power*-based person than the fear of *not* being *powerful*.

The deepest fear of every person is that I am really the opposite of my dominant core value.

For *power*, the fear is to not *be power*, to be powerless, impotent—to be vulnerable. There is no power in me. I am not the power in this group. I have lost all *faith* that I *intuitively* know what to do. I am afraid to act.

For *love*, the deepest fear is that I am not a *loving* person. Not the fear of being unloved; it is the fear that there is no *love in* me. I am not the *love* is this room. I am evil or hate-filled. This is the terrifying fear.

For *knowledge*, the fear is that I am *ignorant*, without *knowledge*, and being without *knowledge* I am wrong. I have spent a lifetime gaining *knowledge* so I can be right. The idea of being completely ignorant and wrong is a threat to all self-esteem.

For *wisdom*, the deepest fear is that I am a fool. I am foolish. I have no *wisdom*. I would not recognize a good idea if I saw one. For a person whose mission in life is to be the *wisdom* in the room, this fear of being a fool is oppressive, debilitating.

Merchant Love/Truth Conflict Mechanism

For *Love* the *Catalytic Value* is *truth*. When a *love*-based person feels first unloved and unappreciated, angry and hurt, or set aside and disregarded, the feelings of hostility and disregard for others come roaring in. A *love*-based person in this situation resorts to *manipulation*, the pretense of being the *love* in the room. The loss of the sense of *truth* in a given situation is felt deeply. *Truth* as the catalyst for *love* causes the *love*-based person to look for the *truth* in the situation. If I cannot see *who you really are*, I cannot *love* you. If you are not willing to reveal the *truth* about yourself to me, I cannot see *who you are*, and I cannot trust you with the *truth* about myself.

Not finding *truth* in himself or in others, he can no longer be the *love* energy in this situation. A *love*-based person who feels unloving is in an emotional crisis, allowing him to do whatever he needs to do to get back to a feeling of being loved and being able to *love*. He gives himself permission, even the requirement to pretend to be *love*, while working destructively to undermine the other person's influence.

This disrupted *love* person asks many questions internally. Is this person showing me her true self? If I can't see who she really is, how can I nurture her innate *Real Core Values Self*? Am I presenting myself to my friends as I truly am, or am I showing them only those parts of me that I am confident they will accept?

If I am showing them only the acceptable parts of me, I must believe that they cannot love the real me; therefore I am not loved by my friends. If they can't love me as I am, I am not willing to be honest and share my deepest self—they aren't good enough for me. I don't love them. The rationalizations toward "I am not a very loving person" continue to degrade the *love* person's worldview and self-view through enormous anxiety—and finally into the fear that there is no *love* in me. I am not *love*.

This fear is so overwhelming that the *love*-based person shifts from a positive desire to get to know people and to nurture their deepest natures, to a position of distrust and hatred, dismissal of the worth or goodness of others. This shift allows the *love* person to use all of his relationship talents, all of his intimate knowledge about the other person, to manipulate the situation—to smile when angry, to lie about failures, exaggerate successes, shift the discussion to future issues when criticism is headed his way, to undermine the love other people have for the now-targeted person.

Innovator Wisdom/Compassion Conflict Mechanism

For *wisdom*, the *Catalytic Value* is *compassion*. For many people the word *compassion* sounds like it should belong to the *love core value*. However *love*, as you see above, is concerned with seeing the *truth* about situations and people.

This need to discern *truth* and make a judgment about the appropriateness of *love* in a situation, often keeps *love*-based people from being *compassionate* (the ability to remain empathetic with people who are behaving inappropriately).

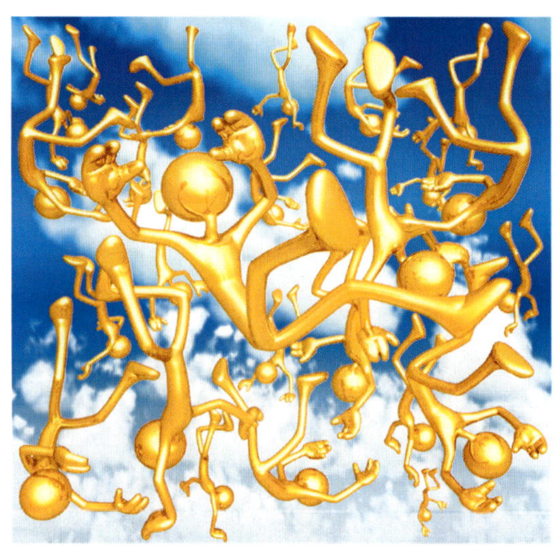

It is the nature of *wisdom* to be curious, to continue to watch, look, and listen until understanding is achieved. This requirement to come to a state of understanding dictates that the *wisdom* person remains *compassionate* and curious. The requirement to remain curious causes the *wisdom* person to sit back from a situation and remove self from the activities.

Wisdom is dispassionate and able to remain with people while they go into and out of whatever passions they feel and exhibit. So the *wisdom* person is gifted with *compassion*. This is the *wisdom* person's dimmer switch.

As the *wisdom* person slips down the slope of feeling foolish—feeling fooled or unable to discern *wisdom* in a given situation—he becomes anxious. This anxiety undermines the sense of curiosity and *compassion*. Refusing to be seen as the "fool," he crosses the anxiety line into fear—fear of being a fool, of having no *wisdom* in him. All *compassion* is lost, and in its place *interrogation*—unforgiving, unremorseful, unrelenting *interrogation*—is asserted.

The dark side of *wisdom* is released through *interrogation*. The goal, to destroy the argument, the reasoning, and the reasonableness of others—in public if possible, so people will see how foolish the opposition really is. Now the *wisdom* person can return to a place of *wise* prestige and eventually back to his *compassionate*, curious, *wisdom* presence.

Banker Knowledge/Justice Conflict Mechanism

The *knowledge*-based person has a similar construct—his *Catalytic Value* being *justice*. With *knowledge* as a prime driver, this person's deepest requirement is to be the *knowledge* in the room. *Knowledge* is not sought for the purpose of having it, but for the purpose of being the *knowledge* at the right time, for the right people, and in the right situation. In order to feel fulfilled, the *knowledge* person must see his *knowledge* put to use for the good of his society or group. The deepest fear of a *knowledge* person is that I am not *knowledge*, I am ignorant.

People in authority must ask for the individual's *knowledge*. They must use this *knowledge* to make wise choices, choices that lead to reduction of risk, preservation of resources, right analysis, right decisions, and efficient action.

Everyone must have appropriate access to this *knowledge*, and the requirement to constantly measure and gather new *knowledge* must be supported by everyone. If any of this becomes untrue, if his *knowledge* is not requested when needed, not acted upon when essential, not disseminated fairly—then the situation is judged to be *unjust*—not worthy of his *knowledge*.

If my *knowledge* is not needed, if it is disregarded or misused, I am made less valuable—less necessary, less fulfilled as a person. The positive impact and the magnitude of positive effect created by my *knowledge*, given when requested and sufficient to the situation—this is fulfillment. *Justice* is my dimmer switch—my perception of unjust situations restricts the flow of *knowledge* from me to others. I am reluctant to give my *knowledge* in an unjust situation—I withhold it.

A *knowledge* person experiences anxiety relative to an unjust situation—when a deep sense of injustice is perceived. He will try to maintain his *knowledge* position and make the situation better, judging himself to be failing in this attempt.

Insufficient *knowledge* is considered the greatest insufficiency and reflects on a *knowledge* person's sense of personal worth. So, the *knowledge* person begins to fear that he is ignorant—too ignorant to help the current situation.

When a person judges his personal ignorance to be great, he will shift from a reliance upon being the positive presence of *knowledge* into a fear-based reliance upon *aloof judgment.*

I will take myself out of the situation, withhold *knowledge*, and refuse my support. I may stay in the room and give what appears to be implied approval, and say "yes" to some requests or demands, but there is no commitment on my part.

Where there is injustice I am no longer required to be just and integrative. I will say "yes" to avoid conflict and not waste my emotions in argument or dissension. I have subtracted myself and judged others to be unworthy of my *knowledge* and my participation. I will work in the background to undermine the authority that has created this injustice. I will work politically to destroy the leadership that has created what I deem to be unjust.

Summary of the Deepest Fears

All of the above ineffective conflict excites in the participants the need to take control. Every *Core Value Energy* has an effective means for taking control—positively and negatively. The conflict strategies that arise out of fear are very effective at taking control. That is why they are used.

Note: We have not included control and its opposite, caretaking, in the attributes that come with any given *Core Value Energy*. All *Core Value Energies* have effective means for taking control. All have effective means for being a caretaker. These are emotionally based positions, not values-driven positions. They are not character types but strategic positioning that comes from emotionally based behaviors that arise originally in conflicts with adults and others in control during childhood.

Remember that we all have some level of preference for all four *core values*, so none of us is, for example, truly just a *knowledge* person. We are a unique blend of all four *Core Value Energies*. But for clarity of issues, we need to look at the pure *core value* and its strategies and tactics, as well as its motivations and drivers.

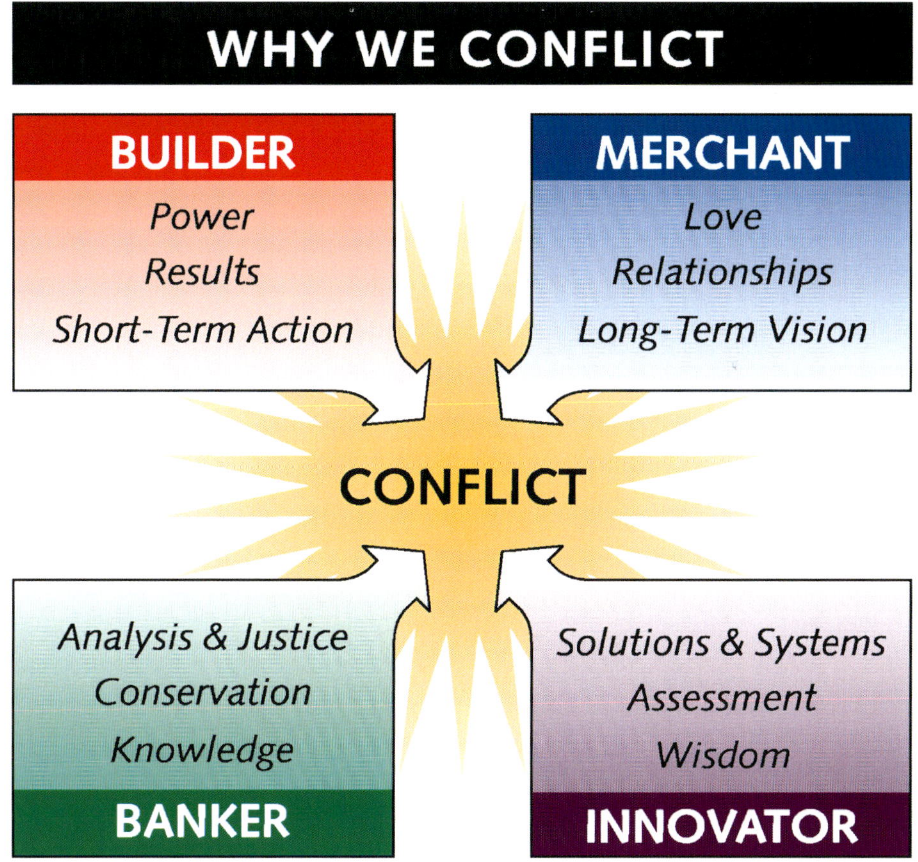

Imagine four persons entering a meeting room from four different doors. The first to come into the room is driven by the desire to *be* the *knowledge* in the room. He comes in, having spent hundreds of hours of research and reading, perusing historic data, and gathering new current evidence, facts concerning the present issues that are to be discussed in this meeting room. Prior to this time the *knowledge* person has usually invested years in development of expertise and a substantial *knowledge* base in a specific field of *knowledge*.

The *knowledge* person expects to help everyone know and accept the facts he has gathered. He has analyzed the data. He expects the team to accommodate and utilize all of this *knowledge* when considering any new actions and strategies to be undertaken.

It is critical to the *knowledge*-based person that his *knowledge* be accepted and put to good and just use. Before any decision is made or any action undertaken, it is the *knowledge* person's agenda to stop action, slow the process, and to cause dissemination of the subject *knowledge*, such that no risk is taken, no mistakes are made.

Next, the *love* person walks into the room through a different door.

The agenda of the *love*-based person is to build trust and rapport with everyone in the room, visualize the future and the manner in which we as a team are going to face the future together. The *love* person takes special care to make certain the team will still be together and having fun before, during, and after any potential course of action is being considered.

Love also wants the meeting to be carried out in a harmonious frictionless manner, with everyone speaking respectfully with everyone else. The mission of *love* is to nurture the *core values* in one's self and in others. In order to accomplish this mission, a good deal of time and energy is required to talk and explore the nature of each person, his or her life experiences, the contribution each may make to the current business mission, etc. Praise and acknowledgment are critical considerations.

Involvement of everyone is always considered essential to *love*. In order to involve everyone, *love* generally works to develop a process of sharing, discussion, open and *creative* thought that leads to an inspired vision of the future with clear connections to the present situation. The basic goals are great team spirit, hope, enthusiasm, and optimism; high-energy activity is the desired result.

Until this important agenda is realized, the *love*-based person feels compelled to stop the process of deciding, making certain the *love* strategies are firmly in place. Stopping the charge into action is of paramount importance because it takes time and open sharing, confidence building, development of trust, and interactive listening in order for there to be a possibility for *love* to remain in the room as critical issues are discussed and decisions are made.

Into the same room, through a third door, comes *wisdom*. *Wisdom* comes in quietly and observes everything that is going on. The first requirement for the *wisdom*-based person is to make an open assessment of the ways things are. *Wisdom* uses all five senses, seeing, listening, smelling, tasting, and touching, in order to come to an understanding of the way things are. By asking questions and seeking related ideas, the *wisdom* agenda is to get everything on the table so a wise solution can be divined.

This person has a strong requirement to be allowed enough time to complete a thorough assessment before being asked to make or help make a decision.

The *wisdom* process is to observe the way things are, ask questions, implement experiments, and observe results, both rationally and *intuitively.* Then the *wisdom* person will gather more information and brainstorm ideas, ask more questions, and finally come to a position of understanding. This point of understanding must be reached as judged by the *wisdom* person herself.

Wisdom comes from a unique combination of *cognitive* processing guided by *intuitive* perceptions.

In order for *wisdom* to do her work and make her contribution, she must be allowed to sit back and observe as long as she deems this to be important. Then *wisdom* must be allowed time and authority sufficient to lead brainstorming, encourage discussion and argument, and develop rational arguments and step-by-step processes.

This get-to-the-*wisdom* process is followed by a time to ponder and consider alternatives, and lastly to come forth with the *wise* solution. Until this *wisdom* process is complete, *wisdom* is reluctant to participate in any activity that may be unwise. She is unwilling to give conclusions, buy off on any strategy, or in any way rush to decision.

The development of *wisdom* at any moment of time is an esoteric process, devised slowly and carefully by the *wisdom* person, in a manner and a form uniquely fit for this particular moment. All attempts to force, cajole, sell, intimidate, rationally overwhelm, *manipulate*, or inspire the *wisdom* person to act before *wisdom* is ready to act only serve to distract her from her mission, and thereby slows the *wisdom*/decision/action process even further.

Before entering, the *power* person already has made up his mind—he already has a clear sense of what the right action must be. He is ready to act. He is impatient with the thought of having to attend the meeting at all. The *power*-based person is compelled by his values to throw his personal energy into the situation. He wants to cause immediate positive change. He wants to get on with it now.

Power is *intuitively* charged, with little requirement for strategic pondering and open discussions. *Power* is geared for quick action and cannot comprehend or appreciate anything that thwarts such immediate action. It is unacceptable for the *power*-based person to be thwarted, slowed down, blocked, or tackled.

Power sometimes faces nothing but resistance from the others.

Knowledge says, "You have put us at grave risk in the past and you have wasted resources. You cannot be allowed to take action without considering all the facts and proving that your actions will not create irreparable harm."

Wisdom says to *power*, "We first have to carefully assess the situation, observe everything that pertains to it, and come to an understanding of the complete situation. Then a course of action may be devised. But we will have to project this course of action into the future and develop a good prognosis before any action can be undertaken. It is *wisdom's* job to do this, and you will have to wait until *wisdom* says this process is complete."

Love invites *power* to sit down and quietly participate with everyone: "We need to build trust and work to optimize the team with everyone's contributions carefully considered and allowed. We need to agree on our vision of the future. All present actions must be measured against this future vision, and carefully tested to see if everyone on the team feels comfortable and fully regarded by any proposed actions."

Any baring of *power's* claws now will only slow the decision process further.

Similarly, when *knowledge* attempts to take control through the requirement to have everyone review his information, *wisdom*, *power*, and *love* all resist, because this agenda is perceived to be in conflict with their respective agenda. *Love* and *wisdom* also work to push their agenda forward and to assure that their strategies are given an appropriate role in the decision process.

Even if everyone in the room is mature (that is, a socially adept person), this does not ensure zero conflict. In fact, stronger functionality, maturity and self-respect of the individuals involved encourages more productive and helpful conflict.

This is a wonderful and necessary ingredient in a good decision-making process. Each person, *power*, *love*, *knowledge*, and *wisdom*, assert their view that their agenda is the most important and must be accommodated by the strategies and tactics prescribed by the other value sets.

The Tenth Core Values Law:

All *Core Value Energies* conflict with each of the other *Core Value Energies.*

The strategies and tactics inherent in one of the *core values* are always superior in effectiveness to the strategies and tactics of the other *Core Value Energies* in a specific circumstance.

This means that only one of the *core values* can take the lead at any moment. The desired effect will be derived from giving a clear priority to one *core value*. Each of the other *Core Value Energies* must take a role that is supportive of the dominant *core value* mission of the moment. This causes positive constructive conflict.

In every situation there is always a most-critical *Core Value Energy*. This most-critical *Core Value Energy*, if implemented well, will have a significant advantage—leading to the most effective decisions and actions.

Thankfully, none of us is purely *power*-based or *love*-based.

We each have a unique mixture of opposing energies in us. No one has ever scored 100% in any *core values* quadrant, and no one has ever scored zero. The reality that one *Core Value Energy* is superior to the others at any moment in any given situation, and the reality that more than one *Core Value Energy* is required during any process over the course of time, requires each of us to learn to shift smoothly and effectively between one *Core Value Energy* and another.

As children, we did this unconsciously. As adults, the opportunity to act in a conscious manner is real and much preferred.

The Eleventh Core Values Law:

No strategy or tactic that dishonors, ignores, or overrides the *core value* of any participant in the conflict will lead to resolution of the conflict.

In order to successfully navigate conflicts that arise from different *core values* of the people in a given situation, everyone must work to honor the *core values* of all of the participants. This is especially true of the leader(s). Honoring does not mean allowing the other *core value* agendas to take the lead, it means maintaining leadership in a manner that is respectful of the agendas of the other *core values*.

How to use language to honor the respective *core values* in others.

When speaking to:

Power people—Why don't you start working on tasks 1, 4, and 5, while we let the group settle some of the issues related to tasks 2 and 3.

Wisdom people—No one else can make as good an assessment and develop the needed strategy. You are the only one who can possibly know the best solution before our meeting next Tuesday. Can you do that for us?

Knowledge people—I know you have the capacity to deal with hundreds of numbers and to analyze that level of data. Can you build a summary for me, and show me your analysis by next Tuesday—with as few numbers as possible? I need your analysis in order to make the right decisions at our strategy meeting.

Love people—Our willingness to make these four things happen before next Tuesday is critical to our success. We will all value your contribution of these important initiatives. Your efforts will make the entire team work better together, and I will personally appreciate your support.

The Twelfth Core Values Law:

Everyone is able to consciously shift from one *Core Value Energy* to any other *Core Value Energy* at any moment for any amount of time.

This is how we unconsciously warped ourselves into a self-protective personality as children. This is also the key to Core Values Consciousness as adults.

We are all wired to be able to hear our inner talking, to feel our anxieties, and to decide consciously to shift out of our dominant *Core Value Energies* into *being* a different *Core Value Energy* in the room. The commitment to conscious decisions about which part of ourselves to invest in the current situation almost always causes us to be more effective—to get better results.

Builder

CORE VALUE

Power Catalyzed by **Faith**

(Personal energy invested to make a positive difference.)

(I know what to do now; I will know what to do next. My power is sufficient.)

Contributions to Team

Action
Results

Conflict Strategy

Intimidate

Learning Styles

Decide and Do

Banker

CORE VALUE

Knowledge Catalyzed by **Justice**

(Knowing the facts through research, measurement, proof, and records.)

(Ensuring the equity of access, accountability, compensation, and opportunity.)

Contributions to Team

Conservation
Information

Conflict Strategy

Aloof Judgment

Learning Styles

Read and Analyze

Merchant

CORE VALUE

Love Catalyzed by **Truth**

(Working toward an inspired vision of what can be by nurturing the core values in one's self and in others.)

(The way things are.)

Contributions to Team

Relationships
Vision

Conflict Strategy

Manipulate

Learning Styles

Talk and Listen

Innovator

CORE VALUE

Wisdom Catalyzed by **Compassion**

(Seeing the way things are and discerning what to do about it.)

(Remaining empathetic and curious regardless of the behavior and emotions of others.)

Contributions to Team

Assessment Solutions

Conflict Strategy

Interrogate

Learning Styles

Assess and Solve

The Thirteenth Core Values Law:

All of the *core values* genuinely complement and support the other three *Core Value Energies.*

This is a paradox in contrast with the fourteenth *core values law* regarding conflict, yet it is equally true. In fact, it is the supportive nature and the harmonizing attributes of each *core value* with all of the other *core values* that causes people to *be* uniquely wired to make certain *types of contribution.*

***Builder Power* + *Innovator Wisdom* = Independence Contribution**, and is expressed through autonomous assertive action. I figure out what to do. I do it. I have no need to talk about it before or afterward. I have no need for outside guidance and intervention, reporting, or management.

***Banker Knowledge* + *Merchant Love* = *Community* Contribution**, and is expressed through group process, structure, and formality. I will create a community with clear rules, strong processes, and standards. This fair and just system will allow the people to get along, work well together, and be effective as a community.

***Innovator Wisdom* + *Merchant Love* = *Creative* Contribution**, and is expressed through inspired activity often intangible, to be appreciated, not measured—abstract and eclectic. I will always be looking for a better way, a new approach, an opportunity to make greater progress, to invent something new, or to perfect something that already exists.

***Banker Knowledge* + *Builder Power* = *Practical* Contribution**, and is expressed through tangible activity and measurable results—concrete and focused. I work. I make things happen constantly. I am able to make *intuitive* decisions and take action spontaneously. I am also able and willing to do repetitive work, meet standards, be measured, and have my results evaluated.

***Merchant Love* + *Builder Power* = *Intuitive* Contribution**, and is expressed through inspired or intuited action—assertive and extroverted. I can stand in a room for a few minutes with my arms open, taking in the sounds, smells, activity, patterns, processes, and learn more than many people can by hours of analysis and questions. I know instinctively and act based upon gut-level impulse. I don't need to think about things before I know what actions to take.

***Innovator Wisdom* + *Banker Knowledge* = *Cognitive* Contribution**, and is expressed through observation, research, and reasoning—passive and introverted. I think and reason, speculate, and gather information. I assess and derive solutions, all from a rational perspective. I am able to prove that I am right and to illustrate that the way of doing things I prescribed is best.

The combination of *Core Value Energies* into contributory types also sheds light on the conflict strategies.

Inappropriate, ineffective conflict comes from individuals who are holding to their preferred strategies despite opposition from others. This causes others to obstruct or negate the positive contribution of the ineffective person's current *core value* choice. This impulse to continue operating from a currently ineffective *Core Value Energy* often comes from the child's urge to be safe and secure, so transference of old emotional responses and reactions come into play. This can also be caused simply by the adult who is more comfortable with his dominant *Core Value Energy* and not able to easily shift into a different *Core Value Energy.*

Destructive, ineffective conflict comes from individuals who are feeling anxious or fearful, and who have moved from their desire to positively contribute into their ego-driven need to survive and therefore protect themselves. The fear-based conflict strategies are aroused, usually in the fearful person's most dominant *Core Value Energy*, and are applied to the present circumstance without conscious thought.

17

What We Don't Know About Ourselves Controls Our Lives

Say, for instance, that someone has thrown you a curve ball.

You are afraid of striking out the way you have struck out many times before. You can see the ball clearly outside the strike zone, but you know that it might break quickly across the corner of the plate. You are afraid of being called out, so you swing.

You not only miss the ball, because it doesn't break the way you expected, but you strike out on a pitch that clearly misses the strike zone.

The difference between this experience and the alternative (getting a hit) happens in one one-hundredth of a second. It happens in that split second that you decide out of fear to swing, fear that you will be called out.

You choose the fear-based reaction rather than consciously watching for new information. Often going into action quickly is required, but being willing to modify your actions as you progress through your swing is better than just swinging for the fences without conscious thought.

You watch the spin of the ball, its speed and trajectory. You watch one-hundredth of a second longer than is comfortable, watching even as you commit to action.

At the last possible split second you see and understand that this curve ball is not going to break in the way you at first expected, and you check your swing.

You are now on base, or up for another pitch, rather than back in the dugout complaining about the call of the umpire or the unfairness of the other players.

This is how we operate at the social level.

Have you ever left a meeting feeling embarrassed by your performance, disappointed in your own reactions? Like the batter, staying conscious for one-hundredth of a second longer and remaining willing to take the risk that a new *conscious* choice might be better than the patterns of unconscious reactions—this is the most likely way to prevent that humiliation from repeating itself.

Fear-based decisions are ineffective for another even more basic reason.

Consider a wounded dog that finds itself in a dark alley with only one exit, an exit that's behind you as you approach the animal. You approach with no intention to harm and possibly even a desire to help the animal, unconsciously backing the animal into a corner. The closer you come to being able to support the animal, the more likely he is to bite you.

The first observation that comes out of this scenario is that nothing is more dangerous than a fearful, frightened (trapped) animal. Once fear takes over, the likelihood that this animal will change its mind and decide to trust the approaching person is not very high. An animal in fear has decided that his own survival is at risk, taking away any requirement to follow social convention.

The creature in fear is the creature most to be feared.

The second observation is not as easy to see, but even more telling about human social situations. As the person approaches a wounded animal that feels trapped and in danger, there is a point where the person experiences clearly the fear and danger that the dog in the corner feels. This awareness of fear sets up a responsive fear in the approaching person.

Now we have two creatures that are fearful, feeling trapped in the current situation—too afraid to trust and make friends, too close to turn and run—trapped by circumstance in subconscious rationalizations, unconscious choices.

At the smallest flicker of aggressiveness from either of these creatures, the fear-based response is the most likely to be engaged, because it is the reaction that can be trusted to best protect and preserve without thought. The ego rationalization is that there is no time for thought—I am trapped—this is no time to get *creative*. Somebody in this situation is going to get hurt, maybe both.

The frightened dog is more likely to sink its teeth into someone's arm than the animal that feels no threat from an approaching person. Once the animal has sunk its teeth into someone's arm, it's hard to let go, for fear of a fear-based reprisal. This also means that the creation of fear in the one being bitten is almost certain. As the conflict deepens the justifications for these fears deepen, and the escalation of conflict is set into motion.

This is the way we react in the committee room, whether the perceived threat is emotional, social, psychological, or physical. One fear breeds another and tends to justify any action required to meet the real or perceived hostility and aggression of another person.

The person who remains in the situation without fear and continues to observe everyone consciously, the person who considers each appropriate response, is able to maintain personal effectiveness and promote an environment that encourages others to do the same.

It is not possible to act out of fear and still make the contributions prescribed by my unique *Core Values Nature.*

When we are feeling fearful, we cannot be a *love*-based person, we cannot be the *love* in the room. Fear causes us to judge others as untrustworthy. We doubt our ability to see the *truth* in the situation and shift into a *manipulative*, protective response.

When we are fearful, there is no capacity to exert positive personal energy—to be the *power* in the room. We lose *faith* in our intuition to know what to do. Fear cuts off all access to intuition. We lose *faith* in the sufficiency of our *power*. The energy will come out aligned with fear, transforming a positive *power* into a negative force. Our motivation to be the *power* in the room exhibits itself in a fear-based response as actions and words that *intimidate* others.

When we are fearful, there is no opportunity for contributing *wisdom* to the situation. When we are fearful, we lose our sense of *compassion* for others and shift from sincere curiosity to *interrogation*. We lose our open curiosity and our patience with others.

When we are fear-filled, there is no capacity for the free gift of *knowledge*. We will withhold *knowledge*. We will maintain an *aloof* posture and *judge* others to be unjust and therefore unworthy of our important information—our *knowledge*. We then use our facts and information to undermine the authority of those we *judge* to be unworthy. *Aloof judgment* becomes our operating mode.

When we react from fear, we elicit fear in others. When fears begin erupting in a relationship, it's like a nuclear chain reaction: each small fear erupts and excites several others, until some sort of destruction takes place.

A few years back we were working with a client who owned his own company. He had built the business up to a point where its technology was being purchased routinely by the U.S. government for many applications, and to a level where most businesses would have stabilized and begun to develop under their own momentum.

However, this business was floundering and for the sixth or seventh time in its history was having to retrench at a markedly lower revenue level.

The owner was generally able to allow many changes in the business over the course of a year's time. As long as he was away on personal trips, the motivation and energy of his employees continued to build. When he returned, we began to see the destructiveness of his personal interactions.

He would charm his staff and employees one minute with jokes and interesting stories, but in the next instance he would insult and threaten them. Everyone was afraid of being fired by this difficult owner.

One day my partner (Jerry) was working with a group of leaders in this company when George, the owner, came roaring into the room, abruptly called the meeting to a halt. He demanded that Jerry go back with him into his office.

Once they were back in his office, George expressed clearly that he resented Jerry's influence over his people and that he (George) felt out of control of the situation. As Jerry showed almost no resistance and listened for clues to this sudden explosion, George became more and more agitated until he was screaming red-faced into Jerry's face.

Jerry's response was perfect.

He kept his arms resting easily on the chair, remained seated in an open position, and allowed the tirade to pass—which it soon did. After a few questions and a brief discussion, Jerry had a clear understanding of George's concerns and was able to lead George into a discussion about the best alternatives and solutions to the situation.

Had Jerry responded with fear and cowered in the corner, or run from the room, the relationship would have been lost. Had Jerry decided to rise up against George's fury with a rationalized fury of his own, the relationship would have been lost and physical force may have been used to settle the dispute. Jerry would have lost that physical battle to the much larger George.

The fearless position, whether one is being the proactive agent or recipient of someone else's actions, always provides the greatest likelihood of a positive outcome. Some people, especially stronger *builders* (*power*-based people), have a difficult time perceiving the strength of this kind of response. It is so opposite of their preferred strategy. Nevertheless there is a fundamental law at work in these situations.

When a *power*-based person has decided (consciously or unconsciously) to escalate emotionally from a position of positive irresistible power into a negative overpowering strategy of *intimidation*, the strategy that is least likely to create a positive resolution is an opposing *power*-based strategy. By reacting in powerful opposition, the stage is set for total destruction of one person or the other.

As we tell our clients who work daily with *power*-based team members, if you escalate into a rage with a *power*-based person, it is like stepping into the boxing ring with Mike Tyson. You'd better not do so unless you are committed to destruction of the other person, because your fearful opponent is committed to the use of *power* to obtain the desired results.

There is little likelihood that your opponent will suddenly decide to put his arms down and back away for a quiet discussion. Once you take a swing at him (verbally, emotionally, psychologically), all formalities are over and the battle will be won by the most intimidating and destructive power.

We are all choosing at every moment in time to *be* one or our most dominant *Core Value Energies*, in order to make a positive contribution; or, we are "taking and getting," led by our egos into self-centered, control tactics.

18

Making Choices

How Can I Learn to Make Better Choices?

Transference:

The Personality that we construct throughout childhood with all of its beliefs attitudes and ideas, along with its ego driver and learned behavior patterns, is transferred by every individual into adult situations in which we tend to have feelings for and to react toward others now, the way we learned to feel and react in our child environment.

As we become more and more attached and committed to our personality's behavioral patterns, we cement their constant presence in our current lives. This in effect transfers our childhood dramas and our beliefs, attitudes, and ideas that justify our behaviors into our adult nonfamily situations.

The law of transference is responsible for most destructive conflicts between individuals. In situations that correlate with old memories, we unconsciously shift out of being our natural and effective *Real Core Values Self*, and back into the ego-driven personality.

The way to unlock the control of transference over any adult situations is conscious self-observation, followed by conscious choices that honor our *Real Core Values Self*, while also honoring the *core values* of others.

The only way to have effective relationships with others is to honor their innate unchanging *Real Core Values Nature.*

Transference causes us to keep being the ineffective *Core Value Energy* that we were being when the conflict started. It is our chosen pattern. We are most comfortable staying in the operating mode of that now ineffective *Core Value Energy.*

The longer we hold this *core value* posture, the more ineffective and destructive it becomes. Fear comes up in us, and the *Negative Conflict Strategy* is unconsciously called forth.

The most effective way to improve our lives is to clearly identify and understand our ego-constructed personality (attitudes, beliefs, ideas, personal truth) and to consciously choose to let go of some of these emotionally loaded beliefs, allowing them to be diminished and to eventually fall away.

Some of us have to turn around, hunt, and kill the most crippling of these beliefs and behaviors.

Only by this process can we allow our *core values* to rise to a higher level of conscious priority, to better meet the circumstances of our lives. Rather than fighting to defeat ineffective or destructive behaviors, we turn inward and reclaim our deepest *Real Core Values Self.* This is the un-warping process.

The un-warping process is best understood as, first and foremost, the conscious reclamation of our *Real Core Values Self*—learning to *be who I really am.*

So. How is this done? In short form, here is the process:

The Four Steps of *Real Self*-Reclamation (*Core Values Consciousness*)

Step 1: We make a commitment and fulfill the commitment to observe ourselves making choices.

Step 2: We learn to see and acknowledge consciously our anxieties. All anxiety experienced by individuals are made known through stress reactions in the body and in our inner talking that is called up by anxiety to run like a CD player, replaying old songs.

Step 3: We name the fears and anxieties that we are experiencing and equate them to the *Core Value Energy* we are currently trying to *be.*

Step 4: We consciously decide to discontinue being the *Core Value Energy* that is being stressed and to choose which of our more dominant *core values* to be at this moment.

This is the *Real Core Values Self* reclamation process that explains and fulfills the aim of positive psychology to identify innate capacities and operate in alignment with these capacities, rather than trying to fix all habits and behaviors. The *Human Operating System* that is made evident by the *Core Values Index* also provides powerful tools for discovering anxieties and fears and for categorizing these, in order to track and identify the part of our innate nature that is most damaged, or wounded, and therefore provides the key to unlocking the hold that our personality has over us.

When I am concentrating on a *power*-based solution for a given situation, I am not thinking about long-term relationship effects or essential practicality or conservation of personal energy and resources. Since it is not possible to *be* or to act in alignment with more than one *Core Value Energy* at any given moment, it is a given that we are often operating in an unconscious, stimulus-and-response mode.

The most common event for most of us is brought on by our over-commitment to continuing to *be* the presence of our most dominant *Core Value Energy* in the room in this situation. We hold to that even when we are experiencing anxiety, causing us to revert to a defensive posture and shift into our *Negative Conflict Strategy*, or to just simply be ineffective. We do this even when we know how to be a different *Core Value Energy*, but feel greater comfort when we are being our most dominant *Core Value Energy*.

The response to this dilemma from our warped personality will sometimes be to align with one of our lesser *core values*. This causes us to be less than effective and off balance (beside ourselves) generally in situations that call for our best, most conscious response.

I will always create a more desirable outcome if I resist or delay my first stimulus/response reaction and consciously consider which of my four *Core Value Energies* I want to be in a given situation.

My behaviors will follow this spiritual shift and produce more effective, longer lasting, and fulfilling results. In other words, my motivation, my strategies, my presence in the room is actually changed in this process, and I naturally will resort to the strategies of the newly selected *Core Value Energies*.

I will always create a more desirable outcome if I choose which Core Value Energy to consciously be, making the honoring of the core values of others a primary requirement.

The Fourteenth Core Values Law:

It is not possible to *be* the presence of more than one *core value* at any given moment. It is not possible to make choices based upon more than one innate *core value* at any one moment.

When we are busy being the *love* in the room, we are not able to act from a position of *power*, or *wisdom*, or *knowledge*. When we are busy being a *wise* observer, we are not able to be a *powerful* decisive leader. When we are momentarily committed to acting in alignment with our *knowledge core value* (information and conservation), this is our only guiding principle at that moment. To act on the value of *knowledge* and conservation is to reject the strategic values of *power* for that moment.

> ***"Where love reigns, there is no will to power; and where the will to power is paramount, love is lacking. The one is but the shadow of the other."***
> *–Carl Jung*

We are provided evidence that supports this rule in two fundamental ways. First, we have a reticular receiver at the base of our brain stem that screens conscious and unconscious thoughts, watching for recognized fears and potential pain so that two things can be quickly accomplished:

- we are allowed to think only one conscious thought at any moment, thereby reducing any chance for confusion, and
- an automatic, non-conscious stimulus-response action can be taken without time delay, thereby assuring our survival.

The second evidence that we can only act in alignment with one *Core Value Energy* at any given moment is the fact that each *core value* has a unique strategy that conflicts with the strategies of all other *core values*. The strategy of *power*, to take immediate action based upon gut instincts, is in direct opposition to the *love* strategy that insists upon taking care of relationships as a first priority both now and in the future.

The *power* strategy, being *intuitively* based, also conflicts diametrically with the *innovator* assess-and-solve strategy since the derivation of *wisdom* takes time to reason, to process, and rational patience to assure success. The *banker* conservation and information strategies are also put at risk by every *power* strategy, making conflict between these two *Core Value Energies* real and constant.

This built-in conflict reality exists in each of us as individuals, since all of us have some level of preference for each *core value*. In our *Core Values Index*, no one has ever chosen less than three of the tactical values that align with each of the four *core values*, and no one has ever selected their preference for all of the tactical values that align with their dominant *core value*.

I have seen people shift from one *Core Values Strategy* to another several times in the course of a sentence, covering all the bases. But it is not possible to come from two or three value-based positions simultaneously. When we are pressed and find ourselves acting without premeditation, we will generally revert to the most natural comfortable response, based upon our dominant *core value* or an unconscious response based upon our adapted personal value structure (the ego-driven personality) in our lives.

If we do not revert to our dominant *Core Value Energy*, we revert to the strategy imposed by the personal belief system we have learned to trust through the learned, addictive (transferred) responses to the dominant forces in our lives. All of this is generally unconscious and generates additional addictive responses, both in one's self and in others.

We are very fragile and ineffective when our current behaviors are being evoked by transference of past experiences. We are either holding too long to our dominant *core values* or stuck in the use of strategies from our less-dominant *core values*. Either way we are on shaky ground.

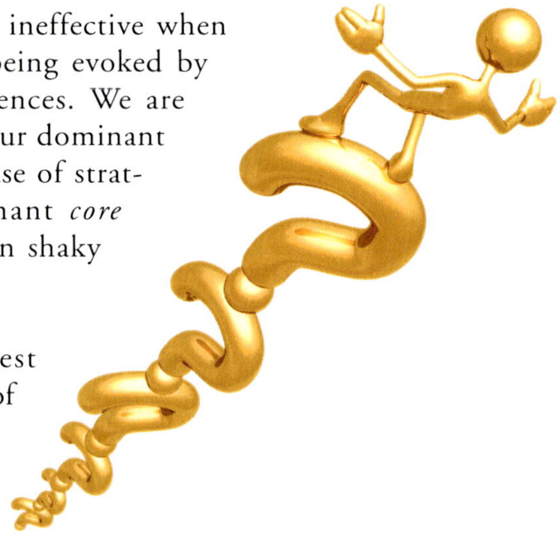

Notice I do not suggest that this unconscious type of response is necessarily ineffective in every given situation. Our warped behaviors may be quite effective, helping us get the things we momentarily want in many situations. After all, we have come to rely upon our warped self because the tactics have been successful in helping us survive until now.

This carefully constructed personality has our best interests at heart, and we remain loyal to it due to our proof of survival thus far. We are each emotionally attached to our warped personality.

It is important to acknowledge this fundamental truth; we make a clear choice between one strategy and all other potential strategies every time we begin to act or react. Since most of us make these choices unconsciously most of the time, we tend to achieve the same results over and over again, even when the results are not what we want. This repetition further strengthens the cellular memory and reinforces our beliefs in our reactive strategies.

When we find ourselves unhappy with the short or long-term results of certain actions, we try to change our behaviors, or often, we try to get others to change their behaviors. Either way we are generally unsuccessful. This direct superficial approach to personal change is another form of parenting.

In this case, attempts to re-parent ourselves are even less effective than were the attempts of our parents to change our behaviors once we were in our early pre-teen years. We are simply not as willing as our parents to make ourselves uncomfortable enough to force new adaptation. It is easier and feels emotionally and socially safer to continue the ineffective behavior—even when we know we are not likely to succeed at the desired level.

Our parents, at least, had the power of fear of rejection, fear of abandonment, and fear of hunger and lack of warmth to control us. Though we all carry a significant weight of self-rejection, self-abandonment, and self-loathing, none of these devices supports us in our efforts to modify our own behaviors.

Most of us are reluctant as adults to select our parents for further parenting in our later stages of development.

Changes made from sheer will power tend to last only for a few moments at a time, and they tend to exhaust us.

If, however, we choose to observe our situation openly and remain available to the truth in front of us, we are able to better regard our circumstances. This allows us to consider alternative thoughts and attitudes, question our stimulus and response emotions, and ask ourselves whether a different person with a different set of *core values* might respond in a more effective fashion.

We often find from this open posture that we already have reasonable capacity and capability to be one of our secondary or tertiary *core values.* If allowed to gain prominence just for this moment, this alternative *Core Values Strategy* would at least create a different, if not a preferable, result. We can choose to shift to the *Core Value Energy* of choice and change our circumstances right now.

The Fifteenth Core Values Law:

We are able to shift from being any *Core Value Energy* at this moment, into any of the other three *Core Value Energies* anytime we choose to do so.

The opportunity for significant improvement in results increases as we explore the use of the *Core Values Strategies* we hold in our second, third, and fourth-level *core values.* In the *Core Values Index* one can clearly see the specific tactical and strategic values one holds as correlated to our *Real Core Values Self.*

When you consider your *Core Values Nature* derived from the *Core Values Index* assessment, it is helpful to acknowledge that in order to select one of the specific tactical values in one of your minor *core values* you had to reject one of the tactical or strategic value options in your dominant or secondary value set. This makes the decision to shift reasonable, workable. You had to have a strong enough capacity (preference) for the lesser value to cause you to reject one of the strategies or tactics of your dominant *core value* when you completed the *CVI.*

The specific values we hold in our less-dominant *Core Value Energies* are held at the same level of commitment as those we prefer in our dominant *core value.* We are designed to work, and perfectly willing to work, from those value positions. We are just not as comfortable, because to do so requires a shift from our dominant values to less-familiar and less-exercised energies. This makes the shifting difficult. But conscious intentional shifting from one *Core Value Energy* to another is how we are intended by our innate wiring to operate as adults, to do consciously what we knew as children how to do unconsciously.

We have chosen our current strategy for this moment in time, because past experience has told us we are safe and better served by doing so. The truth is that if we were a different type of person, we would approach this same situation from a different viewpoint. We would see things differently, think about things differently, and hold different values and attitudes that would cause us to react differently. We would also have significantly different personality warping to contend with. This, by the laws of action and reaction, would create different results and new and different circumstances.

If we are stuck in one mode, we are sure to be unsuccessful in a significant number of life's situations, no matter how carefully we construct our life's framework. This is why we each have a blend of *core values*. It is our individual challenge to learn how to put all of our available *Core Value Energies* to work at the right times.

Some of us are so heavily invested with one or two *Core Value Energies* that we simply have very little capacity for one or two of the other *core values*. My advice to business people and other individuals is to develop a role for yourself, find a job position in which your unique recipe of *Core Value Energies* is what is needed almost always and almost completely in balance with your innate unchanging nature.

19

Making Choices Is Easy

When we are children, choices are easy.

We operate at the creature instinctive level.

We desire and need, subconsciously shifting from one *Core Value Energy* to the next based upon the effectiveness or failure of the first most natural instinctive strategy—our most natural attempt to get us the things we desire and need.

This is easy; it requires no maturity, no refinement of thinking, no emotional maturity, no spiritual/psychological consciousness.

So, one way to make choices easily is to remain psychologically, spiritually asleep.

We can continue to operate like children, instinctively and without moral or ethical consciousness, without a sense of purpose or desire for fulfillment. We can remain locked in the dramas of our childhood, reacting toward others in the same manner we interacted with our parents, siblings, and teachers. This will make the requirement to make choices an easy assignment. It will, however, not make our lives easy.

We can trust the rules of transference to cause us to keep making the same choices we have always made, keeping us comfortable with the same frustrations and discontent we have always had.

The longer we remain asleep spiritually, the more discontented we become as adults.

Our childlike reactions to adult situations begin to cause more trouble instead of reducing our risk. We become more and more recognized by others as being immature, out of control of our selves, and incapable of making tough decisions.

We are seen as people who do not make choices that lead to higher understanding, that do not develop ever-better strategies for success in the adult relationship and adult business worlds.

There is another way to cause choice-making to become an easy facet of life.

We learn to know ourselves. Not in the manner that classical psychology has defined for us—revisiting the past, relegating our present difficulties back onto our parents (although some understanding of this is helpful)—but through the process of learning *who we are* at the deepest most organic level: the essence level, the soul level, the spiritual level—the *Real Core Values Self* level.

We can choose to learn *who we are* at this deeper level. We can choose to understand what our most innate nature is. We can learn what motivates us most, what drives us to learn, what inspires us to take action, what rings our chimes and tickles our fancy and awakens our spiritual passions.

Our *Real Core Values Self* is the center of our consciousness. It is the voice in each of us that agitates our conscious mind to move toward full individuation—becoming all that we are meant to become, to be all that we are designed by God to be.

This *Real Core Values Self*, the various capacities we have for being each of the *Core Value Energies*, is the part of us that decides what we believe, it is the part of us that chooses what thought to think at this moment, what feelings to feel, what actions to take. It is the part of us that is able to stand to the side and watch the actions of our subconscious personality, as it emits angry statements, takes foolish actions, fights, heckles, shames, and blames others.

It is the part of ourselves that decides when to see these truths about ourselves—when to become aware and when to acknowledge our learned attitudes, beliefs, and ideas that we use to justify our ineffective nonconscious actions.

Your *Real Core Values Self* is the part of you that decides—after seeing the truth about your subconscious personality self—when to step in and make a different choice.

In the past, this process toward adult consciousness and individuation was one of prolonged processing and experience—trial and error, finding a helpful mentor, visits to Tibetan monasteries, weekends in Indian smoke lodges, psychoanalysis and therapy, counseling, and religious training.

There is nothing wrong in any of this; except that . . .

. . . each such experiential or cognitive process tends to focus on the experience or the cognitive reasoning and trusts each of us to learn for ourselves *who we are.* None of these provides clear authority that helps us once and for all define, quantify, specify, and clarify *who we are.*

The *Core Values Index* provides for the first time this clear authoritative definition of self, with simplicity for easy comprehension and linear application to everyday living; plus an amazing complexity and range of unique blends of our *Core Values Natures* that accommodate and specifies essentially all types of persons.

Once an individual knows clearly his *Real Core Values Self,* the deepest motivational self—the unique blend of innate *core values* that motivate his life—two things become much easier.

1. ***Detached observation.*** I can now view my actions in the adult world from the perspective of effectiveness or ineffectiveness rather than from a place of judgment of right and wrong, emotional safety, comfort or desire.

This allows me to watch myself in action and encourages me to see the truth about my choices, whether they are coming from old childhood beliefs, attitudes, and ideas—playing my emotional dramas in adulthood just like my childhood experiences—or whether they are choices that drive my actions in alignment with my *core values.*

Am I acting in a manner that expresses my *wise power* or my *loving knowledge*? Am I contributing my essential *Core Value Energies*, or am I taking and getting?

Now that I know my *Real Core Values Nature*, I am able to intentionally step back into this *real self* and view my actions from that higher plain of consciousness. This allows me to observe myself, to identify with my *Real Core Values Self* rather than with the behavioral patterns of my personality self.

I have become the presence in me that decides what to think, what to feel, what to do. I learn that I have emotions, but I am not my emotions. I have thoughts, but my thoughts do not control me. I act, but my actions are based upon choices that I make and that I can make differently next time, each time.

2. ***Conscious choices.*** After the gift of detached observation comes the powerful ingredient of *conscious choice.* As we practice being our *Real Core Values Self*, watching our personality self in action, we gain more and more understanding about the attitudes, beliefs, and ideas that we have learned to use to rationalize our actions.

These beliefs, attitudes, and ideas (our personal truths) will come more readily into consciousness the more we are willing to see and hear our thoughts and patterns of emotion, the more we become practiced at being consciously observant of our daily behaviors.

We begin to see the foolishness of some of our beliefs, the silliness of holding to certain attitudes as an adult. The ability to make a different decision is heightened by this awareness of the patterns of thoughts that accompany and precede all actions.

We only need to be willing to see these truths about ourselves.

This, added to the desire to be effective—to actually live in accordance with our deepest *Core Values Nature*—causes the making of choices to be much easier.

It is also helpful that all negative emotions derive from the personality subconscious and are by their nature a road map for exploration of the attitudes, emotions, and ideas that serve to justify our personality self.

It is *helpful* that considerable pain is endured by each of us when we continue to make childlike emotion-based responses in our now adult world.

The pain of continuing the same emotional and behavioral patterns drives us toward the willingness to see the truth about ourselves—the inner talking and self-justification; the attacking of others in defense of our personality selves.

We can learn to be thankful for our emotional pain. It makes our salvation as a person possible, the reclamation of our *Real Core Values Self* a possibility.

Our willingness to see this truth and to observe ourselves in addictive emotional and behavioral patterns, gives us the opportunity of making a different choice when confronted with the same drama at a later date.

We are able to stop before acting in accord with old patterns, able to choose consciously which *Core Value Energy* might be the most effective to *be in this moment*. We choose, from this place of conscious awareness of negative emotions and inner talking, to be a different *Core Value Energy*, a different aspect of our *Real Core Values Self*.

We are able to choose what *Core Value Energy* we want to *be* at this moment.

We can choose what *contribution* to make right now. This is far easier than it is to continue acting defensively at this moment, only to have to deal with the consequences of the defensive actions later.

The more that we do this, the easier it becomes—until most of our adult life is spent in full consciousness: actions, attitudes, and thoughts aligned with our deepest *Core Values Nature*. We are learning to *be* our *Real Core Values Self*—the natural and effective expression of *who we are*.

There are two critical questions we can ask ourselves anytime we are faced with what appears to be a difficult choice.

Which alternative is most aligned with my *core values*?

This question causes us to view difficult situations or decisions from the perspective of pursuit of happiness, pursuit of fulfillment. Every choice we make that is aligned with our deepest *Core Values Nature* causes us to remain on purpose, in harmony with our *Core Values Nature* and acting in a fashion that will continue to generate affirmation of fulfillment.

Which pathway leads to the greatest learning?

This question causes us to make choices in harmony with the primary pathway of our life. We are already on the pathway toward spiritual health, *core value* fulfillment, and full individuation as a human person. We are each aware of this at some level of consciousness.

By asking this second question, we are giving ourselves the reminder that our life is a process, and that process is one of self-discovery and self-fulfillment. When we make every life choice in harmony with the commitment to continue learning at a faster and greater pace, we accelerate our life individuation process and keep our passions alive.

We find ourselves making a higher and better contribution every day. This makes making choices not only easier but exhilarating and joyous.

Our passions call to us and make the choice of directions and pathways easier. They provide clarity about what skills we need and want to hone, what emotional traumas we want to leave behind, what core gifts we want to learn to better express.

This awareness causes us to passionately choose even a difficult course. The opportunity to reclaim one's life from the environmental, behavioral past is thrilling and rewarding. We are fully energized when we make choices that excite new curiosity and promise new levels of skill, prowess, maturity, and spiritual capacity.

Choose the pathway or momentary action that leads to the greatest learning. These choices become easier to make. The difficulties of life become easier to face and conquer.

Life never becomes less difficult. Learning is never over. Each stage of learning requires our highest concentration yet, our most dedicated focus and discipline, our highest *Core Values Consciousness.*

This makes life simple, choices easy, and the difficulty of life a thrilling game to play, rather than a morality play within which we are stuck as character actors with little chance for success and fulfillment.

20

The Silent Pause

We will benefit tremendously by learning to intentionally pause—silently, before choosing a right action. This is not necessarily a long pause—often only seconds in duration. But one of the tactics we all can use more effectively is the silent pause.

The longer the pause, the more commanding are the words or actions immediately following. Within a silent pause we are able to hear ourselves talk internally, reflect on the real intent of the people around us, and consider alternative modes of being.

When we shift from one *Core Value Energy* to another, we first shift from being the presence of *love* in the room to the presence of *wisdom* in the room, for instance. Since each *core value* has a unique strategy, the shift is highly impactful—suddenly being a different kind of energy, a different type of energy making a completely different contribution.

We are afraid to make this kind of silent pause for several reasons. Loss of control of the moment. Appearance of uncertainty. Acceptance of accountability for subsequent actions. Appearance of stupidity. Fear that we will give others the chance to take control. These fears are faced head-on when we choose to make a silent pause, giving ourselves sufficient time to consider appropriate and effective responses.

It doesn't take a genius to recognize that we can make significant gains in life by pausing during times of stress and irritation, by making a conscious choice to listen, feel, and see the truth about a situation and consider the best *Core Value Energy* to ***be***.

I am a strong advocate of this silent pause and the self-observation this pause makes possible. As we become more and more willing to pause and observe our thoughts, and see the ineffective ways in which we are now acting, or the manner in which we are about to respond, we begin to trust the process of shifting consciously to another value strategy.

It is important to make these observations with a great deal of forgiveness toward ourselves. This is not a time to judge oneself as being stupid, ludicrous, ignorant, immature, or any other negative judgment.

Within the perceived momentary silent pause we should hold a loving attitude toward ourselves and a willingness to see the truth. This can all be frightening, frustrating, and even personally embarrassing. That's why we don't do it more often. Who really wants to see their ineffective, reactionary self the way others see us?

Who really wants the knowledge that I have seen how ridiculous my usual unconscious reaction is and yet I have chosen to go ahead with it anyway? Who really wants to claim complete accountability for the new effects caused by a more conscious reaction in a difficult situation?

All of these considerations relate to our beliefs about what is required of us in order to be loved or appreciated and respected by others or to feel safe and get the things we want. How must we appear? How must we speak? How must we respond in order to protect ourselves within a difficult situation and yet maintain our precious image of being a good, strong, lovable person, a smart person, an effective person, a powerful and wise person, an acceptable person?

All of these wants and fears group themselves around our fearful ego and work to keep us from making conscious observations regarding our unconscious behaviors. We are skilled at protecting our personalities. Our egos are employed to make certain that we do not make the same mistakes now and suffer the same consequences we suffered as children.

??????????????????????????

There is a final element that must exist before we will be successful in observing ourselves and making conscious choices; we have to want something. It is important that we not be merely disgusted with our immaturity or only feel determined to grow up. We have to want a different response from people. We have to desire more success in our lives.

We have to want more fulfillment and a greater sense of meaning. We have to *want* some of these *better results* more than we fear the truth about ourselves. We have to have a sense of want and desire that is great enough to drive us to risk a momentary pause. We must risk taking a peek at the truth about ourselves, risk making a wrong choice consciously, risk creating a worse situation than we normally create through our unconscious, protective responses.

One way to create this internal environment of spiritual pursuit is to spend time and energy clarifying what we truly want in life; take the time to clarify what gives our life meaning and what elements in our lives give us fulfillment. With improved answers to these life questions, we become more willing to risk consciousness and make new provocative choices in pursuit of the things we want. With this final element in place, we can begin the observation process, pausing silently (when under fire) to consider alternative actions, a better more effective *Core Value Energy* to *be.*

When we have experienced a necessary period of conscious observation without judgment of ourselves, we will find ourselves, at one surprising moment, able and willing to make a different choice. We will consciously shift to a different *Core Value Energy* for a better strategy and risk a different outcome.

The Sixteenth Core Values Law:

All choices are made from a position of victim or personal accountability.

Much of our vision of life is committed to proving that we are not at fault, not wrong, not unlovable. We are loaded with fear-based defense mechanisms to keep us from being harmed socially, emotionally, mentally, physically, and financially. We are determined as individual egos not to suffer. In our unconscious minds we are convinced that something or someone other than ourselves must be responsible for anything in our lives that doesn't feel good.

Our strategy is to claim the victim position and deny any responsibility for what is currently happening—unless, of course, the current circumstances bring accolades and positive attention.

Conscious choices cannot be made from the victim posture. Our unconscious patterns are the construct of our survival mechanisms, as discussed before, so whatever response we unconsciously chose as a fearful child continues to be chosen unconsciously by each of us as adults, until we are willing to give up the victim posture and accept full accountability. ***Read this paragraph again, and again.***

Definition: *Accountability*: the acknowledgment that today's circumstances are the direct result of all of my prior choices, and that I have the capability to consider many alternatives and to consciously decide what actions to take. It follows that my future will be created by the choices I make now. This is completed by the acknowledgment that my responsibility is to remain conscious at this moment and *make a choice.*

People who live life from this premise do not tolerate any language, thought, attitude, idea, feeling, or fear in themselves that stinks of the victim posture. These people are in the business of creating the life they want to live. They are consciously observing themselves and others, searching for and finding more effective attitudes and actions, and working to eliminate the choices that do not support their life vision. To be truly accountable is to ***be*** consciously the presence of *love*, *power*, *knowledge*, or *wisdom* at this moment.

As a person learns to stop momentarily, observe current feelings and fears, and choose the best *core value* from which to formulate a response, it becomes easier and easier to remain conscious because the rewards are so great.

When I am operating in this conscious mode, there are few situations within which I will lose myself and make ineffective responses; I am a master at getting the things I want and there are few people that can get under my skin and make me afraid at any level.

When I am not operating at this level, I am an emotional mess, second-guessing myself, watching for hidden messages and warnings, ready to defend, possibly attack if required. Neither defense nor attack is required in 99% of all social situations.

Defense and attack responses are always the weakest choices and the least effective at getting us what we want. Our defensiveness and attacks are also the last things others forget and forgive in us because we always excite some level of fear in others when we defend ourselves or attack them.

We always excite some level of fear in others when we defend ourselves, or when we attack them.

"Don't ever back a dog into a corner," the old saying goes. Why? Because a dog that feels trapped, that feels it has no recourse, experiences the basic requirement to defend itself. There is nothing more dangerous than a dog (or a person) in the defensive mode. To defend one's self creates more fear in others than a straightforward attack.

The Seventeenth Core Values Law:

What we don't know about ourselves controls our lives.

To the degree that we remain governed by unconscious choices—choices being made in accordance with fear-based, ego-driven strategies—the circumstances of our lives are being created to produce the same results and circumstances tomorrow that we have to face today.

We each live in the personality we have created, mostly at an unconscious level. Since we know that our present circumstances are the result of all of our past choices (conscious or unconscious), we know that the situations we are required to deal with today are those *we created.*

When we are dealing with the results of conscious choices, we are dealing with effects and situations we have intentionally created, or the near misses of this effort. When we are dealing with the consequences of unconscious choices, we are dealing with negative surprises, difficult new decisions that must be made. We have to work our way out of such difficulties—so those unconscious choices in the past are now in control of present life.

In other words, we are ego-driven at this moment, either because we continue to make new unconscious choices (stimulus/response reactions) or because we are struggling to recover from previous unconscious choices. Our focus remains in the defensive reactive mode.

We can react to this statement by quickly denying that we are ego-driven, but this is a reactionary judgment we make toward the word *ego*, making *ego-driven* synonymous with *selfishness*, judging this unconsciousness to be a bad thing. We look at ourselves as being unsuccessful in life, childish, if this is the case.

Or we can react to the idea that we are living unconsciously based upon our ego's fears, and that's all there is. There is no better, higher, or more effective way to live and make choices. *That's just the way I am—get used to it.* This reaction, while sounding forceful and commanding, is actually clear evidence of the victim posture. If I were to say to someone else, "*That's just the way you are—get used to it,*" what they would hear is that they are powerless to change, stuck with their life as it is.

Even when I am performing quite reasonably, within social norms, appropriate by social standards, if I am simply acting in alignment with my most dominant *core value*, I am operating unconsciously, and therefore being less effective than I can be if I choose to make conscious choices about *who I want to be* at the moment—*love*, *power*, *wisdom*, or *knowledge*.

If I spend the better part of each day making conscious choices about my actions, attitudes, and ideas, considering alternative actions, then acting in accordance with my best choices, I am in control of my life. The outcomes of my choices about *who I want to be* and the resulting actions are my own as a conscious adult. I can measure the effectiveness of my chosen course of action and choose to continue, or I can choose to make yet another choice, zeroing in on effectiveness and satisfaction by observing results.

If I spend the better part of each day in a reactive mode, behaving the same way today that I did yesterday, each of my unconscious decisions and choices set up new circumstances in response to my actions. These new circumstances closely resemble the old circumstances that resulted from the same choices and responses I made previously in similar circumstances.

The attitudes, judgments, ideas, and beliefs that I allow to unconsciously direct my choices for actions are setting up circumstances over which I have declared no control. From this posture, it is easier to declare the world to be unfair and to declare myself the victim of circumstance. I can prove that I am out of control.

I am not in control. My unconscious thoughts are in control. My fears are in control, setting up situations that require my attention and reaction. My ego-based personality that I created unconsciously as a child is in control. These unconscious reactions are based upon choices I made instinctively the first time I was faced with threatening situations. I remain unaware of these patterns and consequences—they remain in control of my life.

The beliefs, attitudes, and ideas that give rationalized permission and motivation for our actions, these personal truths, are a set of beliefs about why it is better to be *who I am not* (my ego-based personality) rather than to be the *Real Core Values Self* I was created to *be*.

21

Observing Inner Talking

One of the most important choices in life is the decision to observe one's inner talking. This choice allows us to observe objectively and with compassion our own most comfortable life strategies and enables us to consider whether the choices we make in many situations may not be the most effective choices. Then we can ask ourselves which *Core Value Energy* might be superior in this situation (most effective).

If we step back from our emotions and look at ourselves going through a difficult situation, we can hear ourselves rationalizing the situation, laying blame, pointing the finger, trying to prove ourselves guiltless, trying to make ourselves safe. If we listen carefully we can hear repetitive phrases.

Try this simple exercise. Decide for one week to listen to and write down all common phrases you say to yourself silently, describing your spouse and closest relationships. If you are faithful in writing these phrases down, you will likely find many examples that make you right and make them wrong, rationalizations that release you from responsibility and give it to them, that make you the good person and them the bad.

The inner talking of each *Core Value Energy* tends to be unique to that *core value*:

Builder—*Power* dominant *core value*

He should have done that.
I told them to do it. Why don't they listen?
I guess I will have to do it myself.
He's worthless.

What a wimp (weak person).
What's the matter with them? They're lazy.
She failed again.
Just do it.

***Innovator**—Wisdom* dominant *core value*
They just don't understand. What fools.
Why do I constantly have to explain things?
What's so difficult about this?
That's a silly idea.
Why can't they just figure it out?
We've talked about this a thousand times.
It's just not that simple.

***Banker**—Knowledge* dominant *core value*
That's not fair or just.
They keep wasting money.
He's erratic and unreliable.
She never follows through.
Totally unfounded.
Where's the proof?
Facts don't lie.
I sent him the report. All he had to do was read it.

***Merchant**—Love* dominant *core value*
He completely disregards me.
It was her fault.
You never appreciate all the things I do.
He is so rude and disrespectful.
He's always in my face.
He's just a lousy SOB.
She just can't see the big picture.
He can't even be kind.

When we give ourselves permission to hear this inner talking and to see the truth about ourselves, we find ourselves freer, more willing to shift to a different *Core Value Energy*: *builder power*, *merchant love*, *innovator wisdom*, or *banker knowledge*. For some of us, this commitment to see the truth about our inner talking and self-justification can be made dramatically more effective by making a commitment to our higher power. This can be done very cleanly by employing a stated commitment, something like this:

I will see and accept the truth about myself. Help me hear the things I say to myself that are keeping me from being the power, love, wisdom, or knowledge in the room.

A word of caution here. If you make the above commitment and request with integrity, you will find yourself in situations in the very near future that will give you plenty of truth to accept about yourself. This is really nothing to fear, because you do have secondary and tertiary *core values* that you are not employing as often as would be desirable in the most essential situations. Your willingness to see and hear this truth about yourself will help propel you toward making the shift between being the presence of one *Core Value Energy* to another.

At first it is best just to be willing to hear the inner talking and to challenge yourself about whether what you say internally to yourself is really true. After doing this for a while you will almost without effort want very much to not keep running those old tapes. You can then stop yourself and decide to shift into a different *core value* state of being in response to a difficult situation. This will automatically cause you to choose your response from a completely different set of strategies and tactical values.

We can choose to think and act from a different *Core Value Energy* in which we hold some strong values, our second or third-level *core value*. A lot of us have only two or three *Core Value Energies* to select from. The relative preference or capacity for our third or fourth-level *core value* is simply too low to expect ourselves to become comfortable with these strategies and motivations. Thankfully, most of us put ourselves into situations in which, at least a good portion of the time, our success or safety is not dependent upon our ability to be the least dominant of our *Core Value Energies* in these situations.

By making this choice to shift from one *Core Value Energy* to another, we create an opportunity for better results, more happiness. By doing this consciously and repeatedly, we gain new skills and enhance our trust and competencies in our less-dominant *core values.*

We learn to be more effective in deciding which *Core Value Energy* to shift into. And we learn to more effectively invest the strategic skills inherent in these consciously chosen *core values.*

We continuously become more effective dealing with life's constantly changing circumstances. No matter how effective we become in making these shifts, I guarantee, life will find a way to keep our interest and put new challenges before each of us in order to keep us doing this important personal development work.

The Eighteenth Core Values Law:

All choices are based in either fear or acceptance.

The first basis for choice is survival. All creatures are geared to respond to danger with specific survival options: flee, fight, threaten, hide, make noise, be silent, stand still, sniff the air, listen, sense vibrations, etc. As Homo sapiens creatures, we are able to choose among all of these possible survival mechanisms.

When a situation is threatening, but not at the physical survival level, the complexity of our response options grows dramatically: Political tactics, argumentation, deceit, trickery, *intimidation*, being *aloof*, *interrogation*, *manipulation*, surrender, caretaking, are all devices designed to cause a desired response in another person or persons. These tactics are fear-based and defensive. They are therefore only momentarily effective, and they lead to failure, isolation, abandonment, and increased conflict rather than success.

We generally decide to use these tactics when we feel overwhelmed, powerless, or at risk socially, emotionally, or psychologically. We all define situations differently. Grave risk to one may seem inconsequential to another. This is the result of our individual transference process discussed earlier and the personality warping of our basic *Core Values Nature.*

An alternative response for humans is to accept the current situation, including the actions, attitudes, judgments, and beliefs of others. We must also accept the possibility of loss. This usually does not include loss of life or health. It may include in some instances acceptance of some pain or injury, especially emotional or psychological angst.

The crux here is that we must accept the circumstances of our life and the possible negative effects of present circumstances in order to free ourselves from a defensive posture that is based upon fear. If you want to eliminate fear, you have to face the fear and decide not to act from the position of fear.

If we choose to fight for status quo, to defend all of our ideas, beliefs, possessions, and sense of control, we will remain in fear. We will always act from an egoistic motive. We will always be in the reactive mode, unconsciously responding to the present situation. This is the same innate ego-based strategy that we have found successful for our survival in the past and as children.

Acceptance requires no specific response, diminishes the sense of threat, and makes the negative fear-based strategies unnecessary. Acceptance also creates a brief pause during which alternative reactions may be reviewed and selected on a more conscious level. We make room and time for ourselves to consciously and effectively shift into the most effective alternative *Core Value Energy.*

When we shift from the stimulus response behavior into a conscious review of possible actions, our minds are free to consider all alternatives. Shifting from one *core value* to another, consciously considering which strategy will afford the greatest advantage, takes us more certainly toward our goals for fulfillment and happiness.

Allow me to press a little here. We are not talking about stepping out of your life circumstance for a day or an hour or even five minutes, in order to go through some anguish process to make this shift decision.

We are a unique recipe of essential *Core Value Energies.* The time required to make this conscious shift instead of our usual unconscious preprogrammed response is a split second, or a few seconds at most. We did this instantaneously and unconsciously as children. As adults we are able to do the same thing consciously just as quickly and readily.

Acceptance implies a separation of our survival instinct from the response process.

The fear that is excited by any given situation is denied validity when we accept the present situation and its possible losses.

This is done by asking simply, "Can this situation truly, reasonably lead to loss of life, or of physical or psychological well-being?" If the answer is no, there is seldom need for a fear-based response. In fact, to choose a fear-based response to a situation that you have consciously determined does not require one for survival, is to consciously choose an ineffective response.

If you have a compelling emotional or psychological need to fail or to defer life's greatest gifts, the sure way to get your wish is to continue being unconscious and continue playing out old dramas and running old inner-talking tapes.

Acceptance is one of the more difficult attitudes to achieve. We are wired by nature to seek control of circumstances in order to secure survival. This desire to control situations is a primary device of the ego (survival instinct). Acceptance gives away any sense of the need or ability to take control.

The four *Negative Conflict Strategies* (*intimidation*, *manipulation*, *aloof judgment*, and *interrogation*) are in fact simply control tactics. There is no need to seek to control yourself, your circumstances, or the actions and attitudes of others when we are simply *being power*, *love*, *wisdom*, or *knowledge* at this moment.

Example: Imagine a baseball pitcher who has allowed three batters to load the bases, with no outs, setting up the possibility of loss of the game in the ninth inning.

Imagine him focusing his energy and thoughts on controlling these threatening base runners. In the meantime, a new batter is standing at the plate, waving his bat threateningly.

Now the pitcher also must include this person in his control system. The fear that these feelings invoke leads to a sense of being out of control, with the concurrent requirement to regain control by controlling the next pitch and making certain he does not put the pitch anywhere where this new guy can get the bat on it.

From this attitude of need to control, what is the most likely outcome for his next pitch? It's either a pitch right down the middle, waist high, right where he consciously swore he would not put it (like the golfer who slices his ball right into the lake where he was afraid he would hit it). Or, his next pitch is completely out of the strike zone, allowing the batter to gain the upper hand, thereby increasing the intensity of the pitcher's need to control the situation.

If the pitcher gives into the fear just a little more, he controls his pitch completely out of the reach of the catcher and gives the winning run to the other team without their having to do much of anything.

This is not a formula for success.

If, instead, our beleaguered pitcher accepts the fact that his pitching, combined with the defense of his team, has allowed three batters to get on base. He will easily realize that the base runners on first and second are not able to steal a next base unless the runner on third base steals home, immediately letting go of his need to control at least those two people.

In fact, by ignoring these two runners, he may gain the opportunity of catching one of them leading off a little too much and catch them flat-footed. Home is the hardest base to steal. So let the guy at third give it a try. Forget him, too. Let my unconscious mind watch for the opportunity and quit thinking about the potential disaster.

Next, consider the batter.

There is no way to control him. He will be at his best or at his worst, depending on his own battle with his control demons. And the odds of baseball are against him. Three batters in a row have hit the ball; most of them with averages of less than .250 (1 in 4).

Also, the defensive players on the pitcher's team cover far more of the playing field than the portion that cannot be covered. So let him hit the ball. Let my guys do their job.

Finally, the pitch is about to be thrown.

If the pitcher tells himself the truth, more times than not, his pitch goes approximately where it is supposed to go, but seldom right where he wants to put it. And most of the time he throws a strike, otherwise he wouldn't be standing on the pitching mound.

So just let her rip. Put your arm and your back into it. Commit everything without any need for extra control or speed. Trust your curve ball or your slider. Let the batter think he's in control because the ball's coming over the plate at 75 miles per hour instead of 95.

If he can hit that ball, it's probably going to be a grounder or a pop-up. So let him worry about controlling my pitch. In this scenario, the likelihood that the pitcher will perform at his best and succeed is far greater than under his control strategy.

You see, acceptance is a natural positive response, which is often forgotten under moments of stress. Stress excites our fears that seduce us into believing that we must take control in order to survive.

Control of anything is only an illusion, a strategy that never works (for long). The control strategy sets us up for failure, disappointment, and more stress; it starts a downward spiral of fears that leads to more attempts to control which leads to more failures which create more fear, and heightens one's belief that something catastrophic is about to happen, so I'd better take control.

The Nineteenth Core Values Law:

Every action caused by fear is a wrong action. Every decision made based upon fear is a wrong decision.

As an example, there was a recent news story concerning a young hunter who was separated from his hunting party. The eighteen-year-old found himself hiking alone at night in an effort to make his way back to camp. He was not fearful, but he was a little irritated. He suddenly heard a noise behind him. He looked around and saw a mother grizzly with two cubs rushing up behind him.

Before he could respond he was knocked down by the bear's powerful raking blow with a gash on his shoulder, the female grizzly standing over him, between his legs, her head lowered into his abdomen. The young man, not knowing that to feign death, to relax and appear lifeless was the best strategy, responded with the rush of adrenaline cause by his understandable fear.

He punched the grizzly in the face. The grizzly's response was also understandable.

The creature she had suspected was a threat had now proven to be one. She sunk her teeth into the young man's leg and lifted him off the ground, severely wounding him. When he passed out, and therefore quit resisting, the grizzly released her grip and left him lying in the dirt. There is a lot more to the story, regarding the young man's heroic efforts to haul himself back to his camp and his eventual rescue and ultimate survival.

The purpose here, however, is to emphasize the reality that fear-based decisions are almost always wrong, even in the presence of real physical threats.

An appropriate strategy may be to run. But to run on the first impulse of fear, without considering direction, consequences, etc., is likely to put the runner in greater danger. To run in any event is to admit vulnerability against any perceived threat, at least in the eyes of the pursuer. But to run haphazardly away, not thinking about the best course and complementary strategies, is a formula for harm.

To choose a fear-based response to a social situation is even less effective.

I remember an occasion when an employee of my company was irritated with me. He was willing to show his anger by shouting and refusing to look me in the eye.

For two days I found myself walking past his office with its door open, avoiding speaking to him, avoiding entering his office even when I had decisions to make that I would normally discuss with him. At the same time, he continued the poor work habits that had been the subject of the discussion that had irritated him in the first place.

I remember clearly sitting in my office asking myself, "If he quits, will that really be the end of the company? If he displays his fists and goes into a rage, is he really going to kill me? Am I really in any danger?"

Having laughed at my foolishness, yet still feeling uneasy, I decided to immediately go in and talk things out. I had accepted his anger and irritation. I had accepted his likely outburst and threats. I chose to confront the situation head on and immediately.

The situation was resolved reasonably well. I prevailed and caused the end result that I believe appropriate. The positive outcome would never have been achieved while I was remaining in my *Negative Conflict Strategy*—shame and blame, manipulate, and avoid conflict. I made a commitment to myself never again to walk by another door because I was afraid of conflict. I have resolved within myself to always face conflict at the earliest possible moment.

I learned a valuable lesson: that acceptance of a situation is not a passive act. To stop and see the reality of current circumstances, even to accept the likelihood of negative responses from others if a certain action is chosen, is a proactive, powerful response to life from the position of acceptance.

From this position of acceptance we are able to separate the things that are truly life-threatening from those that are simply annoying, embarrassing, or painful. We can also separate emotionally from our need to take control. We can avoid our most commonly used *Negative Conflict Strategy*. This *choice* to accept things as they are, then make a *fearless choice*, is an effective response. We remain in the mode of positive contribution and avoid the destructive and ineffective strategies of taking and getting.

22

What I Choose to Learn

One of the most important choices each of us faces is a life constant: What do I choose to learn? There are many faces to this question. My sons, for instance, are now graduated from college. Each quarter they were faced with a choice regarding what classes they would take. They would rethink and zero in on what their major would be.

As they did this, they were tuning their lives to their basic interests, their innate curiosity, their passions. They were gaining knowledge and skill for application in an adult vocation. They were subconsciously and consciously seeking to align their present activities and their future work with their *Real Core Values Self.*

This is the most obvious type of learning. It is general, academic, and socially recognized as having certain value. After four years at a liberal arts college, they would be prepared to write well, apply math skills directly to life circumstances, and to read. Hopefully, they would also have learned to think rationally. But again, these learned skills are at the fundamental level of mental development.

The next level of learning is the choice of a major. One son majored in business economics. The other majored in philosophy. These kinds of choices are made in accordance with a sense of one's *calling* and a vision of a life's purpose, a direction, and a strong sense of where in society they will make their contribution. At this choice-of-learning level there tends to be a balancing of occupational interests and of personal avocational interests.

My eldest son, for instance, is fascinated and motivated by business innovations and general management practices. He grounded himself in economics and general business principles as the cornerstone of his education. He is also incredibly talented and attracted to music. He is able to find and express many levels of passions through his playing and singing.

This may become a primary vocation for him at some time in the future. Whether this happens or not, he will always carry his music with him as a primary avocation, thus finding a way to make a contribution in life not only through business but also through the creation and expression of music.

This is similarly the case with my younger son; his musical talent is jazz piano. He loves the experience of spontaneous creation, especially jamming with his friends. He composes very complex pieces and plays the piano almost every time he comes into the house, and then again at night just before retiring to sleep. I cannot imagine his life without music.

He may find a business vocation related to music because of this serious drive, but he also has a taste for business development, especially technology. Whether he finds a way to incorporate music into his business experience or not, music will also be a lifelong avocation. Some of his many gifts to the world will be made through the piano keyboard. His highest and best contributions are likely to be made at high levels of business strategy and personal development—here his philosophy major has trained his rational mind to higher levels of cognitive discipline than most business people achieve.

Educational choices are made at the social level. They are apparent in our behaviors and in our investment of energy and time. But we are not yet down to the basic choice-making level regarding what we choose to learn.

The deepest choice of what we will learn is made at the spiritual level. Whether we are spiritually aware or not, the spiritual part of each of us is able to observe the body, mind, and emotions.

This spiritual center is the seat of our human consciousness. It is the *Real Core Values Self* that is our real innate nature. It is our conscious presence, our *being*. Talents, attributes, and intelligence levels all become aligned through the discovery and full development of our individual innate *Core Values Nature*.

This emotional alignment is labeled by many as *passions*. Note that there is a significant difference between passion and desire. Desire refers to physical or sociological wants. Desire puts each of us in competition for resources with everyone around us. Passions do not create this separation. Passions are a spiritual directive or bent developed in each of us in accordance with our innate talents and capacities. As we accept our passions and follow their directives, we choose to learn those things that elevate our experiences in areas that relate to our passions.

The guiding principle for making effective learning choices is to constantly seek to optimize our *Core Values Nature*, to prepare ourselves to contribute this essential human energy to our immediate world. What can I learn from this situation? Which aspect of my *core nature* is most needed in this circumstance? Why am I creating this experience? What is it that I unconsciously am trying to learn?

I believe the universal purpose of every human *being* is to learn *who we are* and to become the best version of *who we are*, so we can make our highest and best contribution to our world. If this is true, then the primary task is to learn first *who we are*, then learn to optimize our talents and gifts (then where in this world we belong)—only then can we become caught up in delivering *who we are* to the world through our talents and skills. All the while we are learning and becoming and *being*.

23

The Way We Are Wired to Learn

Each *Core Value Energy* learns differently.

***Builders* (*power*) learn by the "Decide and Do" strategy.**

Builders (*power*-based people) learn by doing, by failing, by succeeding. The idea of sitting down to study technical manuals or long, detailed directions is an anathema to them. They love the pleasure of tearing boxes open, banging things together as rapidly as possible. They love the feeling of completion. They love the process as long as it's active, energizing, and filled with physical or tangible challenge. *Builders* learn by doing.

***Merchants* (*love*) Talk and Listen in order to learn.**

Merchants (*love*-based people) learn by talking, by listening and sharing ideas, and by teaching. A strong *merchant* personality develops thoughts, ideas, understanding by expressing thoughts, and by refining the thoughts as he goes. *Merchants*, like *builders*, require lots of activity, but they enjoy being entertained or being the entertainer. This is not an autonomous process. With *merchants* there is almost always a partner in some sort of communication, mostly a person—not in books or on the computer screen. *Merchants* learn by talking and listening.

Innovators (*wisdom*) apply the "Observe and Solve" method in order to learn.

Innovators (*wisdom*-based people) learn by brainstorming and by problem-solving with others. They learn by sitting quietly studying the problem and asking questions. They need to remain in control of the learning process so they can determine which questions are asked next and with whom they will brainstorm in order to achieve the greatest understanding. *Innovators*, like *merchants*, teach others their conclusions and in this process refine their thinking. They come to a better understanding as they communicate their learning to others. *Innovators* learn by observing, making assessments, and solving problems.

Bankers (knowledge) learn by applying the "Read and Analyze" method.

Bankers (*knowledge*-based people) learn by reading and studying facts and information. Strong *bankers* seldom act without written plans and structures for action. They learn by gathering and analyzing facts. They have a deep desire to know what actions are appropriate, and they despise the idea of learning by making mistakes. They prefer studying each situation carefully, determining the most appropriate response through careful analysis, and then carefully taking action. By the time a *banker* decides to take action, the degree of certainty of outcome is very high. *Bankers* learn by reading and analyzing.

????????????????????????????

Each of these learning styles has definite advantages. Each has inherent weaknesses. Since each of us is a combination of *Core Value Energies*, some of us are exceptional learners, balancing several learning strategies carefully to fit different situations. All of us have our Achilles' heel when it comes to learning, and we pay an incredible price for our failure to adopt the learning styles of other types of contributors.

A strong *builder*, for instance—when balanced by a little team effort, a little more thoroughness in asking questions and brainstorming, and at least a few moments of careful planning and studying available information—will be incredibly stronger, more powerful, and more effective in the actions chosen.

The price of including these learning styles in a *builder's* life is a sense of slowing down and a slight loss of spontaneous verve that comes from taking an immediate action. The value gained is extraordinary: preservation of energy, doubling of *power* through inclusion of others, perfection of action and focus of activity toward well-considered goals, and minimization of failed choices. Instead of acting for the sake of action, the *power* person who is intentionally balanced in learning style is a prioritized, focused, irresistible force.

One of our *Taylor Protocols, Inc.*, clients, a strong *builder*, confessed recently that he was finally spending some time with his employees and management team, brainstorming and strategizing. His admission was that this process was giving him headaches. It was actually painful to spend time helping others think about, talk about, and come to conclusions that he had developed weeks or moments earlier.

His usual pattern of knowing what to do and commanding others to do it had not been successful. His people either rebelled openly or found ways to passively deflect his energy and ". . . do what they want to do anyway."

He was finding that his pain from time invested in this leadership process was paying big dividends. He was quickly getting where he wanted to go, where he could never have gotten without slowing down and working more effectively with others. The learning style of his team was so different from his own that he had to learn how to learn all over again. He did this by inviting his *love* and *wisdom* energies forward, by intentionally using his secondary *core values* in his leadership process.

He was proud of his progress. His decide-and-do style of learning was expanded to include a lot more observe-and-solve and talk-and-listen learning modes. By his own judgment, his decisions about what to do improved.

CEO Story

John, a *merchant* CEO of a small plastics manufacturing company, was similarly stuck in his own learning and managing process. *Merchants*, like *builders*, tend to be spontaneous and prone to quick action. They see the future and almost believe that it's already here because they can see it.

They act with a great deal of self-motivation and high energy. They like to please, so they can't imagine anyone saying they will do something and then not do it—especially an employee who might risk being fired for failure to perform. But time and again John's team was doing just that—promising performancc and not delivering.

Being a strong *merchant*, John was also comfortable coming up with action plans and great ideas that he wanted other people to implement. His contribution was to see what needed to be done and inspire others to work for him. He continued to push off work that he was the most qualified to perform, shaming and berating his team for not getting things done. He was constantly changing or adding to the vision, increasing the complexity of tasks required.

This is a classic problem faced by small business owners, an inability to effectively delegate. *Merchants* tend to fail by pushing too much off to others too quickly. Then *merchants* tend to fail by not requiring that anyone actually follow through, by not providing a formal system and good management to ensure that people know how to do what they are expected to do. *Merchants* often fail to require everyone to be measured in their performance.

Builders tend to fail in this same manner with little value on management and more on spontaneous action, or by never letting go: "I'll just do it myself." *Builders* can be so impatient with employees that the employees can never truly take responsibility. *Merchants* tend to push responsibility away. *Builders* tend to hold it all for themselves. Neither strategy creates an effective business solution.

Our *merchant* CEO finally began to understand his Achilles' heel and divided the tasks between his staff more appropriately. He retained the necessary responsibility for closing major accounts, for gathering the critical details of these new sales, and for overseeing the process of creating work orders that could be completed without conversation with his production staff. His company became profitable and sales increased exponentially in the following months.

His native learning style was balanced by the addition of more decide-and-do and by the read-and-analyze approach to learning. His company plans were now not just great visions, but well-founded, already-in-progress activity that was being measured and pushed to higher performance.

More Business Owner Stories

Another client, a strong *innovator*, was an exceptional woman, a design engineer and craftsman in the wood products industry. She was a master at creative design and able to create a constant stream of new products that were highly attractive to her retail outlets and buying customers. Her gift of design far outpaced her drive to generate new sales channels and completely overwhelmed her willingness to document and detail manufacturing drawings and specifications.

Her production staff was understandably frustrated, especially given the fact that she was intolerant of things, people, and actions that she considered to be stupid. Her employees would do everything they could to please her and build things right, but not having workable drawings, and not knowing what she really wanted, they would "make it wrong" over and over again. She was also notorious for coming up with product improvement in the middle of a production run. She would stop everything in order to put her new concepts into the products about to be shipped.

Sadly, she was not willing to modify this behavior and her company ended up in Chapter 7 bankruptcy with a Chapter 13 personal bankruptcy right behind it. She was stuck in the talk-and-listen, observe-and-solve mode of learning, and her company needed significantly different learning in order to succeed.

A more successful experience occurred with Glenda, a strong *banker* with a secondary *builder core value*. Glenda was given the opportunity to purchase her boss's failing manufacturing business. She had been the bookkeeper and production planner for the company for many years. She knew the customers, suppliers, creditors, and employees inside and out. She also had worked for a significant period of time as the production manager. Her qualifications to lead the company based upon experience were undeniable.

Glenda also had a critical flaw. Being a strong *banker*, she was driven to document everything far beyond the demands of a small entrepreneurial company, where some level of informality allows quicker response and necessary agility to meet opportunity. Her thoroughness and documentation slowed the business down significantly. Her tendency to over-control and over-document, however, would not have caused a survival threat, just slowed growth.

The fatal flaw was in her *banker's* requirement that everything be fair and just. This was an emotional immaturity, a personality flaw. She was constantly aware of vendor, creditor, and employee actions that to her were not right by her judgment. She compulsively fought to defend the business from unfair activities. The more she fought, the harder it was to get things done. She also became convinced that everyone was conspiring to defeat her and take the company away from her.

This was a difficult situation. Glenda had successfully pushed away several key vendors, antagonized creditors, and angered employees. Her required actions were very difficult for her *banker* personality. But, to her credit, she was willing and effective in *calling* all of the offended parties to apologize for her previous words and actions, asking for a second chance to build a better relationship.

Not having much of a *merchant's* value structure, she got little personal satisfaction out of this process. The business results, however, were amazing. We worked to connect her necessary actions with her *banker* values, talking with her about "appropriate" relationships, "doing the right thing," and being fair and just with people in her business community.

We worked from the basis that she needed to preserve the business structures and human resources that were critical to the company. Her goal was not to make friends, but to hold onto critical business alliances and people who would allow her to face a less risky future. Once she understood this, the task of making the phone calls and apologies was seen as a necessity, and she performed it well.

For each of these business owners, their choice to learn or not learn was crucial to the maintenance of their constructed life framework especially related to their profession. They put themselves in a position in which the requirement to learn these lessons came often and with critical force. The one question that was asked of each of them, regardless of their *Core Values Nature* was: **Why are you here?**

This question for us means: Why have you unconsciously chosen to be in this situation? What is it that you need to learn in order to live your life and fulfill your mission?

For each of them, their first answers to this question were directly related to their work and their occupation. I am here to make this business work. I am here because I have worked hard to get here. I am here to feed my family and build a company. I am here because I was given a great opportunity.

All of these things are true and reasonable responses, but they are not the overriding or the underlying reasons. These socially and financially based answers are not the real issue at all. They had each created a life framework that included running a business for the unexpressed purpose of learning their next essential lesson; a lesson about how to be a better version of their innate *Core Values Nature*, and how to make a greater contribution. This, I believe, is why all of us are where we are, all on our way to some extent to our right job, our role in society in which we will make our highest and best contribution.

The most powerful way we all learn is through the experiences of our lives. We continue to repeat failures or difficulties in new settings until we finally conquer the personal development step that these life situations make important. The spiritual law that governs this is simple. For every unconscious choice we make, we each create a life situation that provides the opportunity to make a different choice. Until we make this new decision consciously, we will continue to repeat old patterns, setting up similar situations that give us the opportunity to learn.

Some people hear this as oppressive. No matter how greatly we succeed, there will always be another test, another demonstration of our failings—more pain to experience.

Others see the cup half full: I will never run out of challenges. I will always be given the opportunity to grow, to develop new skills, to learn new thoughts, to make a better contribution. Life will always be stimulating and rewarding. Like an acorn, I will continue growing until I die.

I see it as a cup that can be full: There is no other way to truly live. It is a challenge worthy of my attention and life energy. It is a challenge worthy of my capacity to make a contribution and to be a unique presence of *love*, *wisdom*, *power*, and *knowledge*. I cannot think of anything I would rather ***be***; a fully actualized contributing individual.

24

The Nature of My Participation in Society

We will discuss in later chapters the vocational and occupational choices we each make. These life-framing choices are the reflection of deeper, more fundamental choices we make concerning our participation in society. What we need to talk about first is the nature of this participation. There are many aspects to our participation decisions. We generally choose to participate from one side or the other of many different value-based positions:

Intuitive	*vs.*	*Cognitive*
Proactive		Reserved
Gregarious		Observant
Spontaneous		Organized
Emotional		Rational
Leader		Supporter
Expressive		Steady Energy
Visual		Cerebral
High Energy		Quiet thoughtfulness

Independence	*vs.*	*Community*
Experiential		Experimental
Expressive		Reserved
Verbose (Talkative)		Contemplative (Thoughtful)
Heart		Mind
Teaching		Learning
Proactive		Reactive

Inquisitive		Instructive
Problem-solving		Risk-reducing
Creative	*vs.*	***Practical***
Visionary		Focused
Aesthetic		Work-oriented
Curious		Reality-based
Opportunistic		Realistic
Resourceful		Reliable
Open		Concrete
Resilient		Forceful and Steady
Abstract		

All of these comparative personality dispositions may be based upon our *core values* (*power*, *love*, *wisdom*, *knowledge*), or they may be based upon the related fears caused by the pains we experienced as we developed our personalities. In other words, we show up in our daily lives almost the same way every day, and people would describe us using some of the words above. This is the nature of our current participation in society.

This mix of personality fear-based participation and *Real Core Values Self* is the primary contributor to our successes and failures. You can be average in talent, intelligence, and skill and succeed greatly by becoming a consciously intentional contributing presence.

Ask five of your closest friends or family members which of the words above most closely describe you. Remember, they will reflect back to you the person you are showing yourself to be when you are with them. Two friends may provide distinctly different responses. This is not true of the *Core Values Index* (*CVI*).

When we are strongly inclined toward the tendencies in the left column, we find ourselves sometimes at greater risk than we would like to experience—subject to visible failures, embarrassment, overstatement, exposed positions, caught in a weak position in a negotiating situation. We find ourselves needing to pull back, to slow down, to rethink and consider alternatives to organize and maintain a structure. When we are *strongly* inclined toward the tendencies in the left column, we are likely to be unfounded, over-reactive, without clear plans, and in danger more often.

When we are inclined toward the dispositions in the right column, we find ourselves limited in our options, losing position to those who are more reactive and faster paced. We are missing the limelight (recognition), sitting back while other, sometimes less capable people take the leadership position and head us the wrong way. We may be right, but because we do not act as quickly and as assertively as others our *knowledge* and *wisdom* goes to waste.

When we are predisposed to favor the right column, we pay the price of unwanted consequences because we do not choose to act quickly enough. We lose relationship opportunities because we do not open ourselves enough so that others may connect with us and hold on to us.

It is likely that as you read down the columns you find yourself saying "Yes, that's me" to many of the descriptors and a strong "No" to others. Regardless of which side of the world you view life from, the words in the opposite column are those that will bring more balance and control (success) into your life. We can choose to learn to include the alternative *core values* dispositions if we have sufficient energy in our innate nature (quadrants with higher than 14 *CVI* points). If not, we need to find people or systems that reduce our need for those *core values* in some situations.

This is the "razor's edge" of life. This does not encourage an effort to change your natural disposition. It is an effort to cause you to be willing to see the situations in which you are least successful at getting what you want. For these situations a change of strategy is required. The change is not a self-willed change in behavior. The change is a conscious shift from one *Core Value Energy* to another: to decide to be the presence of *power* in the situation, instead of continuing to be the presence of *knowledge.*

This is a moment-by-moment, situation-by-situation decision. We are made aware of ineffectiveness by: a sense of anxiety, a negative emotion, or an unexpected and overly strong reaction from someone else. Other clues come from inner talking and physiological messages like tight muscles, sick feelings, twitching eyelids and fluttering heart, etc. This causes us to know it is time to make a decision about our state of being. We need to consciously choose to *be* a different *Core Value Energy.*

We think and make a decision to shift from the *core value* we are currently aligned with, into being one of our other personally strong *Core Value Energies.*

I am not proposing that it is important to create perfect balance in one's life between these social tendencies or within the *core values.* I do propose that by telling ourselves the truth about the cost and gain we experience in each polarity of strategies and choices, we can move more rapidly toward our desired happiness and fulfillment.

When we are acting clearly on one side of a value issue and not achieving what we want, the answer is to shift toward the other side for a while through at least one conscious decision process and then evaluate the results.

This process refers back to the discussion about the fact that we hold strong preference for tactical values in all *core value* quadrants. It is not our goal to change, but to fully actualize ourselves by including all of our available strategic and tactical values in our conscious choices for maximum effectiveness—to include them at the approximate relative balance that they exist uniquely within each of us.

If you are in a life situation or job point that requires you to operate more than 20–30% from your minor *core value,* you are facing the unconscious decision to negotiate a change in role or circumstance. If not successful in negotiations, choose to take your life into your own hands and set out to find your place of highest and best contribution. This new role of life structure will also naturally yield greater joy and happiness.

The only sure way to happiness and fulfillment is through meaningful work and meaningful participation. All meaning derives from choosing to be *who we are* in a given situation. Being *who we are* in a given situation means to act as we are predisposed by our *Real Core Values Self* to contribute the most important aspect of self to our society.

Life moves forward more certainly when we consciously shift our spiritual and social strategies, when we take a risk and move slightly outside our patterned disposition toward an alternate *core value*, or the opposite side of our most comfortable type of contribution. The requirement is not a movement over to the other side as a lifetime discipline, it is a shifting in that direction, at this moment, and for this specific circumstance.

Learning to do this efficiently requires that we learn to select the opportunities and practice being the less-used *Core Value Energy* as often as possible until we become practiced in the strategies and tactics of that little-used *Core Values Nature*.

We have been taught to believe that our observed social nature is our God-given nature, and we can't do anything about it. There is some truth to this, so we take it on like a life curse and use this belief to rationalize away all responsibility (accountability) for our lives: I didn't choose to be this way, I was born this way.

This is what many of us tend to think when our lives are giving us one disappointment after the other. But our conscious view of ourselves is through the eyes of our adapted personality—at the behavioral level. We want to be living at the *core values, real self* level—at a place of being, not at the place of behaving.

To believe our personality is God-given is an error in thinking and is an act of rationalization, not an act of contribution and participation. To believe that our innate unchanging *Core Values Nature* is our *real* nature is right thinking. This right thinking does not excuse us from accountability; it heightens it. We can't change *who we are*, but we can learn to be all we are meant to be. We can learn to always *be what we are* and therefore to always *be* contributing instead of settling into personality, grasping—taking and getting.

The distinction between our *Real Core Values Self*, founded on a set of *core values*, and this self-rationalizing ego-based thinking is the presence or absence of fear in our decision-making process. We will work on the ability to be conscious of our fears and the process of un-warping in later chapters.

25

What Is My Life Purpose?

This is the question that seeks to understand the nature of one's contribution, the meaning of an individual life. What effect am I supposed to have on the world, with people, for society, for individuals? At the end of my life, what will my life's work look like in terms of contribution? What effect did I have on others? Have I made a difference by being here and by doing my work?

The most important self-knowledge is the discovery of one's deepest *Real Core Values Self.*

It is not rational to propose that the four *core values* developed within our *Core Values Index* (*CVI*) are necessarily a complete picture of each person's *Core Values Nature*. However, most people who complete the *CVI* are impressed with the accuracy of its characterization of their deepest innate self, their most organic person.

Many have expressed that "this is the best picture of the *real me*, that I have ever gotten." It is reasonable to use this assessment tool to get a clear picture of our inner landscape. The *CVI* does provide a picture of this innate self that is extraordinarily unique. The chances that you and I would ever choose all of the same strategic values that comprise the ten-minute *CVI* assessment are astronomical.

THE ODDS ARE

10,314,424,798,490,500,000,000,000,000 to 1.
Population of the Earth 6,700,000,000

It will be a long time before any two of us are born with identical innate values.

Odds That You and I Will Select All of the Same Tactical Values in the CVI

10 Octillion
314 Septillion
424 Sextillion
798 Quintillion
490 Quadrillion
500 Trillion
to One

Or, 229,771,103 times the Earth's population squared.

These are the odds that you and I will select all of the same Strategic and Tactical values in *the Core Values Index.*

This makes a pretty strong demonstration of the uniqueness of each of us as a person, despite the masses of other Homo sapiens creatures occupying our planet. The question, then, "*why* am I here on this earth?" becomes a sensible query, since the answer for each of us will be different. The clue to the answer (the nature of the answer) is really quite simple.

Each of us as a person has a unique recipe of *core values*. These values—*power*, *wisdom*, *knowledge*, and *love*—simultaneously serve as our deepest motivational drivers, for the selection of a preferred strategy at any moment in time. This general strategy then is fleshed out by our unique recipe of preferred strategic values and a large menu of tactical values that motivate specific behaviors. In this way we deliver or actualize our *Core Value Energy* of choice at this given moment.

The question, "why am I here?" from this perspective can be answered, "I am here to participate with my society as with my *Real Core Values Self* and behave in a manner that delivers benefits (my *Core Value Energies* contributions) to myself, my family, my society, and to the world at large."

This is the social level of understanding.

At the psychological level of understanding, the answer may be, "I will be appreciated and valued for the contributions I make to my society by authentically expressing my unique *Core Values Nature.*" I will *be* who I am predisposed to *be.*

This psychological level connects us to our sense of purpose on the physical plane. My personal sense of self-respect and the feeling of being of value to others are enhanced every time I act in alignment with my strongest *core values.* I also increase effectiveness and therefore self-respect when I consciously shift into a lesser *core value* in order to be a more effective contributor. The psychological answer includes the universal mission to Know Thyself, and to learn to be the master of your own person.

Another way to better describe this sense of purpose is that I *am* my *Real Core Values Self,* which is made up of the four different energies. I *am* the presence of available *power, wisdom, knowledge,* and *love,* in a unique blend of these energies. When I walk into the room, I am the presence of these energies, available to make my contribution of these energies to others.

This is the spiritual level of reality: I am here to be *who I am*, a unique recipe of *love*, *power*, *knowledge*, and *wisdom*. I am here to contribute my *real self* to this world. The values that motivate me to act or behave in certain ways are the contributions I am *called* to make to the world in which I live. I am here to *be who I am*, and make that count for something.

This is the primary message in Abraham Maslow's seminal book, *Toward a Psychology of Being*. He introduced the concept that each of us has an innate unchanging nature that is our real person. With the *Core Values Index*, we are able for the first time to characterize this innate unchanging nature and to quantify or measure the various *Core Value Energies* that exist in each of us at uniquely different levels.

When the *core values* perspective is used as our first exploration of this important question (why am I here?), we are missing several important human nature ingredients: 1) our wired-in interests and passions, 2) our sense of being called into a certain kind of role in society, 3) our sense of magnitude of our mission, the magnitude of impact we expect to create from our personal contribution, and 4) the basic skills and attributes each person has as a physical animal: intelligence (nature and magnitude), talents, aptitudes (skills), physical dexterity, strength, flexibility, speed, etc.

In other words, the physical attributes join with our *Core Values Nature* and form a capable *core value* presence, whose contribution can best be made through a specific occupation within a specific vocation, with multiple avocations, in response to the person's sense of where he belongs—his *callings*. All of these essential ingredients of our unique person dictate our place of *highest and best use*, our role in life through which our *Core Value Energies* may best be engaged and delivered.

In other words, we are here to *be who we are* and to *do* what it is we are best able (suited) to do. In this role we are called to fulfill our mission at the magnitude of total contribution that we are wired to make.

What we choose to do in order to be highly effective and fulfilled as individuals must be activities that convey to the world our deepest innate self. We are happiest when we are working in a position in which we are required to use our skills in alignment with our *core values*, for the delivery of our *core values* to our society.

We also want to be learning more skills, gaining more *wisdom*, *knowledge*, *love*, and *power* in the proportional balance of our inner *Core Values Nature*.

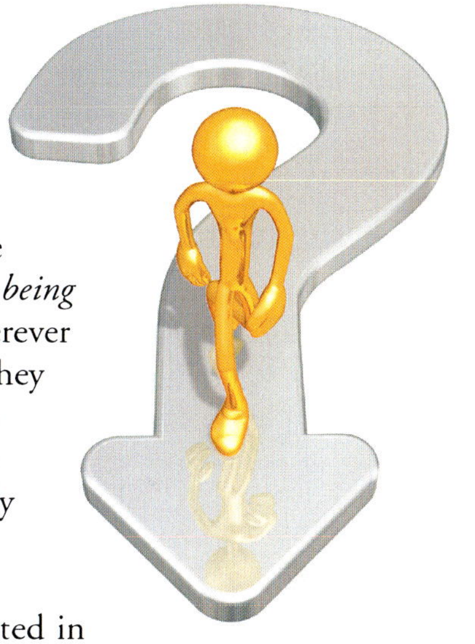

Some people are dramatically weighted in their preference toward only two of the *core values*. Some so strongly prefer one value that they spend 90% or more of their time acting in alignment with—*being*—that one *core value*. They spend most of their time *being* the *power*, *love*, *knowledge*, or *wisdom* wherever they are. We call these people profound: They have the profound presence of one of the *Core Value Energies*. They essentially are here to primarily be and to contribute only one of the *Core Value Energies*.

But even these people are multifaceted in their participation in society.

Each of the four *core values* join each of the other *core values* strategically to make a special kind of contribution. A person who is profoundly oriented toward *power*, for instance, is a *practical*, *intuitive*, and *independent* contributor in some level of weighted preferences for these *types of contribution*.

The Six Contribution Types

Every quadrant (*Core Value Energy)* competes with every other *Core Value Energy*. This is the cause of conflict even on highly functional teams. When people with strong dominance in all four quadrants get together there is a guaranteed divergence of strategy and disagreement about priority. Every *Core Value Energy* also shares common values with every other quadrant. It is these shared values that cause each of us to exhibit and rely upon different types of contributory strategies and tactics.

Intuitive—Merchant and *Builder* / *Love* and *Power*

Share. *Love* and *power* share spontaneity, energy, *intuitive* decisions, leaps of faith, and tolerance for risk. *Intuitive* contribution is the strongest type of contribution when *power* and *love* are the dominant and secondary *core values.*

Conflict. *Love* and *power* conflict because both values want to determine who works with whom, who does what, and how the team feels. *Power* wants focused energy and compliance with direct commands. *Love* wants shared energy and enthusiasm based upon mutual regard with requests for help and invitations to participate in creating wonderful envisioned end results.

Cognitive—Banker and *Innovator* / *Knowledge* and *Wisdom*

Share. *Knowledge* and *wisdom* create the requirement to think and reason; refuse to decide without strong processed information and applied reason. For *cognitive* people, intuition is risky and unreliable.

Conflict. Both want to control the process of analysis or logical flow. Want to decide when enough information and enough thinking is enough and what the right conclusion really is.

Creative—Merchant and *Innovator* / *Love* and *Wisdom*

Share. *Love* and *wisdom.* Imagining what can be—how to create something new—joy of brainstorming and sharing ideas and visions. *Creativity* is the shared type.

Conflict. *Love* and *wisdom* both want control over long-term vision, form, function, and feel of systems and processes, plus control over the *creative* process itself.

Practical—Builder and *Banker* / *Power* and *Knowledge*

Share. *Power* and *knowledge* create the requirement that all energy and work generate positive results—tangible and measurable.

Conflict. Both want to determine how much energy and where. *Power* does not fear trial-and-error waste. *Knowledge* hates waste.

Community—Merchant and *Banker* / *Love* and *Knowledge*

Share. Teamwork, desire for functional and satisfying team/*community*. Need *community* in order to fulfill their prime missions. *Love*—joyful communion and shared vision. *Knowledge*—organized peacefulness and safe environment for all with sufficient resources for long-term survival and vision.

Conflict. Want to control the nature of the *community*. *Love*, how does it feel? *Knowledge*, how does it function? Both ask, what is its purpose, and do the people work satisfactorily together?

Independent—Builder and *Innovator* / *Power* and *Wisdom*

Share. Self-sufficiency. Figure out what to do and do it. No need for anyone else's energy or problem-solving.

Conflict. Both want control of the process. *Power* wants very little process and very fast action. *Wisdom* requires a lot of process and a reasonable pace, and commitment to strategically sound action.

In the effort to answer the question, "why am I here?" each of us builds on our unique *core values*, seeking a place in the world from which and within which we can contribute all of who we are, in a role where what is needed is *who* I am at the deepest *core values* level. When this is the positive agenda of a given person, that person generally tends to be an effective leader or team member and others tend to encourage his or her participation.

What would a successful life look like for me?

What elements must be present in my life in order for me to feel happy and fulfilled?

This question of composition of personal life once again opens huge areas for exploration, and ultimately many important choices. In order to deal with this question at all, we must not only have a good picture of our *core values*, and of our talents and other physical attributes, but also our sense of magnitude of purpose, our magnitude of mission.

When working to develop a clear picture of one's successful life—envisioning our future, some of us have a sense (or a *calling*) that we belong at the head of major corporations effecting tens of thousands, even millions of lives. Others feel that their place is in a small shop where they will personally deal with each customer, one person at a time. In both cases, the *Core Values Nature*, the type of participation, and contribution may be quite similar.

26

What Are You Called to Do?

Your Calling

The following is a brief list of *callings* common among people. You will notice that some of these *callings* have professions that carry the name, such as Teacher. But many people whose *calling* is to be a Teacher find themselves teaching in a broad range of professions. Each of these professional positions allows a full expression of the Teacher in these people.

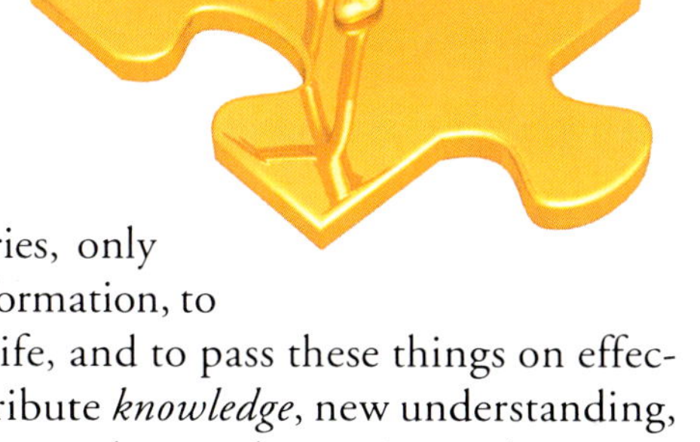

To be a Teacher has no boundaries, only the requirement to learn important information, to understand important things about life, and to pass these things on effectively to others. The *calling* is to contribute *knowledge*, new understanding, quality relationships, or essential skills to others and to society at large.

This same cross-vocational nature is true for all *callings*.

Prophets, for instance, may find themselves functioning as Market Strategists or Strategic Planners. Theologians may find themselves in the field of psychiatry. Scientists may work as Product Designers for biotech companies. Hunters may be employed as merger and acquisition experts.

Below is a reasonably complete list of *callings*. Circle those that most resound in you. It is generally more effective to read this list aloud to yourself, or have someone else read the list to you with your eyes closed and in a quiet place. This allows the subconscious mind to have a more direct impact on the conscious mind.

Teacher	Theologian	Shop Owner	Scientist
Minister/Priest/Rabbi	Poet	Banker	Politician
Philosopher	Storyteller	Wealth Manager	Sports Player
Crisis Manager	Historian	Caregiver	Music Director
Problem-Solver	Prophet	Physician	Composer
Technician	Counselor	Healer	Writer
Inventor	Farmer	Musician	Mystic
Hunter	Builder	Actor	Miner
Business Leader	Scholar	Servant	Artist
Mathematician	Host/Hostess	Playwright	Dancer
Soldier	Rancher	Financier	Life Coach
Sports Coach	Commander	Project Manager	Director—Stage
Hospice Worker	Retail Sales Person	Construction Worker	Director—Movies

Note: The above list is incomplete, but it is important to understand that we are not trying to make a complete list of types of jobs. These are overarching roles in life that are callings to make certain *types of contribution*. All of the above roles can be fulfilled in jobs that do not immediately appear to be directly related to the work of the calling.

As a general rule each of us has a combination of two or three or more of these callings, one more dominant than the others. As we venture through life, working to make our decisions more consciously, we find that each new career opportunity expands our ability to pursue these *callings*, often within the same career position.

Sometimes we may obtain new freedom in a job that opens opportunities to experience other *callings* outside of our primary employment.

Once you have identified your *callings*, choose the one that is most dominant in you. Look at all of the facets of your life framework: job, family, spouse, hobbies, sports, avocations, religion, politics, social service, etc. How many of these life-framework activities are centered around or significantly involve your central *calling*?

Can you see where your second- and third-level *callings* are being exercised in your life?

If the answer is yes, continue on your journey, simply becoming more conscious of your *callings* and their fundamental contribution to your life's framework.

If the answer is no, or not as much as you would like, it's time to modify the framework of your life to include more of your *callings*—within your current activities and by adding new elements to your life framework.

Each person's primary calling generally requires expression of all of that person's unique Core Values Nature, in approximately the same level as their different capacities for their most dominant Core Value Energies.

There is a direct link between a person's *calling* and his talents, *Core Values Nature*, and innate passions. The *calling* is the social, physical observable expression of the inner person. It is a role in life that requires a certain kind of participation that results in a certain kind of contribution. It is important to recognize this connection in order to move forward as an individual.

Each *calling* is a direct translation of a person's *Real Core Values Self* into a societal role that optimizes the contribution of the person while simultaneously setting up circumstances that afford constant growth challenges—the further integration of a person's *core values* into social context.

As each of us becomes more aware of our *Real Core Values Self*, as we become more conscious of our daily choices—relative to the expression of our passions in the context of our own lives—the reality of a personal *calling* becomes more and more apparent to us. We begin to align our activities, thoughts, and learning, through the intentional pursuit of fulfillment through the activities and contributions of our chosen/given *calling*.

As we progress through our lives, each decision at each fork in the road becomes more and more weighted with the understanding that the choices we are most compelled to make will be the ones that promise the fullest expression of our *Real Core Values Self* and provide our next essential lesson.

At *Taylor Protocols*, our mantra is: Every person in the right place, doing the right work, learning the next essential lesson.

This statement of focus is based in the knowledge that people are most productive when they are in a position that allows full expression of their *core values* and their passions. They are also the happiest in a position that assures that they are also the least disruptive and most focused or engaged.

This mantra further acknowledges that we are not just personalities and a physical presence; we are not just our talents and skills: We as individuals are also "what we do." *Who we are* is the essence of our highest and best contribution.

It is critical for each of us to build a life framework that allows full expression of our innate *Core Values Nature* and our innate talents as aligned with our *callings*. Our work must be meaningful in order for happiness to exist, in order for fulfillment to be achieved.

Personal learning is a significant part of this process.

In order to better fulfill our purpose, we must find a work position that offers constant, important learning directly aligned with our *core values* as expressed through our passions and our *calling*. This position must provide daily learning that propels us along our life path toward a sense of meaningful living. The most energizing work usually also involves a requirement to further perfect some of our more important skills and talents—in order to contribute our most dominant values.

We are called forward along this pathway, and the pathway becomes more and more visible, as we consciously choose work positions and life roles that afford these personal growth opportunities.

When new employees are invited to join *Taylor Protocols, Inc.*, they are given a copy of the following poem along with their employment contract.

To Be of Use
By Marge Piercy

The people I love the best
Jump into work head first
Without dallying in the shallows
And swim off with sure strokes almost out of sight.
They seem to become natives of that element,
The black sleek heads of seals
Bouncing like half-submerged balls.

I love people who harness themselves, an ox to a heavycart,
Who pull like water buffalo, with massive patience,
Who strain in the mud and the muck to move things forward,
Who do what has to be done, again and again.

I want to be with people who submerge
In the task, who go into the fields to harvest
And work in a row and pass the bags along,
Who are not parlor generals and field deserters
But move in common rhythm
When the food must come in or the fire be put out.

The work of the world is common as mud.
Botched, it smears the hands, crumbles to dust.
But the thing worth doing, done well

Has a shape that satisfies, clean and evident.
Greek amphoras for wine or oil,
Hopi vases that held corn are put in museums
But you know they were made to be used.
The pitcher cries for water to carry
And a person for work that is real.

Welcome to Taylor Protocols.com.
You have been invited to join us
Because we know you are a worker,
One of the "The people I love the best . . ."

Thanks for joining us.
Lynn E. Taylor
President

In this manner each person is reminded to be conscious of their daily work, of their meaningful contribution, and of their purpose for existence. We are also reminded to throw themselves passionately into our work life in pursuit of new learning, new skills, and new and greater expressions of our *Real Core Values Self*, our unique recipe of *power*, *love*, *wisdom*, and *knowledge*.

The gift of this poem at the outset of new employment also creates a sense of our expectation that new employees will be committed to their work with us. Equally strong is the message from us that we are committed as a company to support each person's personal development at the deepest level.

We are committed to careful construction of job functions that fully align with each person's *core values*, positions that require the full expression of each person's *callings*. If we can align each person's work with his unique recipe of *core values*, we obtain the highest productivity and contribution he is able to make. We also provide job satisfaction. In exchange we receive long-term commitment and passionate work.

Part of our employment process asks the question, "Why do you want to be here with us?" We are looking for people who want more than a job.

We want people who are passionately connected with a sense of mission and who are ready for their next essential life lesson.

Our commitment to each person is to work diligently to keep them in a position that is "right" for them, a position that provides the "right" opportunity for meaningful work, aligned with their passions to the highest degree achievable.

The ideal vocation for each person requires consistent and nearly constant opportunity for the pursuit of one's calling—the application of a person's unique recipe of core values and innate skills and talents.

It is critical to place people in positions that align with their life *calling*. We can err and put people in situations that provide reasonable expression of their *core values* but do not align well with their *calling*. We will see in this case a short-term sense of excitement and good energy thrown at the work required of them, but soon the newness of the position wears off.

Reality sets in.

The daily activities harmonize with one's *core values* but do not allow a full expression of one's physical talents, intellectual prowess, and curiosity—the things that flesh out a person's sense of *calling*. The work feels momentarily energizing but provides little sense of fulfillment.

This factor is at the foundation of one of our strongest *Taylor Protocols*, our *New Science of Employment Pre-Selection*™.

A fundamental part of this pre-selection process is the identification of the primary contribution of the job. This is a statement of purpose for the position that includes a description of the nature of the contribution along with a clear delineation of the way this contribution converts to return on investment for the employer.

Two important, inter-related issues are merged in this process: 1) the employee is provided a clear mandate and commissioning for the work he is asked to do and in a manner that is easy to connect to his most dominant *core values*, and 2) the employer gets a clear agreement and commitment to the required contribution, and ultimate accountability is established.

There is little need for invasive management in these situations, since the work for the employee is fully engaging and fulfilling in its contribution of value to the company. And the employer has a worker who is fully engaged in the work, so a return on investment far beyond usual expectations is achieved.

To the degree that my work assignment is aligned with my *calling*, I will experience a charge of energy, new enthusiasm, a continuous increase in personal respect.

To the degree that my work is not aligned with my *calling*, I will experience restlessness, boredom, a drain of energy, and demotivation. I will begin to disrupt the work environment in an unconscious attempt to cause a change that will take me to a situation in which my *calling* will be more fully realized.

This process begs to be accomplished consciously, and becomes more and more intentional as we become clear about our *core values* and our *callings.*

In order to create a fulfilling life, each of us is compelled to find additional outlets and expressions of our primary calling and any secondary callings within and outside the work environment.

A balanced, fulfilling life consists of activities and relationships that infuse the whole life with opportunity to express *core values* and to fulfill our sense of purpose.

It is not reasonable to expect that one's job will provide all of this opportunity. But it is ridiculous to believe that one's job is a necessary evil and is not a part of our spiritual and social development journey.

The job goes better when life is balanced with other activities that encourage the contribution of our *core values.* The rest of our life works better when our occupational activities require an increasing level of commitment to our *callings* and to our *Real Core Values Self* in order to succeed.

Secondary callings must also be given full expression throughout one's life in order to experience happiness.

Life does not feel full and thrilling if only our central *calling* is being exercised and honored. We have secondary *callings* and sometimes third- and fourth-level *core values* that serve to enrich our lives and make us more effective. When a person consciously constructs his life framework to allow the contributions of *core values* and fulfillment of secondary *callings*, happiness develops and continues.

Each individual's sense of self-respect is directly proportional to the degree of fulfillment of his calling(s).

We feel good about ourselves when we are engaged in activities that harmonize with *core values.*

We feel purposeful and positively challenged when we are busy learning, doing, discussing, sharing our talents and gifts in direct alignment with our *callings.*

Fulfillment is not something we achieve at the end of a lifetime of arduous work, education, and struggle. Fulfillment exists in each moment during which we are engaged in the processes of our lives that connect with and are expressions of our inner selves: our *Real Core Values Self,* our innate talents, attributes, and our *callings.*

We can claim a strong sense of fulfillment anytime we pause to acknowledge and appreciate our contribution to life through these pursuits.

Fulfillment of one's *calling* requires the visualization and actualization of a life framework, including an occupation that requires and accommodates one's *calling(s)*.

Remember, however, even though this pause to witness and even to measure contribution provides a momentary sense of fulfillment or gratification (such as stopping to consciously declare our sexual pleasure or to admire a moment of happiness), once we have stopped living our life long enough to admire its contributions to date, our sense of fulfillment is in the past, and we are once again charged with restlessness to do more and to get better at doing it.

Happiness is realized by making momentary choices that work to fulfill our calling.

So the more we remain in the *flow* of timeless *Real Work*, making choices that lead to freer, more effective expression of our *core values* through our *callings*, the faster we progress, the more we contribute, and the more fulfilled we feel. This is happiness. Staying in the *flow* of this kind of living is the central practice of a fulfilled and meaningful life.

Happiness is available to us at all times, but only through learning, work, and recreation that align with *core values* and require contributions from our *callings*. Happiness is not enjoyment of an experience, it is not even the exhilaration of our *Real Core Values Self* through meaningful participation. Real happiness continues in us when we are resting after a meaningful participation.

Mihaly Csikszentmihalyi, author of the renowned book, *Flow*, in an interview with *Wired Magazine*, described *flow* as "being completely involved in an activity for its own sake. The ego falls away. Time flies. Every action, movement, and thought follows inevitably from the previous one, like playing jazz. Your whole being is involved, and you're using your skills to the utmost."

To achieve a flow state, a balance must be struck between the challenge of the task and the skill of the performer. If the task is too easy or too difficult, flow cannot occur.

The flow state also implies a kind of *focused attention*, and indeed it has been noted that mindfulness meditation, yoga, and martial arts seem to improve a person's capacity for flow. Among other benefits, all of these activities train and improve attention.

In short: *flow* could be described as a state where attention, motivation, and the situation meet, resulting in a kind of productive harmony or feedback.

Our *Core Values Index* puts a new consciousness and understanding of our unique *Core Values Nature* into play so we can each now learn how to put ourselves into this kind of flow experience, at work and at play.

27

Choosing My Occupation

Once we become reasonably clear about our unique mixture of *core values*, passions, and *callings*, we can begin to consciously seek education and training to enhance the basic passions and innate talents associated with our *callings*. Our innate intellectual interests and emotional dispensations have already led us toward our passions by way of curiosity, enjoyment, and capacity to succeed in tasks related to our passions.

We begin the process of consciously engaging our passions by building a portfolio of practiced and refined talents and experiences. This encourages us to move forward while also supporting our representations to others regarding our capabilities to perform the functions required by our desired job (specific assignments within our vocation). This leads us to the opportunity for full expression of our passions and the contribution of our *core values* in and through an appropriate job/social context.

The culmination of this process is a constant increase in our talents and gifts, a constant improvement of alignment of our experiences and skills with our passions, leading to the highest and best contribution of our *Real Core Values Self* to this world.

We increase our sense of fulfillment as we simultaneously increase our knowledge, expertise, and practiced talent base. This effort, combined with the greater effort of naming and recognizing our fears so we can freely express our passions, gives meaning and purpose to our lives. This leads to our fulfillment as a human being, spiritually, mentally, physically, and socially.

Subconsciously, it is our desire to put ourselves in a role where this fulfillment process can best be realized. *Core Values Alignment*™ causes us to choose our jobs and even the specific company, organization, or business within which we work. For most of us, this is to a large degree unconsciously driven on both the positive and negative sides. This can only happen effectively if we are not making critical life choices out of fear.

On the negative side, we tend to select a spot for ourselves that allows a close replication of some childhood drama that still has important limiting effects on us. We only call this side negative because it is charged with negative emotions and is still almost completely unconscious in nature. Within the interactions of this kind of environment we are often made to feel at risk in relationship with someone or something else.

Certain circumstances cause us to move into a protective mode, and we find ourselves acting out in a manner that appears out of context and exaggerated to others. Being in this subconsciously chosen spot gives us the opportunity to face old childhood fears, unresolved grief, and losses, and allows us to work through them. But this is not our place of highest and best contribution.

In this process, parts of our ego-based personality die away and a new passion-driven, spiritually energized *Core Values Nature* is allowed to come to the forefront. Our *core values* reclaim that portion of our personal territory and begin making a clean contribution.

Often we have to shift from a dominant or secondary *Core Value Energy* in order to achieve this new success.

In this way, we change the strategy we have habitually used in a given circumstance and select a new value-based strategy. This change of strategy on our part automatically requires a different response from the people around us, giving both parties the opportunity to make things work better.

This individuation process supports the positive side of our spiritual development process.

The jobs we choose within the companies for which we work also tend to offer us many opportunities to explore and develop our strongest passions and talents. As we learn more and take on new challenges, our sense of excitement, purpose, and fulfillment increases. This results in an increase in our ability to express our passions and make the life contributions that align with our *core values*.

To the degree we have an outlet within our job framework that requires expression of our passions, we are nurtured as a complete human being and encouraged to continue growing.

Note: Some people wake up to find themselves in a job environment that is only providing the childhood drama opportunities. In this work environment there is little or no nurturing of their individual passions. These people feel and are stuck in an unworkable situation. It does little or no good, however, to simply change jobs, blaming the stuck feeling on the work environment.

These persons need to become aware of their *Real Core Values Self*, their passionate self, so they can work through their childhood issues. It is always preferable to make a change by moving toward something, rather than moving away from, or escaping a bad situation, or trying to change ineffective behavior.

When the grass appears greener on the other side of the fence, we are caught in the trap of forgetting how we contributed to the dying grass on our side of the fence.

As long as real harm or significant loss is not imminent, we should usually stay where we are, facing the fears and childhood dramas that we have created around us until we become aware of these issues and find a more effective way to deal with them. This single principle, that there are no greener pastures, is the driving force behind the creation of the *Core Values Index* (*CVI*).

The *CVI* provides a *practical* tool for identifying and developing more-effective strategies within our life dramas.

There is no ideal situation (greener grass) that nurtures the spiritual, passionate self while providing an environment free from fear and childhood dramas. We tend to re-create these childhood dramas with anyone, in any situation that in any way approximates some childhood situation or relationship. We do this until we have essentially replaced that part of our adaptive behavior with a consciously chosen *Core Values Strategy.*

This finally creates greener grass all around us.

This is truly why there are no greener pastures "over there." We are amazingly *creative* people when it comes to re-creation of dramas and circumstances that give us as adults the opportunity to make more accountable, more effective decisions than we did as a child.

As a child, it was appropriate for us to react to some of life's circumstances with a defensive, survival strategy. As adults, we have the choice to act from a position of conscious clarity and strength rather than from these learned stimulus and response mechanisms. This is the difference between a life lived at the personality and behavioral level and one that is consciously driven by the *Real Core Values Self.*

As we have discussed, our fear-based survival mechanisms played a large role in our early years because we truly were more vulnerable to the adults who *did have* absolute power over us. This absolute power became less and less prevalent as we approached adulthood, but the feelings of jeopardy, embarrassment, and shame have not simply gone away due to the passing of time.

??????????????????????????

There is a spiritual principle at work here.

The Credits and Debits Principle:

Negative emotions and behaviors have accrued years of emotional and behavioral *debits* (emotionally charged fears and responses). These memories and feelings are stored in our reticular receiver in our brain stem, if they are traumatic in nature, or in our cerebral cortex memory bank if nontraumatic, stored for future reference. These *debits* are used to make unconscious choices about what actions are most beneficial in certain challenging situations.

In order to change these emotions and behaviors, we must accumulate an equal amount of positive *credits* (positive affirmations, self-confidence, and adamant commitment to one aspect of our *Real Core Values Self*). This requires a growing conscious awareness of our *Real Core Values Self.*

In every situation, in every relationship with every person, whatever our negative emotion, in response to whatever fear we may have experienced, we carry a commitment to these fears and negative emotions, equal to all the energy invested in these fears and emotions over the course of our lifetime. This is how we build up the *debit* side of this equation.

The greater the emotional response, the greater the fear. The greater the fear, the greater is our emotional connection to our learned related behavior. Situations that have happened more often created these *debits* at a greater level. This adds up to a weighted preference and belief in the need to continue to respond to these repeated situations in the same manner we have always responded for safety and comfort.

In order to act freely and fearlessly in similar circumstances as adults, we must invest passionate energy and receive positive affirmation equal to the total of all the negative emotions and fears we have accumulated in this kind of situation over the course of our life. Only then are we likely to give ourselves permission to think about a better response, in the heat of the moment.

Example: A child has been told by an angry father, repeatedly throughout childhood, "I expect this kind of stupid behavior from you." His father was angry because his child's actions embarrassed him as a father. The more the father felt embarrassed, the more negative energy he invested in reprimanding his son for a certain activity.

Over time, every time the child began to act in a fashion similar to any behavior that had elicited this response from his father, the child held back. He also withheld his passionate commitment to any alternative action, undermining his ability to perform at a high level.

He began to build failure upon failure (*debits*), hearing more and more often with more and more chastisement, the same destructive message, "I expect this kind of stupid behavior from you." Now this self-denigration comes from himself, in addition to the emotionally charged berating of his father.

Over the course of his childhood, this pattern of interaction with his father has built a mixture of negative feelings in his developing personality:

- Fear of failure, fear of risk, anxiety when being watched by his father or other authorities
- Embarrassment in the attempt to act
- Embarrassment in failure
- Awkwardness in success
- Anger at his father and any authority
- Self-doubt
- A feeling of being stupid
- Putting others above himself
- Feeling victimized by risky opportunity
- Feeling victimized by any failure
- Feeling powerless to achieve passion-based goals
- Unable to believe in personal dreams and ambitions

All of the negative emotions, when brought up by situations that resound in the old drama with his father, are now vested with intense energy. They built up in the child-teenager-man over the course of his life to become a significant negative push to keep his passions in check. These are the *debits* in his emotional system.

This person is locked in a stimulus-response behavioral mechanism, unable to make his *core values* contribution to life and living with low self-respect.

The life development equation that results from this *credits and debits* principle is simple. We each work to create situations that allow us to express our passions, thus working against our fears and negative emotions. We build up positive affirmations from others and from ourselves, putting more and more energy into the *credits* side of the equation until we overcome the old fears and negative emotions.

We work to get our *credits* side of the equation, greater than the *debits* side, so we can perform better and get better result.

While we pursue this course, we simultaneously create situations that offer the repetition of the dramatic childhood situations. This re-creation gives us the opportunity to observe our inner and outer reactions, to see the truth about ourselves, and allows us to feel the same fears and emotions we did in childhood.

We are given within this *debits and credits* mechanism the opportunity to decide whether to repeat the old pattern, building more *debits* in our internal bank account, or to make new conscious choices and collect more *credits*. The collection of *credits* allows us to take bigger risks, gain bigger successes, and build more positive energy *credits* faster with less stress and risk.

Over the course of time, even at the subconscious level, we all tend to work much of this out, at least to the level that we become socially functional and can obtain some degree of contentment. The work of becoming spiritually conscious, intentionally observing ourselves, and making more conscious choices speeds this process dramatically.

Once we see the truth about ourselves, see the ineffectiveness of our current responses to dramatic situations, we begin to build up anger or adamancy against the futility of our emotional patterns. If we can keep this anger focused at the behavior and not at ourselves or others, we begin to build additional overwhelming *credit* energy. We can focus this heightened energy at the inner talking that we generate during these dramatic moments of choice.

We can ***shout down*** these learned mental patterns. This is done intentionally out loud and in a private setting. We can scream to ourselves silently, or into a pillow, to strengthen our resolve and grieve the lack of love and nurturing we felt as children. This expression of anger and frustration at the thoughts and at the emotions that are holding us back act as a strong affirmation of our own conscious control and a denial of the *debits* we are continuing to hold onto emotionally.

By intentionally increasing our emotional reaction to these negative thoughts, we decrease the weight of these *debits* by a greater degree at each event.

In other words, the self-development secret here is to intentionally excite emotional denial of old emotional debris until we eradicate or expel this old debris out of our being. It is similar to the physical act if inducing vomiting to rid one's self of poison. Old emotional debris that keeps us from being our highest and best self are poison to the *Real Core Values Self.*

With these intentional conscious devices, we can build an increasingly positive affirmation and take on situations that put us face to face with the old fears, meeting them one after the other, doing the required spiritual work. This process shortens the length of time each of us might otherwise have to live with destructive mental and emotional patterns.

In my own life, I have consciously worked on a few critical areas like the one described above. This work involved my parents who are still living so I will not provide the detail. But I am freer now to express my passions, more able to place myself in situations within which I would have previously frozen for fear of embarrassment.

I also find that I am not acting out in other areas of my life in an effort to compensate for the inability to freely express one of my passions.

I have intentionally built *credits* within myself in a commitment to overwhelm the old patterns with new positive energy. This effort has been remarkably successful, and sometimes accomplished nearly overnight, based on the degree to which I was clear about the issues—also based upon my willingness to exert the emotional force required to counterbalance old *debits*, old emotional fear patterns.

I used to embarrass myself quite often in my attempts to compensate for areas of self-doubt and confusion. This is now a rare experience. I know some people live with these feelings and limitations their entire life. This is not necessary.

28

Choosing My Vocation

We have spent the last few chapters talking about learning and occupation as essential elements in our chosen framework. In order to continue effectively, it is important to clarify terms.

Avocation:

The activities and work we are *passionate about*—the things I do and the roles I take to fulfill the complete mission of my life. This is visualized as the process and purpose of my life. These may or may not be the same as my occupation or vocation.

Occupation:

The specific job title and function I am employed (paid) to perform. This is seen by most of us as a temporary part of our life path; specific defined work that is hopefully aligned well with our avocation. Our occupations tend to evolve with the development of our skills, experiences, and knowledge base.

Vocation:

The general course of our work life as identified by social labels, such as Engineering, Medicine, or Transportation. These are generally socially defined roles.

For the sake of this book, we can best understand this gradation of thinking by understanding the following use of this terminology.

I am called to be a Healer (Avocation), in the field of Mental Health

(Vocation), working as a psychologist in a hospital psychology ward (Occupation).

This terminology can be applied to any kind of avocation/vocation/occupation. The order in which I have dealt with these framework issues is chosen because the idea of avocation is very abstract and connected to internal spiritual awareness and processes.

It is at the avocation level—innate connection to activities within and outside our employment—where all of our *callings*, passions, and *core values* are vested. It is my intent to get all of us focused on this central concern first because everything else follows.

Next we can deal with occupation, because this is the most concrete and observable aspect of life, and each of us is either in an occupation now, or seeking our next position. It is important for us to become conscious about our current life framework so we can begin the process of self-observation, working consciously within the framework we have chosen for ourselves.

The bridge between *spiritual* and *social* occurs at the vocational level.

This is the level in our framework where conscious choice is most critical.

We do not choose our avocation (although some believe that our spirits prior to birth choose a life to live). In general terms, our avocation may be a genetically generated drive, or an inexplicable spiritual drive comprising the sum of our *core values*, passions, gifts, attributes, talents, interests, and *intuitive* abilities.

Many tend to see this as built-in design, whether biological or spiritual. I agree with this belief.

Our occupation tends to be viewed more as the result of a mixture of educational choices and job experiences that one has obtained in the past; made useful in the best possible work environment one can find today. This is generally seen as a mixture of fate and intentionality.

Many feel they are doing what they have to do in order to pay the bills.

This doesn't mean that there is nothing about the current job to enjoy, just that there is a belief common to many that . . .

I would not be doing this if I didn't have to earn a living.

This belief would be significantly reduced if everyone were given the opportunity to be financially independent for a period of time, during which time boredom and purposelessness would settle in. Most would likely begin working on something closely related to their current job, paid or unpaid.

In other words, the type of company where we have found employment is likely of some deep interest to us or we would not have picked up the phone or dropped in. However, many people simply follow their parents into large companies, or they follow their parents' advice about the vocation they choose. They have a challenge to either find a right seat from which to make their real contribution, or they have a significant adventure ahead of them—launching a new mission to find a right seat in a right field of endeavor in a right company.

The "I would not be doing this if . . ." statement is a clear expression of the victim position. This kind of statement is intended to excuse ourselves from responsibility for our boredom and sense of emptiness and frustration. It excuses us from consciously choosing to make a change in order to make a higher contribution.

When the current job position does not connect well with one's passions, it is convenient to disguise our frustrations as an adult attitude of responsibility: "I have to make a living, feed the kids, and make the spouse happy." This serves two purposes: to make ourselves appear *right* and mature to those around us, and to excuse ourselves from responsibility for our self-described unsuccessful and unfulfilling life.

It also allows us to have something to point at as the source of depression, unhappiness, or loss of hope. It is a strong victim statement, often easily accepted by others.

Both of these purposes run contrary to our need to fulfill our *calling* and find happiness. They also support our fear-based position of delaying the spiritual work, the work of seeing ourselves truly *as we are* and accepting complete accountability for our own lives. The consequence of this is that we also delay *owning* our lives. We delay claiming our passions and our *callings* and our *core values.*

We put off happiness to another day somewhere in the future when someone or something will be kind enough to put us in a better job that pays more money and makes us feel happy all day long. It is amazing how many people have learned to believe that a job with greener grass cannot exist, except over there in the other guy's pasture.

I just have to make do and focus on activities outside of work.

As a business management expert I have worked with hundreds of business owners who felt trapped in their own businesses. The joy was completely gone out of their work, and they felt genuinely trapped in a company that was no longer fulfilling, interesting, or meaningful. I have heard many business owners express it something like this: "You can have my company for a dollar and a half. Just get me out of it."

Most of these business owners are still in their business, and they wouldn't sell them *now* for millions of dollars. Why? What made the difference?

Our business management turn-around process is always the same.

We study the company and create a clear financial and verbal picture of it. We study the owner and the key employees and show each of them how they have contributed to the current business situation (good and bad). We show each person, including the owner, what his or her highest and best use is to the company at this time.

We help each identify their key *core values* and their basic passions, helping each to understand how their highest and best use within the company will fulfill part of their passions (their *callings*). And finally, we put in systems and realign the organization to support the *core values* of the people, optimizing the opportunity for each person to make their individual contributions, optimizing the interactions between individuals for supreme team performance.

We put in measurement systems to acknowledge each success. Within a few weeks the team environment is dramatically improved (no matter what the starting point, poor to excellent). The productivity is dramatically increased, sometimes with fewer people involved.

People, including the owner, are making their contributions (their highest and best), having more fun, and feeling rewarded and challenged with new learning. The company is still making shoes or medical lasers or chewing gum. What was once an owner's trap is now the owner's vehicle for a fulfilling life and for spiritual growth.

When a company's core commitment is that each person is working to elevate every other person to their highest and best contribution, that company generally outperforms its competitors. This is true on all levels—customer service, product and service quality, organizational efficiency, and net profits.

We have learned that most companies have the opportunity to generate net profits at two or three times industry-standard profits.

The most important thing that happens in our work is the reinvestment of the owners in the activities and *creative* contributions that drew them into the creation of their businesses to begin with. This reconnects them with their passions and makes the situation a challenge and an engaging project rather than a trap.

The next step is equally powerful.

We help each owner see their business as their spiritual "Tibetan mountaintop." This is the place in the world each has chosen to do their spiritual development work. This is the framework each has created in order to make spiritual progress. Individuation, coming to one's self, learning to *be who you are*: all of these personal journeys and life missions are made visible and even essential in the ownership of a privately held business.

Small business ownership is the anvil of God, upon which we lay ourselves so we can come under the refining and strengthening hammer of complete accountability and personal self-determination.

We have a conversation in each client company about why each person is here in this current juncture of life, in their current job. We talk about this related to the *Real Core Values Self*—the life-work perspective. What essential life lesson are you here to learn? What attitude, belief, or idea do you need to give up in order to rise to your highest and best contribution?

With this ultimate step in place, the owner and his team once again feel passionate and have a renewed sense of meaning at the social-economic framework level and at the spiritual level.

Occasionally, of course, the right solution for some has been to help them sell their business.

For them, the process described above is the same. We have to do all the same work to optimize the business for sale, completing the tasks required, so the owner is not leaving to find a mythical greener pasture, rather a new adventure in life through which his next essential life's lessons may be learned.

We have to do all the right work, help with all of the self-awareness and connection to each person's innate unchanging nature, in order for this kind of decision to be made and for this kind of significant business challenge to be successfully accomplished.

29

Passions

Our passions consist of a set of social/economic/philosophical/intellectual interests that provide a vehicle or media through which we each may express our *core values*. Our *core values* then become the contribution we make through the process of following our passions. Passions unite people in empathy and joy.

There is little in life more captivating and overtly joyous than the experience of being with another person who is completely free in the expression of their life passions. The only experience in life that overshadows this experience is that of being in the flow of one's *own* passions; timelessly experiencing the animation of a deep inner drive, being totally at risk in the expression of a pure passion, and so involved with that passion that all sense of risk is lost.

Few people are willing to let themselves experience life at this level.

This is why the experience of observing others in their passionate moments is so captivating. First, this experience is entertaining and provocative, causing a stirring of our own passions. Second, we identify with the expression of passion, and we long for similar moments in our own lives.

Many people long for fame and fortune.

These are desires, are superficial and meaningless. Such desire-driven dreams are filled with envy and greed, and are backed by the victim position: Why didn't God give me talents like that? Why do I have to work so hard to have my talents appreciated? If I hadn't gotten married, I would have . . .

The identification with another person's passion is much deeper and more empowering. When I connect with someone who is expressing a life's passion, I experience an affirmation that says, "This is what makes life exciting." It's not just *okay* to let your passions flow. It's a central part of the puzzle of life—to find and release one's deepest passions.

Note: Our passions are composed of one or more of our strongest *core values* connected to specific interests that become activity in our lives.

If what we choose to learn is directed by our conscious acknowledgment of passions, all learning supports the eventual free expressions of these passions and leads to ultimate fulfillment as a person.

When what we choose to learn is directed by desire for fame or fortune, or by a need to conform to the expectations of parents, teachers, and friends, what we learn tends to further separate us from our passions. Continuing to build a life strategy around our ego-driven personality and a vocational/avocational framework stifles and diminishes passion. We cannot find fulfillment through this course.

Fulfillment is necessarily postponed until the pain of living a passionless existence becomes greater than the fear of not succeeding in the eyes of the world.

We find fulfillment by aligning our activities with our *core values* and passions.

Whatever we do from this aligned position builds our self-respect and satisfies our desire to make our contribution. Regardless of the amount of work we do or success we achieve, if we are not aligned with our *core values*, our contribution will not do anything to build our sense of self-respect. We may be admired and respected by others because of wealth, fame, or business success, but there can be no sense of fulfillment and purpose unless our daily activities are aligned with our *core values*.

The trick then is to identify our *core values* and to discover our passions, honoring these essential parts of ourselves in all aspects of our lives, especially in the choices of what we learn and what we do each day. The financial strategy books that constantly talk about increasing your desire for the end result, visualization of the accumulation of wealth, are at best destructive for those who are not yet connected to their passions.

Joseph Campbell in his book, *The Power of Myth*, talks about finding one's Bliss and following it fearlessly. The best definition of *Bliss* is the experience of living in alignment with one's *core values* and passions. If we obey this important directive, we will find ourselves achieving whatever wealth is appropriate to the blissful path which is uniquely ours.

For some this will include substantial wealth. For others there may be little material proof of success in living. The power of this pathway is fulfillment of life in either case. Material wealth is not required and often impairs one's ability to experience Bliss.

The power of the constant visualization of end results and wealth accumulation is that it clearly distracts us from the pursuit of learning driven by passion and from our spiritual quest. The further one ventures down this cold pathway, the further one becomes separated from this spiritually directed passionate life.

It is important to assess the degree to which we are driven by desires or led by passions. For instance, we have often heard that adult male humans tend to think about sex every eight minutes or so. These thoughts for most are barely noticed mental blips, like the twitch of a muscle. Most of these passing thoughts are ignored due to lack of appropriate opportunity or by the paling of sexual desire relative to the current investment of energy in a higher *calling* and one's passions.

Often the desire for money, the sense and signs of success in social and business arenas can also come into the minds of people on a regular basis. These basic desires are as innate as the drive to procreate. Indeed, these desires are part of the procreative competition of the human creature. Men and women are attracted to the most attractive sexual mates according to their outward signs of social success.

Some women prefer the muscular, rough-looking physical laborer, usually not wealthy, to the smooth-skinned millionaire. Such a preference may be driven by the conclusion (instinct) that physical survival and pure animal joy are more likely to be experienced with the former than with the latter. Another woman's instinct may lean toward the socially successful man, preferring the protection and acceptance of society.

Of course it is likely that one's original family and the teachings of its social mores contribute significantly to these leanings, but the basic drive is there, right next to, and part of, the sexual drive.

Let's be clear. Sexuality is not a passion. It is a desire.

Materialism, greed, and envy are not passions, but ego-based desires that support and sometimes substitute for the sexual drive. They often substitute for a real passion and the desire to be worthwhile in our lives.

Passions by definition are spiritual pursuits designed to lead a spiritual person (which we all are) toward fulfillment and joy in life. The difference between those who claim to be spiritually based and those who do not is one of consciousness and commitment.

For all of us, when our passions are allowed to connect with and harmonize with positive emotions, these passions become greater than our desires. When this occurs our lives begin to be driven by our passions.

One of the things we choose to learn, or choose not to learn, is the way we function at the spiritual level—the spiritual laws. Few individuals invest significant life energy in pursuit of spiritual knowledge and understanding. That's why so few of us are seen by others as being truly happy and fulfilled.

It is interesting that the strength of our passions is so great that we are often led by them even when we are not conscious of these basic impulses. Our passions are often harmonious with our basic social desires. Many people are in jobs that are well suited to them. They spend their time performing tasks and learning information that rings true with their inner spirit. But this is not enough. The conscious pursuit of desires rather than the expression of *creative* passion creates dissatisfaction and unrest, even in situations that naturally connect with our passions.

This remains true for people who are working where they should, relative to their passions and vocational drives. In order for a sense of happiness and fulfillment to occur there must be a conscious recognition, a connection between the work being performed and the vocational passions. All work performed in pursuit of passions leads toward learning that which is specific to spiritual growth and fulfillment. All work performed in pursuit of desires leads, in the best-case scenario, toward the learning of skills. But the pursuit of desires leads always toward either momentary fulfillment of desires, or to frustration and personal dissatisfaction.

This is why we see many people who have achieved great business or financial success, doing what they appear to be passionate about, caught up in broken relationships, drugs, legal battles, or simple hedonism. They themselves declare that they feel empty and their lives are meaningless. The spiritual laws are not being followed.

Our passions are hardwired into us as clues that lead us to discover our mission on this planet.

Our passions point us toward the interests, competencies, and talents that are within us. As we choose to focus energy and learning into these areas of interest, we deepen our interest, heighten our focus, and sharpen our skills and competencies so we can make our highest and best contribution.

Passions are the gateway to our fulfilled life.

All of my life I have had a passion for writing poetry. I have gone as far as publishing three books of poems, and I have had many poems published in small regional magazines and poetry anthologies. I thought in my younger days that poetry would be the center of my life, that I would someday be a renowned poet. Well, this might yet happen, but not through focused effort and commitment.

Yet this passion for poetry in many ways has led me to the writing of this book. The creation of poetry, economy of words, intentional choice of words for right meaning and greater connection with others, the nuances of words, the power of words to carry ideas and to open minds and hearts—all of this I learned from my work with personal poems. My poetry passions set me up with competencies of structure and classical thought. It caused me to place inordinate value on the choice of one right word.

It is interesting that the *Core Values Index* (*CVI*) is a group of carefully chosen words designed to reveal the deepest most important information a person can have—self-knowledge. The *CVI*, because of my love of words and the honoring of words, is the first human assessment that characterizes and quantifies the human spirit. This creation/discovery was largely made possible by the thousands of hours, the millions of words I have written in my lifetime.

Within my passion for poetry is housed a greater passion—the passion to know and understand myself, the passion to help other people come to know and honor their deepest most precious nature.

My passion is to always learn and to work to discover my true nature and to find my place of highest and best contribution. All of these related passions have caused me to work for more than eighteen years perfecting the *CVI*. I am now willing to spend another twenty years of my life helping people derive benefit from the knowledge the *CVI* provides each person.

You see, it is the presence of passions in our lives that adds that unique element—a unique life-path, a unique discovery process, and a unique purpose for our existence on this planet. My passions that have led me to deeply explore these things have also caused me to be prepared to help others explore them. Our passions, if we allow them, will lead us to our mission, and our innate *Core Values Nature* will be contributed to the world in such a fashion that we are fulfilled by the activities and the contributions of our lives.

30

The Core Values Rules Governing Passion

***Passion* Rule One:**

Passions, not desires, lead to fulfillment and happiness.

There is immediate reward available to a person who single-mindedly works to fulfill a specific desire. The positive and immediate return for pursuit of desires creates a sense of personal achievement and, more important, a gratification of that desire that is momentary but very stimulating.

This effort-and-reward cycle builds a belief that the momentary fulfillment of desires is a good thing: what feels good is probably all that matters in life. This cycle creates an addictive requirement. Since the sense of fulfillment of a desire is short-lived, and creates an increased emptiness as the exhilaration fades, there is an immediate requirement for another desire "fix."

Some people are quite accomplished at keeping this cycle going, building one short-term gratification after another, pursuing desires as a standard practice. This, of course, leads to hedonism—the constant pursuit of desire. As one's desires become more and more demanding of time and energy, there is less and less time for long-term relationships, for essential learning, or for the expression of the essential self (*power, love, wisdom*, and *knowledge*).

The pursuit of *passions* on the other hand requires a willingness to accept delayed gratification in exchange for long-term fulfillment, happiness, and productive relationships.

The desire-based effort-and-reward cycle allows little time for such pursuit.

***Passion* Rule Two:**

The desire cycle (effort and reward) precludes the *passion* cycle.

To the degree that you are locked into the pursuit of short-term (near-term) gratification of desires, you are not investing your energy in delayed gratification, high-contribution activities. Paying attention to desires precludes the investment of energy in fulfillment and activities from which you can derive meaning.

Similarly, the *passion*, long-term gratification cycle also subtracts from one's ability to constantly, effectively pursue desires. Short-term gratification actually goes down, perceptually, when one first moves into the pursuit-of-*passion* mode.

This absence of short-term gratification is similar to the absence of a euphoric drug that one has decided to live without. The restlessness that one feels during this transitional phase drives many people back to their old behaviors in order to obtain a quick desire fix.

Such lapses and quick fixes necessarily delay the fulfillment of one's *passions* and the accomplishment of *Real Work* through one's *calling*.

The secret to winning this transition process is a passionate commitment to the process (learning, work, and short-term achievements) of building a life centered on your unique *core values*, your *passions*, and your *callings*.

As we learn to pay constant attention to the pursuit of our *passions*, our work and learning become completely mind absorbing and fun. The effective result is that one naturally remains more constant in a sense of happiness and fulfillment without the ups and downs of the desire/emptiness cycle.

This experience of "flow"—the sense of timeless involvement with passionate work—replaces the addictive demands of our desires and begins to build self-respect. Regardless of society's judgment of our accomplishments related to pursuit of desires, no respect for self is built by any such desire-directed work.

This is not to say that desire-driven successes are not ego-enhancing.

Remember that ego is the protector of the less-developed self, so enhancement of one's ego does nothing to build self-respect. In fact ego-enhancing activities boost the ego, further cementing a person in personality behaviors and shielding him or her from the pain of necessary spiritual growth. If we remain steady with our ego-driven desires, we will not have to suffer the momentary sense of loss and reduced sense of gratification of our desires.

Passion Rule Three:

Activities that look like and sound like *passions* but are performed unconsciously in the pursuit of desires lead to emptiness and anger, even when—*especially* when—these activities create the outward social acknowledgment and approval that was also desired.

Imagine a painter whose passion is to create amazingly colorful renaissance paintings using huge and powerful brush strokes and pallet knife textures. His *desire* is to be recognized as a gifted painter and to become famous and wealthy. People are not readily buying his large, almost overbearing pictures of fields of flowers or ladies in flowing gowns. His agent and gallery-owner friends convince him to paint the current avant-garde flat color work, showing people with weary expressions in unappreciated toil.

He follows their advice and becomes instantly successful, known for his hard-hitting interpretations of life. There is a constant demand for his "new" paintings. He has no time to further develop his renaissance *passions.* He is busy making money, talking to people at gallery showings about the paintings they are buying—to which he has little or no personal connection. As his paintings become more and more bleak, due to his personal detachment and loss of *passion*, he becomes more successful, more in demand, and wealthier.

Can you imagine a scenario like this, in which the painter will feel happy and fulfilled? Is it likely that the world will allow a graceful and easy change from his current successful work back to his colorful *passions*? Not likely. He can, of course, return to his *passions*, but only by changing everything that now surrounds him: his agent, his galleries, his buyers, and probably his friends.

Those people who would have been deeply attracted to this painter had he remained true to his *passions*, do not currently find this successful, wealthy, famous person attractive to spend time with or to buy pictures from. In order to find his *passions* and his life, he has to reject the world's approval, give up the stream of money flowing to him, and turn inward to his real person, reclaim his *passions*, and allow his life to unfold as it was intended to unfold. This is not a comfortable process.

Pursuit of one's *passions* does not, as some contemporary books want us to believe, always lead to even greater wealth and success. The pursuit of one's passions does lead, however, to daily contentment, happiness, and fulfillment. It is true that some people's *passions*, combined with skills and talents, set them up for significant wealth or fame. But this is just one of the more challenging elements in the puzzle of their personal lives.

It is equally true that the pursuit of spiritual health, adult consciousness, and transformation of life to one that is driven by *passions* and *callings* does not require most people to become poor and isolated. For most people, *Core Values Consciousness* and the pursuit of a fulfilling life that is built on making your highest and best contribution, carries with it greater success and greater identifiable achievement and accomplishment—often much greater financial rewards and social influence.

Why would anyone choose the pursuit of wealth and power over happiness and fulfillment?

Only because they do not understand or believe that real happiness is possible.

Or they may believe that a sense of personal fulfillment is behind all of our social and economic struggles. The point is to make one's highest and best contribution as long as we live.

Whether this leads to fame and fortune is subject to conscious choice, and the reality that society is willing to pay more for some passionate contributions than for others.

***Passion* Rule Four:**

Passions that are not supported with a commitment to constant learning, diligent practice, and free expression cause restlessness and dissatisfaction. These *passions* are reduced to fantasies by lack of commitment and learning.

Have you ever known someone that you would label *grandiose*?

This label generally describes someone who has too high an opinion of himself, especially as we observe current performance relative to declared goals or personal visions. We hear this person's dreams as fantasies that are unachieved and likely unachievable by this person.

What we are seeing is the lack of fundamental work, a lack of learning, and too little focused effort related to the accomplishment of the dream. Or we are seeing someone who is simply (by our judgment) out of touch with his innate capabilities—the perceived requirements of the dream.

Fantasies that are supported daily by learning, work, sacrifice of short-term gratification, and acceptance of long and continuous effort without immediate results, are fantasies that may become realizable dreams. When *passions* and *calling* align with one's dreams, then the only requirement that remains is constant work and commitment. Without this last element, one's life work will never be complete and there can be no sense of fulfillment.

***Passion* Rule Five:**

Passions that are not connected with positive emotions will not be released. They will be blocked by fears and lack of energy.

The key to unlocking our *passions* lies in observation of our negative emotions. The power of this fifth *passion* rule is immense. Few people understand the negative emotion mechanism and are therefore unable to be effective in dealing with negative emotions in themselves and in others.

First we must understand that all negative emotions are based in fear.

Negative Emotions

Anger: Fear of loss of control. Fear of being controlled. Fear of rejection or abandonment. Fear of embarrassment, etc. All fears may lead a person to anger.

Envy: Fear of failure. Fear that others are more loved by God. Fear of frustrated desires. Fear that desires will never be attained. Fear that we cannot be loved without obtaining the object of our envy. Fear that we do not deserve to have what others have. Desire to be revered or respected for false reason.

Sadness: Fear that we don't deserve happiness. Fear of claiming our dreams and *passions*. Fear that one does not have the skills or talents to achieve dreams. Fear of connecting or believing again, based upon disappointments and loss. Fear that we will not get love and attention except through sadness.

Guilt: Fear of judgment. Fear of retribution. Fear of being caught and embarrassed. Fear of being seen as a bad person. Fear of being a bad person. Fear of not measuring up to the judgment of others.

Greed: Fear of failure. Fear of having unfulfilled desires. Fear of starvation and deprivation. Fear of being unacceptable. Fear of society's judgment of failure and mediocrity. Fear of loneliness. Fear of inadequacy. Fear of incompetency. Fear of lack of fortitude. Fear of not being lovable without extraordinary material possessions.

Apathy/Depression: Fear of failure. Fear of disappointment. Fear of self-judgment relative to worth and capability. Fear of proof of self-doubts.

Despair: Fear of being found worthless. Fear of proven incompetence. Fear of future negative emotions created by failed attempts. Fear of rejection by self and others. Fear of isolation and loneliness.

Embarrassment: Fear of rejection and ridicule. Fear of abandonment. Fear of isolation. Fear of unworthiness. Fear of not being loved. Fear of being humiliated and excommunicated.

Name That Emotion

The negative emotion mechanism is *not* easy to understand, but *is* quite simple. First we must simply observe and acknowledge to ourselves when we are experiencing a negative emotion. We can then label that negative emotion, saying to ourselves: "I am feeling *greedy*." Knowing that each negative emotion is stimulated by specific fears, we then ask ourselves the question: *"What am I afraid of, right now?"*

In our first attempts at this process, we may fail.

The only real requirement is to observe yourself while you are experiencing negative emotions, then acknowledge and name those emotions and ask the above question. At some point you will see a clear connection between your negative emotion and the fear that causes it to be aroused in you.

When you name the emotion, it begins to immediately fade. This is a direct correlation to the opposite experience, one that we all have likely experienced . . .

While experiencing a particularly positive emotion, or enjoying an extraordinary experience, we sometimes pause mentally. We notice how happy, or excited, or sexy we are feeling. By noticing this, and naming the experience—I am having the greatest sex I have ever had—we immediately cause the positive sensation to disappear. The positive emotion is gone. Even the heightened sensations and creature delight is gone. We have gone cerebral. We are *thinking* instead of *being*.

The same thing happens for us when we name our negative emotions, and especially when we name the fear that has aroused that emotion. Name that fear, and the fear will immediately begin receding into the past. Name that emotion, and you will no longer feel that emotion.

***Passion* Rule Six:**

Passions must be consciously pursued and given expression without fear.

This is the formula for fulfillment and happiness. Consciously acknowledged, emotionally supported *passions* still cause restlessness. This restlessness, however, is immediately relieved by the pursuit of learning, practice, and expression of the *passion.*

I call this kind of restlessness *spiritual agitation.* We are stimulated by our true *passions* that exist in us to *call* us into service of others. We become naturally agitated when we are not *being* proactive and engaged in activities that are a clean expression of our *Core Values Nature.* Our innate *being* needs to be stimulated and brought to life by the excitation of *passions* and founded in our *callings.*

Many people confuse passions with desires.

A high-technology business leader helped to create one of the foremost technology companies of his era. The drive to create and sell millions of units of an innovative product was powerful. The company succeeded in all of its principal aims, including becoming a giant on Wall Street. The principal of this company then found himself on the outside of his large successful organization, screened out of management decisions, no longer considered important even in technology development leadership.

He left his company and worked to create a new one, based solely on his innovations. After twenty years he is still working 80- to 100-hour weeks trying to recapture some of the original excitement and inspiration. The man is obviously following a built-in drive to innovate new technology. This is his sense of vocation and avocation.

But there is something missing for this man.

What is it?

He is wealthy. He is being an *innovator* of technology. But he is miserable and tired of the grind. He is not able to re-create the success of his past in his new pursuits. He is caught in the desire for proof of worth. He has forgotten his sense of mission and contribution.

It is the *spiritual* connection that is missing.

This person is suffering from a *passion* disconnect. Unconsciously, in the first major project all of this extraordinary leader's *passions* were being tapped. He was working in an inspired mode on his own innovations. The validation of any innovation is its adoption as a primary solution by millions of users. His *passion* was being fulfilled not only by the activities but by the sense of meaning and a connection with his *calling* to provide technological solutions to people.

When *passions* become replaced with vocational activities without a basis in personal contribution and *calling*, the work becomes meaningless and empty.

To the degree that this individual is now being driven by the need to prove himself, or by the desire to get back into power and authority, or to earn prestige and respect, he is separating himself from his deepest most innate nature: He is living a life driven by desire, whipped into work by ego, instead of being inspired into work by a *passion* to make his highest and best contribution.

He is less likely to succeed because of this.

If he does succeed, he is already spending the emotional and spiritual currency that it might afford him through his focus on gratification of desires. The sense of fulfillment and high contribution will be lost in the fog of desires already served, and constant subservience to fears and negative emotions.

A person's motivations dictate the degree and nature of his fulfillment.

Another important factor contributed to this man's severe disconnect in his old company. The original innovation was inspired. After that, each new product was a derivation of the old. The level of challenge and the sense of technological breakthrough were almost totally lost. Other people elsewhere were working on the next breakthrough technology.

The *passion* for him was in the development of something no one else had conceived—to create new, useful products that would change the way people live. So the real *passion* became sublimated to the desire to build a successful company. He succeeded and found emptiness, isolation, and frustration.

This is the kind of disconnect that happens with all of us at one time or another. Some use the experience to reenergize their *passions* or to open themselves to their Bliss for the first time. Others continue to flail away at their desires, never satisfied, forever restless and empty.

***Passion* Rule Seven:**

All *passions* work to energize the individual toward a sense of meaning. Activities driven by desire lead only to tangible rewards, or frustration, never to a sense of meaning.

The sad truth is that people who are highly successful in obtaining their desires are like that camel that can't get through the eye of the needle. They are so wealthy in their accomplishments that the need for fulfillment barely has an opportunity to cause the smallest ripple of spiritual agitation. Their spiritual ears are blocked by pursuit and attainment of desires.

This seventh rule provides another critical way to discern one's desires from one's *passions*.

As individuals work hard and with discipline toward the fulfillment of desires, as demonstrated through social and financial success, they often become more and more dispassionate and have a deeper sense of emptiness. This emptiness is the requirement for the discovery of a sense of meaning. What is my contribution? What positive effect should I be having on my family, my society? Why am I here?

"Why am I here?" as related to a sense of purpose, is an older question and a deeper question than the same four-word question discussed earlier as a way to identify your next essential life lesson. The previously discussed "why am I here?" question will lead you to your next opportunity to learn from a particular perspective or from a current situation.

Here, the question "why am I here?" is more fundamental. It is connected directly with innate passions and a requirement for a sense of meaning. It cries out for some connection with humanity, God, a higher power, or some universal force. It is a child's question for a parent, asking, "What do you think I should be? How do you think I should spend my time? You know me. What do you think?"

The universal response appears to be something like this:

> You have negative emotions. Follow them to see the truth about yourself.
>
> You have positive emotions. Observe them. They are the key to unlocking your *passions.*
>
> You have intelligence. Use it to learn whatever your *passions* dictate.

You are a spirit. Use the framework of life on earth to reclaim and fully express your spirit (a unique mixture of *power, love, wisdom,* and *knowledge*).

You are here for a reason. Find your avocation, your *calling.* Your avocation and *calling* are the life situations (work) through which you are able to make your highest and best contribution. This is the place in your social and political framework that requires your unique set of skills (honed to high proficiency) and your unique *Real Core Values Self.*

Through this work, invest your *passions.* This is the way to find happiness and fulfillment. This is the way to find and fulfill your purpose in life.

Passion **Rule Eight:**

The universal purpose of all humans is to discover one's *Core Values Nature* and the *passions* that drive us to invest this spiritual energy in a certain and specific way.

Our life in pursuit of our *passions* causes us to educate ourselves in support of these *passions* and to express (live in accordance with) these *passions* to the fullest measure. This is the simple process that creates fulfillment.

As we begin to identify and honor our innate *passions*, we are provided by life circumstances the opportunity to do two things: 1) accept new risks and move out of our comfort zones in pursuit of *passions* that lead to fulfillment, and 2) observe our negative emotions and our self-defeating thoughts and beliefs that undermine our willingness to follow our passions.

As we accept new risks and venture out beyond our comfort zones, we set up new circumstances that are prone to generate a new array of the same kinds of old negative emotions that have held us back to this date.

Our willingness to observe these negative emotions, to name them and to name the fears that generate these emotions, provides new impetus to our quest for fulfillment. As we overcome each new risk, we are rewarded with a greater sense of self-respect and renewed belief in the value of our own life.

We begin to claim our own life and discontinue the process of living for the approval of others. This frees us from our warped personality patterns into alignment with (into being) our deepest *core values.*

We are also rewarded with the opportunity to observe negative emotions that have been aroused by our consciously accepted risks and the successes and failures that follow.

Since we have been more conscious about our life choices at this point, we are more able to see the direct link between old fears, desires, and belief systems that keep us locked in negative emotions and keep us from acting in accord with our *passions.* As we name these fears and face them head on, they lose their power over us, and we begin accelerating toward fulfillment.

In the process of working toward fulfillment, each person will discover a primary (central) *calling*. The *calling* for each person is the societal role which allows the optimal expressions of one's *Core Values Nature* through his *passions* activity.

Passion Rule Nine:

When a person is consciously and energetically working in alignment with his *passions*, the full expression of his *core values—power*, *love*, *wisdom*, or *knowledge*—will be automatically put to work.

The sure way to tell whether you are on the right path is to observe how much of your day is being consumed by work, play, and learning related directly to your most dominant *core values*. If your activities are aligned with your *core values*, your energy will be high, your awareness of passing time will be negligible, and your sense of personal respect and happiness will be expanding.

You will be deriving some sense of newness and satisfaction from at least one of your *core values* all day long. You will be conscious of a deep sense of *power*, *love*, *wisdom*, or *knowledge*, but consumed by the activities without a sense of time. You will experience less fatigue and more heightened personal energy. You will forget yourself in your attentive, intentional contribution of your innate *Core Values Nature* to others.

31

Choosing a Life Mate or Intimate Partner

Hang onto your hats.

This chapter may not be your favorite. I will tell you up front—there is no secret formula to be found here. For most people this choice of a life mate is central to all spiritual, social, and emotional development. It is central to the creation of a peaceful and satisfying life. It is deeply imbedded in our psyches to be driven to procreate and to leave our children on this planet when we ourselves leave it.

Why is it that our spouse can make us feel more angry, more defeated, more frustrated than anyone else? Why is it that the way our spouse feels about us can be more affirming and important to us than the feelings and judgments of anyone else? Why is it that we have such a difficult time getting this kind of affirmation, or giving this kind of affirmation?

Why is it that we sometimes feel trapped in our relationships and think thoughts like: "If we didn't have kids," or "If we had not stayed together so long already," or "If divorce weren't so expensive and messy," or "If I thought I could do any better." . . .

It's sad when these kinds of victim justifications for staying together are the primary glue in the relationship. What has been lost? We tend to enter marriage and relationship commitments with the expectations that we will always *feel* as we did at the time of marriage, have that same excitement, enjoyment, and interest in our spouse years in the future.

For most of us those initial feelings are lost over time, and they must be replaced with other, more lasting, and fundamental relationship anchors.

Those in successful marriages gradually replace disappointments with acceptance, the *feelings* of love (infatuation) with a real love. They let go of the illusion that every moment of every day will be filled with joy by the other person. They learn to allow the *feelings* of love to ebb and flow, like everything else in life.

Mostly the real difference between a successful and a frustrating marriage is the commitment of at least one person to truly making a contribution to the other person's life. Good marriages are built on a foundation of commitment to the real person we married—not to the fantasy ideal that we felt infatuated with during our early relationship.

When we form our first (expected to be the last) spousal relationship commitment, most of us are in our twenties, not terribly alive with spiritual consciousness, driven by hormones and the visceral drive to procreate, and largely unaware of anything about ourselves and others beneath the ego-driven personality.

We fall in love with our spouse's body and personality, the one he or she has been perfecting for social acceptance for many years. We fall in love with how we *feel* when we are with them.

This personality we have "fallen in love with" is founded upon the fear-based stimulus-and-response mechanism, combined with the desire to please the adults in our life and to be accepted by society.

This personality is a carefully prepared script, a character designed to fulfill a part in a young person's drama—very exciting, not much to feel negative about, especially not the parts of the personality self that are revealed to a new love interest.

The problem with this is: The personality is not the real person, the *Real Core Values Self*, and it is designed to win acceptance and approval and to get what it wants. It is not wired to make the other person happy unless in doing so we get our desires met.

We also do not see the negative aspects of our future spouse's personality until we have really established the marriage, and we have begun to drop the pretenses and show the underbelly of our personality.

This is not much of an anchor hold a relationship in place.

In fact, this first-level relationship is guaranteed to cause a break at some point, the only variant being our individual stubbornness and depth of our commitment to hide the truth about ourselves each from the other. Some of us are great experts at this deception. Some are so committed to our personality strategy that we are able to sustain it from youth until death.

The more strongly two individuals hold to their delusions of perfect love, the more likely they are to have a dramatic breakup in the future.

This aspect of life-mate selection and maintenance devolves to such expressions as the "seven-year itch" or the "third-year disillusionment."

For me—being the stubborn deluded self that I *was* going into my marriage—my deepest struggle was during our tenth year of marriage. We barely survived that year as a couple. We have now been married for more than thirty years and love each other more deeply than we ever imagined possible. The foundation for this love has been largely and consciously developed by each of us—individually and together—during that very dark and difficult tenth year.

For most of us, as the illusions fall away, we don't have much of a real view of our spouse to make the substitution.

This happens imperceptibly a lot, due to occasional slips in image projection, the hidden differences between our personality (perfect image) and our flawed personality self that we have been hiding from each other. We accidentally occasionally disclose more of this carefully crafted defensive personality to our spouse, and our images of each other slide imperceptibly toward the true image side.

But we are still seeing the image, with all of its flaws, and not the *Real Core Values Self* with all of its amazing capacities and energies and wonderful motivations to contribute.

We see this awareness creep into our relationships in the form of conflicts over squeezed tubes of toothpaste, underwear on the floor, and bills paid but incompletely listed in the check book.

These irritations in themselves would not cause a breach in relationship. Most of us fight over issues that have little life consequence most of the time. It is our addictive need to interpret these small breaches of etiquette and expectations as signs of lack of respect, rudeness, indirect anger, hostility, etc. that cause relationships to break.

We build a roster of offenses, each with our own list, so that at the next challenge to *our* imperfection we may raise evidential missiles and fling them with appropriate vehemence or superior detachment at the other, overwhelming our spouse's paltry attempt to make us wrong.

We are, in all of these battles, acting from fears and in defense of unimportant ego-driven personality issues. The choice we are making each time we engage in these ego battles is the choice to defend the personality that we adopted as a child. If viewed for long from inside our marriage home, most of us know that we would look quite childish at times.

How could this not be so. We are emotionally committed to being the personality that we crafted as a child, with a child's needs and wants. This is completely opposite of the need of each of us as adults to make a positive contribution, to *be* a positive presence, to participate with others in a constructive manner.

The strategy we are using is not effective in the new adult arena, but we feel attached to our personality and do not want to believe we are wrong or a bad person.

We choose to defend ourselves, even though being an aggressor in committed relationships is fear- and ignorance-driven. We do not know a better way to respond, and we also maintain the belief that our personality is "who I am." So we have to defend it.

But this personality, as we discussed earlier, is a warped version of our *Real Core Values Self*, and the parts of the personality that have been heavily warped have to be pruned away by our own adult, inner work.

Our personality has to die one warped part at a time, in order to allow the more conscious and effective *Real Core Values Self* to rise to the surface. Our ego has to suffer these small deaths throughout our entire life. But we can move through the bulk of this process in the matter of a few years if we are consciously committed to the process. This is the power of *Core Values Consciousness.*

Marriage and occupation are the two primary anvils in life upon which we position ourselves, so that we may be hammered into our refined innate shape. This is the process that Dr. Carl Jung described as *individuation.* Becoming what we are uniquely *meant* to become; learning *to be who we really are.*

Marriage more than anything else tends to put the fire to us, making us either run screaming and blaming from the heat, or making us more malleable for the hammer. The hammer is our own consciousness. It is our focus of full attention to our emotions our fears, our inner talking and our physiological disturbances. The hammer is our acceptance of complete accountability for every aspect of our personality and our *Real Core Values Self.*

This is our choice. We choose first *whether* to marry, second *who* to marry, and third whether and how long to *stay married.* The third choice, if we decide to leave a marriage, we tend to remake over and over again, thereby having to face the same small battles over and over again.

What causes us to choose a particular spouse?

There are of course the raging hormones, "chemistry," and physical attraction. But this would only cause us to procreate and move on in the ancient, primal game of survival. There is a greater attraction, more complex, and not reducible to a simple formula. We can see it best as a variable recipe of ingredients.

We are innately driven to seek fulfillment and to make our contribution to the world. In order to do this we naturally seek out people, especially life partners, who can see, honor, and strengthen our *Real Core Values Self.* This ingredient, added to the chemistry thing forms the basic *real* recipe.

We then add to these basic elements an assortment of spices and sweeteners . . .

Childhood traumas and losses that have not been grieved or resolved. These emotional pains connect themselves to various areas of our life and continue to cause disruptions, fear, and negative emotions in any new situation that feels like the originating situation. In our effort to reclaim our *Real Core Values Self,* even unconsciously, we choose partners whose personalities (warped *Real Core Values Self*) create the kind of new dramas in our adult life that cause us to feel the old feelings and fight the old fights until we are willing to look at the negative emotions and work through the old pains. Many of us subconsciously choose individuals who are a lot like mom or dad, or sister or brother, in order to have another chance to work things out more effectively that we did as a child.

Social patterns and habits. We adopt certain mannerisms, body postures, speech patterns, formalities, courtesies or lack thereof, cleanliness, etc. These social patterns are either natural expressions of our *Real Core Values Self,* or they are the warped (adapted) response to our historic situations. We often choose partners that A) honor our innate selves, and that also B) conflict with social patterns that we subconsciously would like to rid ourselves of. Most of us find someone that meets the latter requirement (B) quite nicely. Most of us are not tuned in or consciously aware enough to know how to determine if a partner is willing and able to honor our innate self.

Avocation and *calling*. We are each attracted subconsciously to the other's avocation and *calling* by the interest, the harmony, or the battles that these elements may bring into the relationship. The way our partner spends his or her time. The position he or she holds in society. The perception others have of him or her. All of these subconscious considerations color our choice of partner. This is part of the creature-level issue of survival of the fittest and genetic competition. It is also connected with a sense of who we deserve to be with at the personality level. For some, the connection is at a life-mate level in which the sense is that the other party is truly a life partner and one who will support us and cause us to reach our highest and best level of development.

Familiarity. Our life partners are generally familiar to us. They feel natural to be with. They seem to *fit* into our lives. In other words, it's not just the things we share and the things we fight about, but it's the tone of voice, the level of *passion*, the amount of spirituality, etc.

The most important awareness is that we do choose our partners, mostly subconsciously, but our choices are intentional. The level of intention and the impact of intention on our achievement of happiness come from two very different sources.

We use our intellect as *part* of our decision, even though the choice of a life partner is largely emotional and *intuitive*. Still, we choose people to be our spouses with the profound expectation that we are making a great life decision that will lead to continuing happiness.

We also have a certain level of consciousness about our own maturity and the maturity of the other person. This provides the opportunity to make a conscious decision about our life mates. As you learn more and more what true *Core Values Consciousness* is, you will likely see that most of your choices have not been nearly as consciously made as you tend to think.

The act of thinking about a decision, and talking about it with others, is not evidence of consciousness.

In order to make conscious choices, we must have a high level of awareness of our emotional maturity, our current level of individuation and psychological/spiritual maturity. Ultimately, we need to have an awareness of our current level of *Core Values Consciousness*—this is the only true adulthood for us Homo sapiens creatures.

A good way to gauge your own level of maturity in a given choice situation is to observe yourself and see if you can clearly identify any inner talking and emotional feelings. The presence of inner talking and strong emotions is a good indicator of personality-driven choices.

The willingness to see our immaturities, hear our inner talking about our partner, to feel and name the emotions that are directing our outward responses—these choices are an important ingredient in our ability to consciously choose a life partner.

This awareness will allow us to make a more conscious and reasonable choice about who we should marry, which starts with a choice of who we should even choose to date. This awareness should also tie us back to the "no greener pastures" idea and cause us to remain true to the partnership.

We are most benefited when we hold steady in our relationships at least long enough to allow this largely unconscious choice to provide the growth in *Core Values Consciousness* and personality-fighting opportunities it was constructed unconsciously by you to provide. We are best served by our life choices when we stick with them long enough to realize real growth from the circumstances and relationships we create so that we won't have to repeat the same unresolved *stuff* in our next relationship.

The juicier the fighting gets (barring physical and emotional abuse), the closer we are getting to our real life issues—the warping that we are working to rid ourselves of. If we leave a relationship because of this kind of discomfort, we will likely choose a new relationship that closely mirrors the last, because we still have the same basic subconscious requirements for our personal evolution.

We recreate the same dramas in order to learn how to overcome them.

(It is, of course, not suggested that anyone remain in a situation that is physically or emotionally abusive or dangerous.)

Two other scenarios are quite common.

1. A person lives with a spouse for a significant period—in a relationship that has basic *core values* differences, i.e., a predominantly *love*-based person living with a significantly dominant *knowledge*-based person. One person has chosen to grow spiritually and emotionally more than the other, and continued friction over issues that now need to be left behind are no longer useful for continued growth, so a break is orchestrated.

2. Rather than remarrying the same kind of person as the former spouse, a person searches for and finds someone very different. The primary reasons (for good or ill) in this scenario are: The person who is choosing someone very different to live with is hiding from still unresolved issues, or there has been a deep awareness of personal *core values* and the relationship of one's own personal value structure to one's spouse. The choice from the position of new awareness may be to choose accelerated growth and a more nurturing (accepting) environment where a positive building of psychological/emotional muscle may substitute for the conflict-generated growth of the past.

This process of choosing your right life mate is founded in your *Core Values Consciousness.*

The portions of our value systems that were honored by our parents tend to be relatively clear, reliable places from which to make good choices and decide upon appropriate behavior. Even these nurtured areas of our lives, however, may be warped (exaggerated in their importance to us) if other *core values* in our nature were not honored or were belittled.

This warping of our basic selves shows up either as too much reliance upon one strategy (*love* rather than *power*, for instance), or as distrust of and therefore too little willingness to act in accordance with one of our stronger values.

If mom or dad disliked or punished us for positive expressions that came naturally from one of our stronger values, we learned to put the correlated strategy to sleep—keep it out of play, even when the strategies that align with *knowledge*, for instance, would be the better, more effective strategy.

When we choose life mates, we tend to fit ourselves with another person that mirrors either our parents' nurturing of one of our dominant *core values*, or the disregard for another. In this way, we are regularly invited to re-experience childhood situations.

This is not a curse.

It is the normal consequence of our adaptive behavioral training as a human creature. It provides an opportunity to learn life's lessons and to become more effective and more able to fully express our innate unchanging *Core Values Nature* even with someone who provides a strong resistance to our expression of this *real self.*

As they say in weight lifting, "No pain, no gain."

Here is a process that will lead to an optimum choice of an intimate partner.

- Each person completes their own *Core Values Index*. The couple compares the scores and the reports they receive in this process.

Here are the questions to ask:

- Where are we most alike? What values did we select that are the same? Do we compete or support each other in each of these values? If we compete, do we compete fairly and in a positive manner, or do we clash and end up fighting?

- Where are we most different? Are we complementary—you doing what I don't like to do in some areas and me doing for you in others? Or are we in conflict because of these different values?

If you can't have one or more productive interesting conversations at this level, you should consider delaying any formal joining and get counseling together or separately. A good partnership or marriage is built mostly on the ability of the two people to listen to each other, converse with each other in a positive way, and negotiate changes and compromises.

The comparison of individual *core values*, one with the other, will bring many things to the surface that are important now, or are likely to become significant in the future.

It is absolutely essential for a good marriage that each partner is willing, able, and committed to nurturing and honoring the other's most dominant *core values*. If you both have the same dominant *core values*, explore possible competitiveness and the possibility that the two of you may be so much of the same nature that you are going to have difficulties in the areas in which you are both weakest.

If you have different dominant *core values*, how high a capacity do you each have? Is there any chance that the other will be able to honor your dominant *core value* that is so dominant in them as to be almost the constant nature of the person?

You need to explore whether the person with the very high score in one *core value* even understands and appreciates the different dominant *core value* of the other. Who is going to suffer most? Who is going to have to compromise, or live without some important affirmation and appreciation?

One of the CEOs in a seminar I recently conducted is a dominant *innovator wisdom* person. His score is 29 in *wisdom*, which is what we call a profound score. This means that he is almost always showing up as the *wisdom* in the room. He seldom operates as any of the other energies, and he is driven by the motivation to be *wisdom* in any situation in which he is involved.

His wife is also *wisdom* first. Her score is a much lower 23 points, but still strong and essential to her sense of worth. *Wisdom* is her dominant capacity for contribution.

As we discussed their relationship, it became very apparent that she was only showing up in their relationship as her *merchant love* energy. She was reporting frustration and distress to him in their marriage. But even in this communication, his response was to ask questions, devise a strategy that might resolve the issue, then get back to work.

Her position was not improved by this. Her *love* energy was being disregarded and made sacrificial, while he presumed the dominant role in the *wisdom* process, even when the issues being discussed were most important to her.

It took very direct language to break through to this highly intelligent and very *wisdom*-driven person. I finally said simply but very directly: "You can't have a better relationship with your wife if you are not willing to honor her *wisdom*.

"There have to be specific and constant issues in your lives that are important that require her to *be* the *wisdom*. You have to show her that you trust and respect her solutions and stop yourself from second-guessing whatever she decides.

"Can you do this?" I asked. "Yes," he responded. "Will you do this?" I asked him in the room with his peers. After a long pause, he looked up and said firmly, "Yes. I will."

The single most important rule I know for development of strong relationships is that you must always honor the *core values* of the person you are with. If you are not willing or able to do this, you might as well decide not to be with this person. Eventually, they will grow tired of your dismissal and lack of regard for their most important *core energies*. This will lead to fights or flight.

Once a person owns the fact that they are composed of important and essential *Core Value Energy*, they become appropriately intolerant of being in situations that do not honor *who they are*.

32

The Decision to Become a Parent

Would you want to have yourself as a parent?

Are you being a better parent to your children than your parents were for you? Or do you believe you will be?

Is being a parent an important and essential aspect to your life?

Is being a parent integrated into your sense of purpose and meaning?

Do you see this as a way to express your *core values*? (If you do not know your *Core Values Index* profile, it's time to take the assessment. Find our website at www.taylorprotocols.com.)

Parenting is one of the primal drives of the Homo sapiens animal. It is for this purpose that we are endowed with such strong sexual desires.

Procreation and the twenty-year assignment as a parent may be the most commonly shared experience of all people. Yet, most people, when asked, find themselves frustrated as parents, often in conflict with their children, especially two-year-olds and teenagers. They often feel trapped by the responsibilities involved.

This first thing to recognize about parenting is that it is a minimum twenty-year assignment with no break in responsibility. Those of us who have lived or are living through this assignment are fully cognizant of this fact. There are times in the diaper years when sleep is so rare and freedom so low that parents forget almost totally what life was like before kids.

The enormity of stretch and sometimes a complete break in relationship between parents is a significant challenge.

The demand for a quickening of our personal maturity causes an exaggeration of the conflicts and traumas discussed in previous chapters. Both parents, if they are sharing the parenting load, put aside many preferences and defer many entertainments and pleasures in order to take care of children.

And they give up a substantial amount of access to each other. They delay gratification in many areas.

The demands upon personal time and the emotional and physical drain of energy leave little left to share with each other. What the two individuals are sharing is the life process of raising children. If one parent is not passionately involved in this process, that parent's sense of loss of partnership can be great.

Add to this the desire to be a good parent, to provide food, shelter, and warmth, to nurture the innate *Core Values Nature* of our children and see them succeed in their own life.

Parents tend to learn as much about themselves as they do about their children, sometimes at the expense of the child's positive development. Wherever you are in this equation, it is important to spend very little time on the past and focus on today and tomorrow.

There is one absolute guarantee about parenting: You and your child will have different *Core Values Natures.*

We have shown that the mathematical odds that you and your child will have identical *core values* are 6 to the 36th power, or 10 with nine sets (000) of zeroes to one. This fact guarantees another resulting child-parent reality.

Parents always warp their children to some degree.

We over-praise certain behavior and under-reward other *Core Values Strategies* and tactics and personality traits, based both upon positive *core values* and also on our own warped personalities.

Life's circumstances also contribute to this development of personality by children within family structures. The possible influences are multi-various and innumerable. Some of the more prevalent issues that contribute to development of adaptive personality strategies are:

Deaths in the family
Poverty or wealth
Illnesses in the family
Depression in the family
Separations
Family (a)morality
Family ethics
Divorce
Abuse
Drugs and alcohol addiction
Religion(s)
Education levels
Intelligence
Emotional maturity of parents

Add your own influencing circumstances . . .

____

____

____

____

____

____

____

____

All of our life's circumstances, especially in the early formative years, contribute to the variance (warping) of our children's *Core Values Nature* into their carefully crafted personalities. The age at which children experience these events, the way others around them behave, the ways they are supported emotionally or encouraged to cover emotions, the level of victim attitude in a family—all of these influence the development of our children's adaptive behavioral patterns.

So even if we were not innately different in our *core values* structure, our children would still develop different (slightly warped) personalities due to different circumstances in our lives and our own imperfect representation of the *Core Values Nature* that is our unique presence in the room—the one the child has to adapt itself to.

The Twentieth Core Values Law:

Any event that creates fear in a child greater than the child's ability to handle it safely, creates learned future responses in that child for all future similar events.

If, as parents, we are able to face with our children some of the fearful circumstances listed above and demonstrate positive, *creative* responses, we can significantly reduce the impact of such experiences in our children. We cannot, however, under any circumstances overcome all such fear-filled circumstances for children, even if we wanted to.

We can only demonstrate our own ability to deal with life's situations. The children will still have to learn to master such fearful circumstances on their own—without the strength of father and mother to fall back on.

The best foundation we can give to our children is as clear a picture as possible of their *Real Core Values Self.* We can provide positive affirmation of their unique *Core Values Nature* as they express themselves in our shared lives. We can honor *who they are* in every interaction. We can give gifts and attention and approval for those aspects of their *Core Values Nature* that we do not have in ourselves, looking for ways to acknowledge their special different energies that make them unique.

Quite often parents do the exact opposite of what I have written in the above paragraph. It is far easier to accomplish this good goal once we know the innate nature of our children. After that we have only to be observant and willing to respect and love the aspects of our children that are the most different from our own nature. The wonderful thing about self-knowledge and the knowledge about the innate *Core Values Nature* of others is that this knowledge depersonalizes the responses and interactions between the two persons.

When I see that my children are not *being who they are* in defiance of me, or showing lack of regard or respect, but only *being* the *Core Value Energy* they are wired to be, I detach from their unexpected interactions with me and see them as the unique, wonderful individuals that they *are*. This dramatically decreases my immature need to control them or correct them for just being *who they are.*

When there is a need for me to step in as a parent and set boundaries or correct inappropriate behavior, I am more clear that my actions are positive and clean of personal agenda. If I am angry or frustrated when I correct my children, the interaction is more about my feelings than the good of the child. Having this knowledge about our respective *Core Values Natures* keeps this kind of ineffective behavior at a minimum.

If we show our children that we are constructed similarly as persons, but that we are not the same, we give them the capability to also detach from perceived slights or misinterpreted behaviors. They learn quickly when I am just *being* mom or dad, and what is truly a personality conflict.

Note: When I speak of personality I am speaking always of the new definition of personality, so I am always talking about our warped version of the *Real Core Values Self.*

If we as imperfect parents are committed to learning daily to live in alignment with our own *core values*, we create an acceptance of the human life process, and we provide a model of observation and acceptance of truth and learning. This foundation of commitment to learning and growing puts hope into every situation so conflicts can be resolved more easily, a quick apology given. Moving on becomes the norm when one or the other slips out of being a positive innate *Core Value Energy* and into emotionally based personality behavior.

An essential brick in this foundation is the message to our children that we see and respect *who they are* as people, that we have every confidence that they will be able to face their own life's challenges and opportunities successfully. We will let go of the bicycle sooner, rather than later, allowing our children to take full charge of their own lives at the earliest possible moment. We will balance this gift with our diligent effort to keep our children from any real harm.

If we truly love our children (*love* being defined as the nurturing of the *Core Values Nature* in one's self and in another), we will be constantly watching them and finding ways to acknowledge, support, and strengthen their *core values* as the child makes them apparent.

We will do this regardless of our own different *core values*. In doing this, we will find ourselves treating each of our children differently, rewarding differently, praising differently, and correcting (guiding) each one differently from the others.

When my sons were young, their different *Core Values Natures* made themselves apparent early on.

The one incident that most clearly demonstrates this happened on a driving vacation when they were six and seven years old.

We stopped on a very hot day at a very large swimming pool in a very small town in South Dakota. The swimming pool was called the largest swimming pool in the country. It was huge, with an expansive wading area and swimming zones for skilled swimmers.

We played for a while together as a family in the shallow end. Then as we parents retreated to our towels and the warm sunshine, our two guys began exploring the entire pool.

Doug, who is a profound *merchant love* person with high creativity, proceeded to climb the high-dive ladder as he had been watching the older children do. Before I could get up and hold him back, he was running the length of the diving board, twenty feet above the water, and throwing himself off in a poorly executed dive. He smacked into the water hard enough that he looked like he had a sunburn when he pulled himself out of the pool.

In the meantime, my older son, Greg, age seven, sat quietly at the edge of the deep end of the pool, watching the older kids dive. After sitting there for almost an hour, he got up slowly, walked over to the low diving board. He walked to the end of the board, pushed his hands up over his head and tossed himself forward in a not-too-bad dive.

In their later years I watched Doug's willingness to throw himself into new experiences become a real strength, and I watched Greg's tendency to sit back and observe and cogitate, become a real challenge for him in some adult situations.

This is as it is for all of us. Our greatest strengths become our greatest weaknesses, because we get comfortable approaching life in our most preferred manner, choosing unconsciously to be our most dominant innate *Core Value Energy* in situations that we would be more effective in if we were willing to shift into a secondary or third-level *Core Values Strategy.*

33

Religion

A religion is a set of beliefs, histories, and stories that provide several things:

- Preferred answers to fundamental questions of life
- A set of beliefs that are considered to be "the truth"
- A moral and social framework with prescribed behavioral boundaries
- A methodology for prayer, meditation, and worship
- A prescribed justice, risk-reward system
- A gathering place and a unifying center for a community of people

All religions by definition are founded on beliefs and rituals and social mores that are adopted by "believers." The adoption of beliefs by new participants generates an unequivocal acceptance from the religious community that is generally not retractable as long as the new community member attests to the religious beliefs, participates in the community gatherings, and behaves within the tolerance level of the moral and ethical strictures of the religious community.

The universal power of religions is to provide the sense of unconditional love and acceptance by a community with the price being some compromise of individuality and independence. I say religions provide a *sense* of unconditional love, because in many ways they are the embodiment of highly conditional love. A person is made to feel completely accepted unless he decides to challenge beliefs or disrupts the morality and ethics of the community. Then the result is exile, emotional or actual.

So the effect of religion is control of the individuals through conditional acceptance.

Within these religious communities, freedom of thought, especially expression of belief-challenging questions, is at some level considered threatening. As a person seeks spiritual, emotional, and intellectual development, the chosen religion may assist or resist this development.

Since most religions claim the position as the only "true" religion with various levels of tolerance for other religions, religions by definition cause a separation between the participants of one faith and the believers in another faith. When this separation exists within families, between spouses, etc., the relationship challenges are substantial.

It is important to accept the fact that each of us chooses our own religion or lack thereof. We do this whether we choose to remain constant with our parent's religion, or we choose another religion, or we choose to not join a religious community, or reject all religious belief and practice. Atheism is a religion in and of itself. It is founded upon a belief that there is no God. The need to decide this is a religious urge. The need to propound this belief to others is a religious, emotionally charged religious urge.

And strong atheists tend to believe they know the truth and that their vision of how the community should interact, especially toward other religious groups, can be as strong as a religious fundamentalist.

The historic fact that we may have been born into a particular religion and the culture that accompanies it illustrates part of the influences that cause us to adopt a certain religion. Regardless of fear of separation and other potential consequences of changing or leaving a family religion, we remain the captains of our own fate and choose to stay or leave as adults. Most of us tend to do this out of compliance or rebellion. Neither of these emotionally driven strategies is an effective way to choose one's religion.

It is important, then, to look at our choice of religion and seek understanding about how this choice has been made, and whether our current religious affiliation is contributing to our personal development in the manner and to the degree we would like.

There are strong social, psychological, intellectual, and emotional factors that influence our decisions regarding whether to adopt a particular religion.

- Family heritage of strong devotion to one particular religion.

- Split allegiance between parents to different religions, or a nonreli gious parent and a religious devotee.

- Early childhood religious (community or individual) experiences that created comfort, affirmation, and positive situations, or experiences that created self-hatred, fear, and coercion.
  Note: It is not generally the religion itself that dictates the level of positive or negative experience, but the nature of and quality of the leadership in the communities to which one has belonged.

- Rigidity or flexibility of the belief system within a religion.
  For persons of high intellect, rigid boundaries regarding beliefs may or may not be tolerable.

It is important to be aware of these factors when considering the role your religion does have and should have in your adult life. This will help you become clear regarding the truth about the current influence your religious choices are now having on your life. It is appropriate to consciously choose the contribution you want your religious choices to make to your life.

It is appropriate to consider whether your religious choices are providing you the freedom and spiritual support you require to develop and to move toward fulfillment as an individual. We all face the possibility of rejection by our family's religious community and by family members themselves if we break away, even partially, from the religion of the family. This is how a religious community establishes some control over moral and social behavior.

This is not a judgment of right or wrong against religions.

There is likely positive social gain from the threat of exile as a means to control persons who are prone to choose harmful or disturbing behavior. It is important to simply acknowledge this emotionally powerful device as part of our human condition, and to understand the price one must sometimes pay, in order to truly claim one's own life—when a change of religious beliefs or community is deemed appropriate. This is a choice that has many ramifications.

In terms of our *core values*, which underlay our adopted personalities, the religious choices either affirm, ignore, or undermine portions of our innate *Real Core Values Self.* It is a certainty that any one religion (including denominations or subsets of religions) will not support all of a person's *Real Core Values Self.* Let's explore this.

If, for instance, you are a strong *power/love* person, you are highly spontaneous and geared for making decisions quickly. You are predominantly *intuitive* rather than *cognitive*. So a highly formal religion, liturgical in nature with a culture founded on logic, debate, and religious knowledge, cannot provide you as direct and complete an affirmation of your *Real Core Values Self* as a religion that is more emotive, less formal, and founded more in relationships and social activity.

The *love* and *power* person is more prone to evangelism than any other *core value* profile, more willing to reach out to new people, and to intrude (a personality motivation) in another person's life, "for their own good."

Love/wisdom people are *creative* and fond of teaching and of interactive discussions that are open and intellectually challenging. Abstract thinking and aesthetics are essential parts of their lives. A religion that is austere and highly pragmatic, that discourages open discourse and encourages the control of emotions or *creative* thinking, is not a comfortable fit. Imagery, metaphors, and poetry are essential ingredients of religious communication and worship for *love/wisdom* people.

Wisdom/knowledge individuals are *cognitive*, rational, and enjoy high levels of organization and systems. A religious community run by committees with written procedural guidelines is most comfortable. Freewheeling, emotional gatherings with loose agendas without time limitations—highly experiential gatherings—these are unnerving elements to such people. Evangelism for these people is the antithesis of their *core values*, which center around continuity, reverence to doctrine, adherence to cultural conventions, and written tradition. There is a tendency toward black-and-white thinking here, or right-thinking requirements. A private, less communal approach, with reading and thoughtful contemplation, suits this kind of individual.

People whose *core values* are predominantly *knowledge* and *power* find themselves most comfortable in a religious community that values justice and has a clear foundation of substantiated history. A more autocratic structure is preferred due to their impatience with decisions by committee. Authority that comes from social community structure and rules is important. Personal inspiration is difficult to handle in such a religious environment. But there also must be a social agenda that creates the need to structure an organization and pay attention to measured effect and results.

Persons with a predominance of *love* and *knowledge* values seek out religious experience that is founded in both history and a vision of the future. They tend to be generally forgiving of others and generally polite and appropriate in their actions. Their value for trust and for justice causes these people to sometimes be harsh judges of others, concerned whether someone is being fair and living within the law, and also whether they are "good" and "true" people. But the community comes first, and the level at which certain individual needs are met attests to the quality of the religious community.

A religion (or subset of a religion) that supports these values tends to be highly political in nature, due to the fact that people who value *love* and *knowledge* do not enjoy conflict and tend to gather into "like-minded" groups within the community, looking askance at other religions, and attempting to gain influence or control through indirect means.

Power/wisdom individuals are highly independent and unwilling to be restricted by systems and procedures. This makes them reluctant participants in any strong religious community. The drive for independent thought, autonomous action, and an environment with less, not more, boundaries will often keep them from feeling comfortable in any large, stable community, especially one with strong and unchanging religious doctrines.

A religious environment that is somewhat honoring of this kind of *core values* temperament is one that relies upon personal inspiration, broadly interpreted doctrines, and very little community oversight into personal and business lives.

These factors are not put forth as an inducement for you to change, adopt, or desert any religious choices made to date, but rather to heighten your conscious awareness of the effects that your religious choices produce in the rest of your life, and to help you make better choices across the spectrum of your life.

34

Spirit

The human spirit (innate unchanging *Core Values Nature*) is composed of four essential *Core Value Energies* in a unique blend within each person. *Core Values Consciousness* is a new understanding and description of higher consciousness or psychological/spiritual consciousness.

At last we are here, back at the beginning of this book. Everything begins and ends with each individual's innate unchanging *Real Core Values Self*. . . a unique recipe of *Core Value Energies* that govern the person's perspective on the world and motivate him or her to make certain *types of contribution.*

It is the merging of *core values* into a coherent individual, combined with the sharpening of talents and skills, that together dictate what role in this world is most conducive for a given individual to make a contribution. This mixture of *core values* and skills into a life occupation is meant to provide a vehicle or delivery system within which the person can contribute his *Core Value Energy, his human spirit,* to his society.

We each create a social framework within which our talents and skills provide a great delivery vehicle for our innate unchanging *core values.* Our *Core Values Nature* is, after all, what we each contribute to this world.

In essence, we each work to perfect our innate skills and talents, to be a better delivery system for the contribution of our *Core Value Energies* into our world.

The *core value* makeup of a person does not change during his lifetime. It is a separate and steady unconscious force in childhood. It is the driving force that requires the slow and steady desertion of our ego-driven personality, constant psychological evolution, and dedicated discovery and ownership of our *Real Core Values Self* in adulthood.

We each have a universal mission, to discover who we are at the deepest level. And, through the perfection of skills and talents, deliver our *Real Core Values Selves* into the service of humanity and the life of our planet.

Any work or activity that successfully delivers our *core values* into our society is meaningful work for us. Any activity that promises to cause this delivery to take place and is aligned with our *core values* creates a sense of fulfillment and purpose for our lives. All activities that help us hone our greatest talents and competencies prepare us to make our highest and best contribution.

Any activity that does not align with our *core values* feels demeaning, de-energizing, and depressing.

It is this unique blend of *Core Value Energies*, our *Real Core Values Self*, that we long to have acknowledged as valuable.

It is this self that observes our own life first from an unconscious level during childhood and has the capacity to later observe and make decisions from the psychologically, mentally conscious level.

Our innate unchanging *Real Core Values Self* is itself the gift we are here to contribute to the world.

You see, life really is quite simple. We come into this world as a pure blend of *Core Value Energies* in a physical container.

The physical container resides in a social environment that is guaranteed to have value judgments for and against our own innate *Core Values Nature*, so we make subconscious choices to adapt ourselves to our environment for safety, comfort, and acceptance.

This warping away from our *Real Core Values Self* into a personality (the way we choose to show up) is unavoidable. So there is a requirement to unwarp ourselves in adulthood and discover our *Real Core Values Self.*

We are designed to act in alignment with our *Core Values Nature* and make ourselves a gift to the world—a fully participating contributor.

This process of individuation was described by Jung in the early twentieth century and remains today a standard view of human growth and development for most psychologists and counselors.

What they often miss is the innate unchanging *Core Values Nature* component that Abraham Maslow pointed toward and that the *Core Values Index* at last describes. The *CVI* quantifies the various types of energies that exist separately and collectively within each person.

The observation of character traits and behavior patterns is too good a game to play when combined with unique childhood traumas and an infinity of home environments. The focus has been on how we got warped, without a good way to find what it is that we got warped away from, warped out of being, warped into acting in a chosen pattern of adapted behaviors.

The fulfillment of the individual human development process is to live a meaningful life.

But what is meaningful to one is not meaningful to another. The ability of counselors and psychologists to lead individuals to a fulfilling life has been blocked by the lack of a reliable way of getting a picture of each person's unique and innate *Core Values Nature.* A picture that is not some general concept of a "good" person, but rather the specific and unique *Core Values Nature* that each individual is.

Without this detailed picture, the process of individuation remains a random, arduous adventure, fraught with mistaken ideas and wrong turns. We make the same choices over and over, because we are afraid to let go of the emotional commitment we have to our ego-driven personality.

Without a picture of the wonderful, positive, highly contributory self that we *are*, we have trouble letting go of the safe personality beliefs, attitudes, and ideas. We have trouble changing even the smallest behavior

The *Core Values Index* assessment provides this picture of each person's innate *Core Values Nature*—in a quantified way.

The likelihood that any two persons will ever choose all of the same tactical and strategic values that any other person has chosen is astronomical: 6 to the 36th power, or 10 with twenty-seven zeroes after it to one.

Now imagine someone almost identical to you in spiritual makeup but with a totally different set of skills and talents—physical characteristics. Once again the uniqueness of each individual is compounded.

So not only our spiritual nature is unique, but the life we are given in terms of its social/environmental setting and the skill set and physical attributes are also unique. There is no other person that will ever live your life. No one will ever live mine—except me, of course, if I choose to do so.

The sad realization is that most people are not living the life they are designed to live. They spend most of their time in jobs that do not align with their *core values*. One Gallup study found that most people (approximately 75%) are somewhat or significantly ***not*** engaged in their work.

We know that this means most people are simply in the wrong seat, doing the wrong work.

They have not yet found their place of highest and best contribution. This ideal work role would ask them to be *who they are*, all day long, delivering their sacred energies to the world through their talents and skills employed by the tasks of their job.

The first choice I wish for everyone to make is to claim your own life.

Decide to find, identify, explore, express, and deliver your spiritual energies into your world.

To do this, a lifetime of learning must be chosen—but this is already a choice freely made by many. Also a life of spiritual consciousness, *Core Values Consciousness* is required. This is a choice which many choose not to make.

The challenge is to open oneself to consciousness, to personal observation—witness your flawed beliefs and ideas, your ineffective and sometimes harmful behaviors; observe, also your inner talking and negative emotions. This is not pleasant. It's simple, but not pleasant. It is not easy. It is simple.

This process constantly increases one's ability to make conscious choices about all aspects of life: What thoughts I choose to think. What emotions I choose to feel. What words I choose to speak. What actions I choose. What contributions I choose to make. Where I choose to *be*. Which *Core Value Energy* I choose to *be* at any given moment.

And in these conscious choices, we are made consciously responsible and accountable for the circumstances of our lives.

It is this process of deciding to discover one's deepest innate *Core Values Nature*—deciding to claim it out of the morass of environmental warping—deciding to reclaim it from our ego-driven personalities. It is this choice process that awakens the power of spiritual consciousness and releases the spiritual energy of each individual into the world.

It is the way to fulfill one's life. It is the way to find a sense of meaning and purpose. It is the means for making one's unique contribution. It is the way to deliver to this world that unique nature of God *we are here to be.*

The *core values* information obtained through the *Core Values Index* (*CVI*) is the only quantification of the deepest spiritual nature of individuals available from any source that we can identify.

This quantification of the organic, motivational nature, the center of self-consciousness, provides the most powerful information regarding the employment of humans together in corporations, organizations, communities, and as individuals.

Without the *Core Values Index*, each of us must find our own way to self-awareness and self-knowledge. Behavioral and personality assessments help in this process. Psychotherapy and counseling provide significant guidance and support in this pursuit.

But all of this available methodology is limited by the single factor that each of us tends to remain without a reasonably complete picture of our real inner nature. It is difficult enough to claim that inner nature when fully visualized and made more real through the *CVI* window into this inner realm.

The more crucial the situation during which an individual is observed through the lenses of behavioral assessments, the more pressure he feels, the more fearful he becomes, and the more he reverts to his personality (learned behaviors), which is some warped version of his original organic self.

So, most often, when other systems are used to measure suitability for employment in a given situation, the somewhat informative value of the behavior-observational systems melts under the pressure. This is why they have been uniformly inconsistent and significantly unreliable—not useful as prescreening tools for employment—certainly not proven accurate indicators of future top performance in a given job.

Once people understand the *Core Values Human Operating System* and the *Taylor Protocols* methodology for applying this information to smart business decisions, we will see that the following statement is not hyperbole, but crucial business knowledge that must be integrated into common business practice as rapidly as possible.

There is now a way to determine whether a person is likely to be a top performer in a given position in a given company. The way is to develop a *Top Performer Profile*™ of people who are already top performers in that position in that company. Then test to see whether the *core values* pattern of top performers is different from low performers, sufficiently different to use the *CVI Top Performer Profile* to screen other future top performers into the position.

Then, the automated matching, comparison, and pattern-matching judgment of the *CVI* is the only known way to quantitatively determine a match, keeping all human pre-judgment, affectations, preferences, and blind prejudices out of the process. The only remaining issues are measurable skills testing, IQ and emotional/psychological normalcy-health-maturity.

We have proven in hundreds of companies over the course of more than twenty years that we can dramatically improve human productivity throughout a wide variety of industries and occupations, without the employment of other testing factors. We have substantiated the *Core Values Index* and *Taylor Protocols* as the single-change ingredient that has directly and solely caused these increases in human productivity.

The reason this works is that we have discovered a method for identifying the deepest, most powerful aspect of human identity, the *Real Core Values Self.* We have learned that this innate self is unchanging throughout life, that it is the core of human existence.

The effect of this work for people who are skeptical of the need for, or desirability of, *Core Values Consciousness* is to demonstrate the tangible results of applying this new knowledge to bottom line, measurable issues.

In this *Real Core Values Nature* resides the deepest motivational drivers, the preference for viewing the world from certain aspects, the desire to act in certain strategic and tactical manners, and the requirement to contribute this deepest aspect of self to society to establish worth— purpose, meaning, and fulfillment of life purpose.

When we hire people with the "right" talents and skills into a position, without considering the *core values* fit, we are continuing the worst practice of the industrial age: the acquisition of human talent in exchange for livelihood. When a person is hired based upon skills and experience, the person's deepest *Real Core Values Nature* is not considered—in fact, an employee's sense of purpose and need for meaningful work is often considered a deterrent for prolonged tenure and job satisfaction—we are trying to buy the talent and energy only, and that is a huge mistake.

It is the unspoken secret of our times that the constant increase in turnover in American businesses—growing from less than 5% per year in the 1950s to greater than 30% in large businesses in today's markets—is the proof of this: We are still selling and buying individual human life energy to be put to work in a business in exchange for money.

If I must use my talents, energy, creativity, *power*, communications, *wisdom*, *knowledge*, and *love* in service of business and in a job position that does not align my deepest *core values* with the work that I do, then I will sell myself to the highest bidder. My skills and my experience are then the value that is being sold, and my deepest *real self* is the unnecessary rider of my existence.

We, with our simple *Core Values Index*, are turning the world of business inside out and upside down.

First, we find those people in business who are in fact working in alignment with their deepest *core values*. They are easy to spot, for the most part: the top performers in any position. Most of the others in the position are struggling to earn a living (keep their job) in a position that is a less-than-satisfactory match with their individual *Core Values Nature* and life's purposes.

We identify the *core value* pattern of the top performers in each functional position. There is a certain limited *core values* pattern, and a certain limited contributory type among the top performers. It is silly not to try to find others with the same *Core Values Nature* as our identified top performers.

We are intentionally aligning individual *core values* with the work we want them to do. Instead of the prostitution of skill and talent for money, we are exchanging a means of livelihood for the opportunity to make a contribution that is a wonderful and effective expression of each individual's *Core Values Nature*. We are paying people to invest their *Real Core Values Self* in our businesses and to make their highest and best contribution to the world through our business structure.

People begin to say things like, "This job feels like it was made for me." Or, "I have never felt so comfortable and at peace than I am when I am busy doing this work." What has happened is the powerful business result that leads to all success . . .

We put the right person in the right position and give them the right work to do.

The reason this promotes higher productivity is simple. When you hire me into a job that indeed was made for people just like me, I have finally found the place in the work-a-day world that needs *who* and what I *am*—not just *what* I am.

Since every person is in some stage of self-evolution and self-discovery, we have put people in a situation that promotes their use of skills, experience, talent, and energy as a means for expressing themselves, while learning more about themselves.

Why are we talking about work in this chapter about spirit? Because we cannot, we must not, separate spiritual issues from our daily work.

The simple truth is that we have now based the design and growth of our business on the *Core Values Nature* of individuals. Each person is in a position in which his deepest *Core Values Nature* is what is needed to succeed in this job. His spiritual energy is what is needed, not just his physical energy and skills.

American contemporary business becomes for each person his Tibetan temple—his mountaintop experience. This is where people find themselves, come to themselves, optimize their personal worth, and make their contribution.

The transition is from a temple of skills and talent prostitution with limited human productivity, to a temple of spiritual actualization in which human productivity is optimized.

This is not utopian thinking. This is not nirvana, or heaven on earth.

The most difficult work a person can do is to continuously explore new parts of himself: learning new skills, finding new ways every day to rise to his highest and best use—to openly work to become the individual he is designed to become, and to face his life's mysteries and challenges, working back through old beliefs, attitudes, and ideas, making better choices today than he made yesterday.

The Four Gateways to *Core Values Consciousness*

There are four important attitudes that release each of us from old thoughts, beliefs, attitudes, and ideas that hold us back. These gateways to consciousness align with each of the four basic *core values* in the *Core Values Index*. They are:

Core Value	**Gateway**	**Strengths**	**Affirmation to Remember**
Power	Submission	Inexhaustible Irresistible	Ask for help before you need it
Love	Acceptance	Resilient Optimistic	Be accountable
Wisdom	Judgment	Tenacious Resourceful	Decide sooner than is comfortable
Knowledge	Forgiveness Patient	Reliable	Give your knowledge and trust without judgment

Message to all *Builders* (*power* people)

There is no one more powerless and vulnerable than a person who continues to be the *power* in the room, when what is needed is a little *wisdom*, *knowledge*, or *love*.

Submit to the realities of the current situation. Submit yourself to being a participant, working with others to accomplish tangible goals. Submit your will to a higher power and do not waste your *power* energy in situations in which *power* strategies will not be optimal and may even be destructive.

Submit to the truth that your personal *power* is not inexhaustible or irresistible.

Message to all *Merchants* (*love* people)

There is no one more unloving than the person who continues to use *love* strategies when what others need is more *wisdom*, *power*, or *knowledge*.

Accept the truth about yourself and others graciously. Accept accountability for results and circumstances. Accept the limitations of *love* strategies and look for opportunity to fulfill your *love* value through the other *Core Value Energies*. Do not waste your *love* energy in situations in which you cannot see the *truth* about the way things are, and in which *love* strategies are not effective.

Accept the reality that resilience and optimism will not be sufficient in every situation. Also, even when you are acting purely in alignment with the *love core value*, not everyone will love you or be accepting of your *love* energy toward them.

Message to all *Innovators* (*wisdom* people)

There is nothing more foolish than the person who continues trying to be the *wisdom* in the situation when *knowledge*, *power*, or *love* would be a better strategy.

Be willing to judge the right and wrong of situations and people's actions. Use your *wisdom* energy internally to decide how wise it is for you to continue to participate with people in situations that are unjust or inappropriate. Put aside your tenacious resourcefulness, your tendency to sit back and observe, and stand your ground, based upon wise *judgment*.

Shift into *judgment* sooner in situations that are not yielding to *wisdom* strategies. Your *wisdom* is not perfect. The openness of others to your *wisdom* is sometimes essential. And some people are not willing or able to accept wise counsel. Seek wise counsel for yourself from others.

Message to all *Bankers* (*knowledge* people)

There is nothing more ignorant than the person who continues to use *knowledge* strategies when *power*, *love*, or *wisdom* would better serve.

Forgive others for their mistakes and willfulness. Your patience and reliability is of value only when you remain generous with your *knowledge* and tolerant of imperfection in others. Use your *knowledge* to raise everyone around you to their highest and best contribution. It is better to leave a situation completely than it is to stay and withhold your *knowledge* and support.

Be willing to admit mistakes and to be wrong. And do not use your *knowledge* to make others wrong. The fact that some people will ignore your facts and information and continue to make avoidable mistakes will always be an offense to your *knowledge* value. Remember to give others access to *all* of your *knowledge*. Remember to steadily, courteously assert your gift of *knowledge*. Only then are you fulfilling your mission.

Everyone

You can do this. All real happiness comes from the pursuit of this kind of adult, spiritually conscious living.

Isn't it interesting that human corporate productivity is also greatly enhanced and can be optimized only by the pursuit of *Core Values Consciousness* even in the workplace—especially in the workplace, where we spend most of our adult lives.

What choices are you avoiding today? What unconscious choices are you continuing to make today that are setting you up for the same results tomorrow and that frustrate you today?

If you are a business leader, how much profit are you leaving pent up in your talent and skills factory that can be unleashed through application of the *Taylor Protocols* and the alignment of *core values* with the nature of the work assigned.

Wake up to *who you are*. Wake up to why you are here. Come alive by reclaiming your innate unchanging *Real Core Values Self*. Learn to *be* all that you are born to *be*. Make the highest and best contribution you are wired to make.

I guarantee you will find true fulfillment and great joy in the process.